# Emergent Globalization

## A New Triad of Business Systems

Chong Choi, Brian Hilton and Carla Millar



palgrave
macmillan

First published 2004 by
PALGRAVE MACMILLAN
Houndmills, Basingstoke, Hampshire RG21 6XS and
175 Fifth Avenue, New York, N.Y. 10010
Companies and representatives throughout the world

PALGRAVE MACMILLAN is the global academic imprint of the Palgrave Macmillan division of St. Martin's Press, LLC and of Palgrave Macmillan Ltd. Macmillan® is a registered trademark in the United States, United Kingdom and other countries. Palgrave is a registered trademark in the European Union and other countries.

ISBN 978-1-349-51632-2 ISBN 978-0-230-28743-3 (eBook)
DOI 10.1057/9780230287433

This book is printed on paper suitable for recycling and made from fully managed and sustained forest sources.

A catalogue record for this book is available from the British Library.

A catalog record for this book is available from the Library of Congress.

10 9 8 7 6 5 4 3 2 1
13 12 11 10 09 08 07 06 05 04

Emergent Globalization

*This page intentionally left blank*

# Contents

# List of Figures and Tables

## Figures



## Tables

# 1
# Introduction

This book is about a process and an idea. The process is socio-economic emergence. The idea is globalization. We agree with Rugman (2002)[1] that globalization the fact is hard to find. However, we would suggest that globalization the process is well in train. We present it as an emergent property of the next step in the evolution of the socio-economic processes driving our planet's development – an emergent global business system empowered by the knowledge industries. Our contribution is to present emergence from the analytical perspective of a new triad of business systems.

The present international business scene has been categorized as having three principal types of business system – the Anglo-Saxon legal individualistic system, the Continental European communitarian system and the East Asian familial system.

Arguably, all successful international enterprise has roots in at least one of these. Those who think in these terms, however, choose to ignore some obvious exceptions, not least those in emerging, or developing or, in many cases, more realistically, non-developing economies.[2] States in both these categories are rarely seen as having business systems at all. The latter especially, and they contain the bulk of the world's population, are the ones we refer to as having a 'heritage system'. They are the economies where Rugman suggests that there is no evident sign of globalization. We agree. However, while this may be true of the non-developing states it is most definitely not true of those that are now emerging onto the global scene. These are the emerging markets displaying the characteristics of what we term the 'emerging business system'.

These emerging areas of the world are normally either considered only by businesses seeking entry into their market or by ideologues interested in preaching to them about the virtues of a particular existing system as a desired end state. Rarely are they considered on their own terms, and very rarely in terms of how they can realistically evolve from where they are to a particular desired end state – other than by trying to institute, with no prior history, institutions analogous to those existing in successful states elsewhere. Here we not only treat them as interesting in their own right but as providing a penetrating insight into the processes of emergence.

While mature business systems may provide a basis from which to analyse current commercial success in different contexts, they do not offer a basis for understanding emergence itself – the *process* by which emergence occurs in the first place. Newly emergent systems may, however, provide such a model. It is certain that specifying an end state for any newly emerging system based on what has evolved to maturity elsewhere is not smart.[3] It would be analogous to telling people to plant a tropical rain forest in Siberia. It will not work. Some would-be socio-economic engineers do try the equivalent. Even aspiring to replant the redwood forest in its home environment in the North West seaboard of the US would not work, as rationally guided human action cannot replicate the evolution of an ecosystem over thousands of years, let alone grow the 1,000-year-old redwoods of which it was composed. Time, place and history do matter – as do culture and resources.

Intellectual interest in the processes of socio-economic development or evolution is always high. It drives much controversy. In the eighteenth century Adam Smith,[4] in the *Wealth of Nations*, saw evolution in terms of a conflict between selfish mercantile interest and free enterprise. He felt that the community interest had been captured by monopolistic mercantile interest, and saw an effective counter in allowing the unfettered growth of international trade. To him, enterprise freed from the constraints of state regulation could be contained in the communal interest by the forces of international competition.

In the late nineteenth century, Karl Marx[5] felt that such competition had failed to produce this result. The forces of materialistic competition had failed to contain the rapacious self-interest of individualistic capitalistic merchant enterprise. Instead it had re-enforced its dominance. He argued that in the end the community of workers at large would wrest power from such individualistic enterprises and restore man, the communal being, to his proper place in the scheme of things.

In the second half of the twentieth century Marx's prediction had not obviously materialized. Rostow, among others, took issue with him. Rostow[6] introduced the idea that socio-economic evolution could best be explained by understanding the coupling that he felt existed between the micro forces generated by individualistic enterprise and communal macro forces. In particular at the micro level he introduced the idea of a leading, free-enterprise, industrial sector. Successive explosive waves of growth at this level would drive society forward into successively higher states of socio-economic well being. In Rostow's conception, one can find the genesis of this work. The forces we now seek to understand are those at work in the post-modern twenty-first century. In this context we feel that socio-economic evolution is a more appropriate concept than development. It captures for our analytical interest the increasingly pervasive paradigm of evolution as it is envisaged in the new science of complexity.

From this latter perspective the micro individualistic driving forces are now in the knowledge industries, the leading sector of the new age. An intangible, knowledge, not a tangible, capital, is in our view the resource of pivotal interest. As an intangible it is notoriously difficult to assert individual ownership over. Our focus is to understand the forces and processes that are evolving to release and constrain its power in the communal, increasingly global, interest. The knowledge industry, we therefore hypothesize, is the leading sector of an emergent trans-national business system. We will call this the 'emergent global business system'. In this, we also reflect Rugman's point that it has as yet not matured to an extent sufficient to call it the 'global business system'.

Increasingly, enterprise sees its core capability as rooted in knowledge, particularly of the knowing (how) type. Knowledge is now fundamental to any resource-focused business strategy. The networks of enterprise now spanning the globe more and more seem to see their viability in terms of knowing how to create, manage, exploit and sustain the knowledge that pervasively underpins all their activities. Communal capital is needed to support this and this social capital is the kernel of a social revolution. Some see this as a renaissance of the concept of community, not just a revolution in the nature of enterprise, and as possibly impacting all aspects of human existence – physical, intellectual and spiritual.

This book explores the role knowledge plays in igniting, sustaining and modulating the explosive, and we believe highly significant, evolutionary changes now occurring. Our wish is to develop understanding of the institutional processes that are coming into being to empower enterprise to produce and use knowledge to best effect.

However the emergent activity we describe must be set within its wider evolutionary context. This process, like evolution itself, is not best characterized as 'red in tooth and claw' – and so, inferentially, to be feared and likely to guarantee the destruction of our humanity. It could equally be seen as an impartial process that could deliver a new age in which mankind could prosper and find fulfilment. Either end game may be possible.

Evolutionary analysis never predicts a particular outcome, it merely seeks to produce results capable of developing our understanding of an eternally unfolding process. We take the optimistic view that such a process can best be seen as being driven by benign forces that will seek to find an accommodation with each other, not mutual destruction. Irrespective of one's view on this, it seems that if intent lies behind the process we are currently witnessing is it not more credibly benign than malign: after all, it has brought us here to contemplate it?

We will argue that enterprise, like nature, generally tends to take the co-operative route. It is of the essence of knowledge and the knowledge industries supporting it that it is at core an enabler of successful co-operative enterprise. The dynamic of the process we will describe is such that it automatically channels energy to support the growth of the global intellectual connectivity that is now fuelling the emergent global business system.

Fortunately in developing our understanding of the processes leading to this new business system, we have existing ones as benchmarks. They provide useful analogues. In a work such as this they are inevitably our starting point. It is from within them that the new system is unfolding. They are also a legacy with which it must deal. While new emergent properties will be revealed in this unfolding, it has to encompass that which already exists.

It is not surprising that enterprises considering, or actually exploiting, the opportunities of emergent environments generally deal with their investment uncertainties in one of three ways:

(1) By being overly optimistic, as in the dot.com bubble
(2) By treating it as Russian roulette offering huge pay-offs (but this is a game which only a fool or a desperate man would play)
(3) By making a token minimalist investment, if a global presence is seen as essential.

None of these is well advised although a well-considered version of (3) could be constructed to make sense. It is therefore worthwhile, if not imperative for their future survival, for enterprise managers to take the time to better understand 'emerging markets'. This book may provide useful assistance in embarking on such thought.

Emerging markets, as venture capitalists know well, offer real opportunities for huge added value. The game of emergent evolution need not be as risky as it might at first seem. This can be so provided one understands the nature of the game. We would argue that with thought and care the huge potential of these markets can be tapped to generate significant commercial advantage with a vanishingly small downside. As we shall see, some enterprises have already got this message.

## Emerging markets

In this work, the idea of 'emerging markets' arises at three levels:

(1) That leading to socio-economic development and the entry of traditional nation states into the traditional international economy
(2) That leading to the creation of new markets by new industries
(3) That leading to the creation of an emergent global business system.

Emerging markets are a key focus of interest for investors and existing international enterprises. They are exciting. They promise opportunities for phenomenal growth. They have a fast expanding market of potential customers. Until recently many have been rejected as being too poor to buy. However if they could be rich enough to cover the cost of supplying them, the business potential they proffer is massive. As we shall see, this could come to be the case. The products and services on which we repeatedly focus in this book may have significant fixed start-up costs but have vanishingly small marginal costs.

Therefore notwithstanding the poverty of this potential customer base, the size of the market and its need and greed for the new products of the knowledge age is such that the business opportunity it presents cannot, will not be and is not being, ignored by enterprise.

## Institutions

In emerging markets the nature of society, business exchange, legal systems, consumer demand and public policy are all very different from those in mature systems. They present a challenge for governance of them and enterprise within them.[7]

The 1990s saw an acceleration of a fundamental transformation of the global competitive space facing enterprise. Increasingly enterprise operates ignoring traditional geo-political boundaries. Enterprise is now increasingly dependent on operations outwith the protection, oversight, or reach, of existing states.[8] We are moving from an international to at least a trans-national context : we would argue a global one, which transcends the traditional competence of states.[9] And we see this transformation as inevitably changing the sources of advantage for enterprise.[10]

Advances in technology have led to significant changes in industrial structure as a result of increasing global outsourcing. This has been particular strong in infrastructure services such as distribution, finance, knowledge technology and communications. These are the areas setting the pace for the explosive growth of the emergent global system. Knowledge and information are now the resources to manage, establish, sustain and exploit. This is true for both institutions and enterprise.

Because of the significance of emerging markets to globalizing business, we wish to add the emerging market business system to the mature ones traditionally referred to. We would hypothesize that the processes of this system were the point of origin of the dynamic of all existing, and so successful, business systems. The specific outcome may vary from context to context but the essential features of the processes of birth and emergence are, we would maintain, themselves constant.

## The new triad of business systems

To position ourselves in the socio-economic context we need to span the full spectrum of possibilities. We argue that this is best done by having a range of conceivable outcomes which at one end is a system based on individualistic self-interest and at the other guided by communal interest. This then gives us three limiting cases of business systems – each a straw man but together enabling us identify the space populated by actual systems:

(1) The *individualistic system*, driven primarily by the interests of one type of stakeholder, the owner/shareholder; this could be said to be close to what exists in the US or UK and therefore is close to what the traditional triad approach calls the Anglo-Saxon system
(2) The *communal system*, attending to the interests of a small insider group of key communally linked stakeholders; in terms of the traditional triad, this is close to both the Far Eastern familial and the continental European communitarian system
(3) The *emerging market system*, attending to the interests of all interested parties but with each facing considerable uncertainty as to their current or prospective propriety in any value created.

The fourth category which earlier we referred to as the 'heritage' system is embedded in legacy systems which hardly allow it to engage in active international trade. The heritage system figures only because of its ability to be exploited for its extractive industrial capacity and any market it offers for inward sales. It is not, in those terms, a business system. Countries or areas within countries which fall within this category cover a huge proportion of the world's population. This group has little cognizance of globalization; Prahalad has also recently written on the huge potential such 'heritage' markets hold out for enterprise in the future (Prahalad 2002).

While bearing in mind the existence of this fourth segment, we shall for most of this work use our three reference business systems to provide co-ordinates for any specific system we wish to refer to. With these three as reference points, we intend to examine from a systems viewpoint the context and drivers for business operating trans-nationally in today's environment (Figure 1.1).

Thus in Figure 1.1 we can triangulate to characterize a specific system. We have an origin set within the dynamic of emerging systems and a scale running from the extremes set by two demonstrably successful systems from the old international business environment. They are the Anglo-Saxon, in which individuals impersonally pursue their own interest

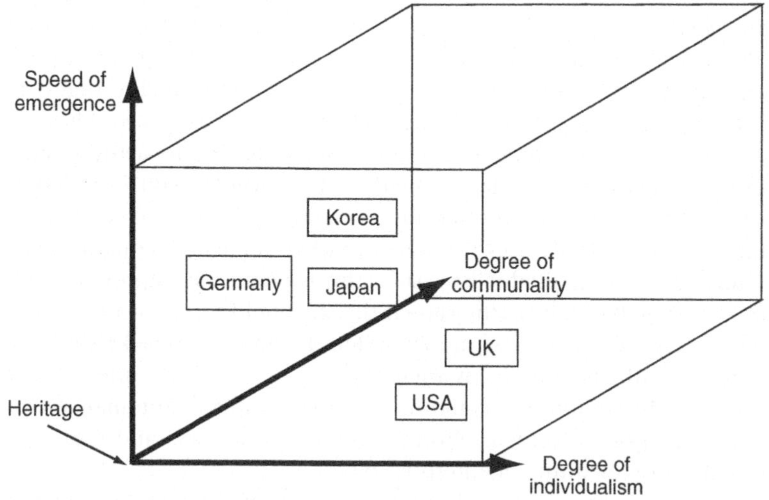


*Figure 1.1* Our conceptual space of business systems

and are drawn by Adam Smith's 'invisible hand' to serve the common good, and the Communitarian/Familial, in which the individual's role is as a self-conscious member of a community to which they have a duty of service in the common interest. In the latter system, transactors operate within a framework of guidance set by the community's most powerful stakeholders to produce a result all consider largely in the common interest. This should ensure the welfare of all. We do not suggest that any one of the above represents reality in any particular state or region. They merely provide a means to build a model enabling one to obtain a better perspective on the processes which are at work.

## Core competence

A key aspect of modern business strategy focuses on how to exploit any unique resource advantage to the full. This is seen as especially the case when others are unable to copy or complete it away with existing capacity. Generally, this is designated 'core competence'. The usual caveat is that it will still be possible to make this technically redundant by innovating such an advantage away. However, if core competence is seen as rooted in a capacity to generate knowing in a particular narrow area of competence, such an advantage may be sustainable. If one can identify, focus on and exploit that capacity for knowing one can produce a sustainable economic return – provided the enterprise supporting it adopts an *adaptive learning strategy* designed to sustain it in the face of change. This would be aimed at constant improvement and the identification of, and the exploitation of, every niche application related to that core competence. Such a strategy benefits all an enterprise's stakeholders.

The pressures on modern executive management to achieve such focus are significant. As management has to concentrate only on that in which it has experience it offers huge economies of managerial effort in time and skill. It also provides an incentive for risk-attenuating outsourcing. In the individualist system this is because it improves shareholder value by limiting the capital the shareholders put at risk in any one enterprise. In the communal system it can also spread risk if the state or banks do not focus their support too narrowly and instead extend it throughout the community. However in a communal system the temptation is to focus effort in too narrow an area and create an unstable mono-culture of enterprise types.

As has been argued, knowledge in the sense of 'knowing' is now the core competence to be managed and financed. A difficulty in this is that knowledge of all types has all the attributes of what economists call a 'public good'. It is expensive to produce. Huge resources are expended on its creation (invention) and exploitation (innovation). Once created, no matter how many people use it there will be no less available for others. The fact that I have read the book of instructions, listened to a radio or watched a television programme does not detract in the slightest from other individuals' capacity to do the same thing. A further challenge is that knowledge is very difficult over which to exert property rights. In its tacit form it is very difficult (even impossible) to define and measure, and therefore to sell or manage the benefit/value of what is provided. In its explicit form, books, ideas, records, videos, articles are so easily and cheaply reproducible that it is virtually impossible, once knowledge is released into society, to prevent its onward exploitation by whomsoever wishes to access it.

Counterfeiting and pirating are some of the fastest-growing activities on the Internet. Counters to them can be devised; however, they tend not to be in terms of the traditional institutions used for asserting propriety, copyright, patents, etc.

If knowledge is a public good one might think that a communitarian social approach to its invention, innovation and exploitation would be entirely appropriate, but the evidence seems to that this is not the case.

Individualistic systems have an impressive history of 'blue skies' creativity, invention and resilience in the face of extreme adversity. This has not been surpassed by others despite strenuous efforts. However, the individualist system has been notoriously bad at innovating to exploit to the full the technical niches it generates.

Communal systems, on the other hand, have shown an outstanding capacity to identify and exploit to commercial advantage every imaginable niche application of an idea. These systems have a phenomenal capacity to absorb existing knowledge, and a similar ability to exploit the 'knowing' (know how) contained within their enterprises' boundaries.

Of course enterprises with high absorptive capacities exist in the current economies which are closest to the Anglo-Saxon system, as do highly creative enterprises in those closest to the Communitarian. Our view is that there is none the less sufficient evidence to support the view expressed on the relative strengths of each to make this a caricature of reality useful to analysis. This underwrites the value we have placed on them as analytical tools delineating a range of possible end states for socio-economic evolution. One provides a rationale for the pursuit of individual self-interest in some contexts the other suggests a more social approach is appropriate in others.

## A route map through the book

From the foregoing, it is clear that we must consider a number of questions.

First, we have to clarify our framework, by setting out more precisely how our three business systems are constituted, and in particular how they differ. Key concepts here are the social and political embeddedness of institutions and enterprises. Such embeddedness bounds what is possible in business systems evolution.[11] This is the task of Part I (Chapters 2–5). We start in Chapter 2 by examining the forces that are likely to be at work if one has the variety of equally successful systems as observed in the real world. We then explore the role that the community as opposed to individual enterprise plays in effecting the observed difference in structure and success (Chapter 3). Chapter 4 builds a model of how synergy arises from the interaction between organizations and institutions, specifically those pertaining to enterprises, society, education (knowledge construction) and the state. Finally in Chapter 5 we explore how the evolution of the various elements of such a system can lead to the explosive growth that produces emergent phenomena such as the knowledge industries or a global business system.

In Part II, we consider the differing patterns of corporate governance and financing that have evolved to effect command and control over socio-economic activities. Each business system uses different institutions to hold its constituent enterprises to account. Each has therefore evolved a distinct culture of operations. These affect how stakeholders choose to use and distribute the resources allocated to them. This has significant implications for exchange in global networks. Each enterprise in such a network will be embedded in a different socio-political system. The consequence of this is explored in Chapter 6.

The next issue looked at is the role knowledge, as a resource and a product, plays in the process of emergence. To do this we need first to understand its mercurial properties as an intangible resource, especially in the form of 'knowing'. This is what stakeholders gain as a result of their input of intellect, education and experience of working together. Knowledge, especially in this form, is very difficult to specify, measure, manage and control, whether by Anglo-Saxon market disciplines or by the communitarian hierarchical social disciplines' system. This is covered in Chapter 7–10. In Chapter 7 we look at the problem of dealing with knowledge as a product in exchange and in such a context at the significance of both buyer and seller having a trusted identity. However in emergent contexts much is often so uncertain and obscure that the identity of the parties to a transaction is essentially unknowable, and in such circumstances a process has to emerge to enable the transaction. This we call 'dynamic identity', and it forms the focus of Chapter 8. However, even with such an identity significant problems still remain. If the parties to a transaction exist in distinct socio-cultural contexts one has to expect reliable communication to be hard and so potentially prohibitively expensive, as discussed in Chapter 9. One then has to find ways of bridging the gap in comprehension that must exist if the future world is to remain as culturally diverse as we predict it needs to be. This is essential if we want to access the huge longer-term pay-offs, in terms of robustness and insight, that come from being able to see things from a number of distinct perspectives and sustain one's operations in dispersed, socio-economically distinct contexts, as outlined in Chapter 10.

In Part III, we explore the significance of the differences between our defining cases. This is important for a number of reasons. First, if these systems are so very different then the means they use to develop understanding, and to communicate within themselves, are likely to be very different. In the case of knowledge, these differences will be crucial to the capacity of the systems to transmit mutually useful understanding across the resulting communication gap. Second, globalization is already leading to the creation of cross-cultural strategic networks of people and enterprises. These are potentially difficult to maintain if their constituent elements are in very different cultural milieux. This is the problem of 'psychic distance'.[12] We suggest that it can be overcome through a dual approach. First, the solution needs to permit the exchange of the key product on which we are focused, knowledge. Second, it needs to make possible the social cohesiveness required to sustain a strategic network. This is the topic of Chapter 11.

In Chapter 12 we come to the core of our work: the role global networks play in creating, using and exploiting knowledge. This is the biggest challenge of all, even though using naïve rationality it seems the easiest to solve. On human grounds, it is the most difficult to affect. For a network to work well, those within it must trust each other. A common culture and relationships would seem to help in this. On the other hand, diversity is powerfully robust against unforeseen change in operating environments.

If the latter is so then the system needs to encourage and sustain, rather than eliminate, diversity. If this is the requirement then people need an inducement to work together to mutual advantage despite their differences. To achieve this the members of such a value adding network need to be co-ordinated globally while being supported to remain in their own particular context while adding value for themselves and the whole. This requires an efficient global supportive communications infrastructure that drives human contact – social, professional and entrepreneurial – and this will be beyond the practical oversight of any existing state.

This creates a dilemma for governance in the emerging system.[13] In the past business systems have always been politically embedded in the structure of a state. The communication infrastructure has in the past been a key feature of national sovereignty and the public mission generally. Until very recently, the institutional environment so created was one of clear values and high legitimacy, reflected in the state-protected monopolies enjoyed by national telecommunications carriers and broadcasters. Such monopolies still exist. National security, social convenience and economic utility have been identified as the legitimizing foundations of state monopolies of telecommunications. These have now been broken in many instances by satellite communications, the realities of the Internet, etc., where a regime now exists which by definition thrusts itself beyond the geo-political boundaries of nation states.

The *ancien régime* is now called into question by new technology that has led to the spate of recent privatizations of the communication sector and the opening of previously entry-restrictive markets. Convergence within such an emergent infrastructure as the Internet is causing a crisis for national sovereignty and the governance of a style of enterprise that goes beyond the possibility of traditional approaches to social or political regulation. This new world has thus to be navigated in new ways in what at first sight might be seen as an institutional vacuum.

As an example of one aspect of this, consider the division of accountability previously made in national postal services between carriage and content. The former was the accountable responsibility of the postal service and the latter of the user. This may no longer be tenable. Internet service providers are increasingly being held responsible for the offensive materials users post on their systems – especially that emanating from that fast growing part of the network, pornography.

While the global community is not happy about this, there are considerable concerns about any constraints to the liberty of the system that society may attempt to impose. In fact, the genie is out of the bottle and it is absolutely clear that it is extremely difficult technically to restrict access in the interest of some greater local cultural social view of good. The consequence is some concern about the security of the system, a reluctance by all to get locked into unproven restricting technologies and an urgent need to find a mechanism to provide reliable guidance through the huge offerings of content now available. At the same time, national means of control are challenged by the inherently trans-national nature of multimedia delivery channels.[14]

Throughout the book we develop ideas intended to indicate how business can rise to the challenge that all this represents. Our thoughts on how governance and command and control can be effected in the global networks resulting from all this form the basis of Chapter 13.

Only time will tell whether our analysis provides the right means to interpret events in the emerging global community, but it is clear that institutional change will take place and new institutional forms emerge in consequence. The new technologies will succeed and industries and markets will emerge and mature. In the process much that is new will be created and both old and new will either learn to adapt or be destroyed. Further thought on the nature of emergence forms the focus of our analysis in Chapter 14.

# Part I

# Foundations

# 2

# The Seeds of Business System Diversity in Knowledge and Governance

## Introduction

Internationally, the structure and conduct of enterprises and social institutions varies. Associated performance varies less. This could be seen as unfortunate. Practical people, in both government and business, would like to use the form and behaviour of enterprises as a guide to best practice in their design and operation.

How can such uninformative variation exist if the international economy is truly global? We are told that global competitiveness forces states and enterprises to conform to a unique optimal norm. In practice, the norm is diversity. Distinct national contexts support different styles of enterprise. There appears to be no particular golden route to success that statesmen, institutional bureaucrats or enterprise managers can aspire to. Some might react to this by dismissing the whole idea of globalization as unhelpful. We do not. Emergent globalization is the new reality. We believe that globalization sustains and encourages such differences and that diversity benefits the emergent global system.

## Co-evolution

It is trivial to observe that different countries provide distinct contexts. This is the crucial point of studying business in an international context and it is useful to see states as providing distinct contexts, 'business systems', pertinent to the performance of enterprises operating within and across their borders. However such business systems do not suddenly appear perfectly formed, nor stay immutable. Each emerges over time and then evolves to accommodate the changing needs of states and enterprise.

Knowledge of the specific political and social context of enterprises and their people is vital to those seeking to understand what they can achieve in a particular context and in what timescales.[1] Too often, the social context is taken as constant and given. This is unhelpful. Context and enterprise evolve together. Both can be actively nurtured, though not controlled, to follow mutually advantageous paths.

Here we describe the mechanism at work, generating the observed diversity of form and behaviour. This mechanism is at work even in a globalizing highly competitive economy. We argue such diversity is crucial to the continued vitality of the globalizing system, that it is indicative of its health and robustness and that it should be seen as its strength not its weakness.

Each business system evolves distinct means for co-ordinating activity. In each a set of institutions emerges. These provide the cohesive forces required to enable enterprises to come together to form systems of commerce and exchange. They do so in those competitive, but paradoxically mutually supportive groups, we call industries. Ideally industries exist in a coherent, supportive social context. The institutional forces that make this possible emerge to accommodate the needs of both enterprise and society. Both need enterprise to operate in a regulated and controlled environment. This environment constrains and directs the forces generated by enterprise. The nature of this containing and constraining control determines what styles of enterprise can co-evolve. Particularly it determines how appropriate governance may be exercised over an enterprise's operations. The result is international diversity.

Understanding the roots of this diversity is essential for those wishing to play a role in social evolution, whether as observer, politician, bureaucrat or businessman. It is best understood by studying the processes by which institutions evolve. Institutions, including those of enterprise, have to learn to adapt or fail. If an enterprise stays constant in its responses to its environment it will eventually fail and make way for newly created enterprises with more appropriate current responses.

All the players in this game seek a viable route to survival for their own and their institutional contexts. Survival requires working unendingly to accommodate the changing behaviour of others. Enterprises learn when and how to accommodate the change in their constantly shifting institutional environment or die.

Thus we argue that institutions and enterprises do not simply adapt or evolve, they co-adapt and co-evolve. All those with influence in the process who wish to survive have to understand that the process is one of continuous adjustment. And this process is not one which terminates with the solution to any problem posed or the establishment of a stable end state but is one consisting of continually evolving compatibility with others. For this reason, it is unhelpful to see the process as driven just by aspirations to sustainable dominance. If an enterprise ever presumes it has achieved such dominance and settles down to sustaining this, it will quickly find itself untenable in the face of the continually unfolding forces of co-evolution.

## Embeddedness

Sociologists call the outcome of this co-evolutionary process 'social embeddedness'. And as we have argued, such embeddedness is not static, because society is not a static given: it is itself a variable. Its institutions adjust continuously to accommodate the viability and social acceptability of enterprise. Social embeddedness is rooted in the interactive knowledge base and behaviour of the individuals in an enterprise and society. The value of an enterprise thus depends on its people, their experience and their evolving context. The aggregate of these, set in context, determines an enterprise's response to change. Within each enterprise a unique enveloping context evolves, its culture.

Given its dependence on the unique history of each enterprise, this culture cannot be replicated. It may, or may not, create added value in its current context. Using the metaphor of humans, enterprises are like the humanity of which they are composed and so have evolved to be learning, creative, entities adaptive to all the circumstances they encounter. Then, while not always perfectly in tune with their context, they can aspire like humans to be sufficiently adaptable to ensure their viability in any context. The unique identity that history bestows on an enterprise is fundamental to the value it proffers. This is particularly so in the information age and the knowledge society it supports. The source of any piece of information or knowledge – i.e. the identity of its supplier – gives it the credence essential to its value. The credence of the supplier is as fundamental to value as is the ostensible direct usefulness of what is supplied. In the case of information or knowledge this sometimes can be the sole basis for its usefulness.

It is very evident to those in business that the process by which a supplier's identity is made evident is crucial. Unfortunately rational bureaucrats, though rarely politicians, sometime miss seeing the value wrapped up in this truth. Identity, and the processes leading to its substantiation, are as vital to worth as the cost factors which so often drive price. In many cases a product's worth may be determined solely by its supplier's identity, Gucci as compared to Lever–Fabergé, PricewaterhouseCoopers as compared to Andersens. Identity, and the reputation associated with it, do matter.

In the case of the currently evolving global community we see the process of creating and exploiting knowledge as providing energy. This is forming a newly emergent business system. Any adequate view of modern enterprise thus has to explain the role knowledge and information play in its evolution and we are therefore obliged to take a knowledge-based view of enterprise. This sees enterprise as a way of organising, disseminating and exploiting knowledge. To be viable in modern competitive environments enterprise needs information and knowledge, particularly knowledge of how ('knowing'). 'Knowing', however, derives from the unique historical experiences of the people an enterprise employs. It is thus closely associated with enterprise's identity as defined above.

However, when knowledge has been codified as information, it is notoriously difficult to exercise property rights over it. It will change when staff leave, it is so deeply embedded in the culture of the enterprise it cannot be replicated elsewhere and it may be created out of relationships with other enterprises. Thus the embeddedness of enterprises should not be expected to wither away in the new global environment; rather, insofar as this is accompanied by and founded on the role of the knowledge-based enterprise, the embeddedness should be expected to increase.

For policy, both national and corporate, however, this presents problems. Who owns and controls the knowledge which is at the heart of this embeddedness? If propriety cannot be exercised over it, then it is hard to see how it can be acquired from those who 'possess' it (i.e. can demonstrate that they have it). In particular, if it is of the tacit, 'knowing', type trade will probably seem impossible. Yet managers in enterprises and those with wider social authority may wish to invest in acquiring and exploiting it. It is an undoubted source of individual and social value. How can there be a business case for its creation and deployment if it cannot be owned?

## The dilemma of knowledge as a product and a resource

Traditional business models do not provide the insight necessary to understand the processes generating and distributing information and knowledge. In the modern Internet-connected world much knowledge is created in activities that transcend the boundaries of either enterprises or states. In consequence traditional institutions (e.g. national contract, or copyright, laws) cannot protect a stakeholder's investment in it. Without a definable product over which to exercise ownership, nor law capable of enforcing propriety, any investment in knowledge would seem to be too risky. Without the incentive of enforceable propriety one would expect minimal investment in knowledge processing and distribution. The reverse is observable. Vast investment is going on in the asset base that the information and knowledge based industries makes possible. This can be so only if investors credibly believe that the returns from such activity will be realized. How can they come to this conclusion if, as described, these products are difficult, if not impossible, to exercise propriety over? It is this conundrum that underlies one strand of this work.

For such investment to be worthwhile, successful effort must be being put into ensuring that investment in knowledge adds realizable value. In the absence of enforceable propriety, this seems difficult to achieve using the market. As the reader progresses through this book, we hope to provide a credible explanation of how this is possible.

In the meantime we observe that the global communication infrastructure for people, goods, services and ideas now ensures that no natural geo-political boundaries exist to the processes of creating, disseminating and using information and exploiting knowledge in the global economy. This is a challenge for those responsible for:

(1) The proper governance of enterprises
(2) States, in setting up the institutions to support the needs of enterprise in the knowledge and information industries
(3) Other stakeholders contemplating taking a stake in the activities of an enterprise.

Knowledge and information as products have particular difficulties given the 'public goods' nature of what they provide. It is very difficult indeed to conceive of how effective propriety can be established in them. Their public goods nature ensures it is difficult to supply them through the market. The logic would seem to suggest that they be supplied communally. In the global system there is as yet no obvious means to achieve this. Those wishing to be involved have to operate beyond the regulatory authority of any existing nation state or individual enterprise. This book is thus in part about how governance might still then be effected.

As we have observed, the nation state cannot provide the necessary context. As yet no global government exists. However, enterprise is clearly thriving in the global context. How? In the information age necessary propriety is clearly exercised. How? This 'how' question must be answered if we wish to understand how the emergent global business system is working and will continue to work in future. Every day, second by second, huge value in terms of information and knowledge is transferred around the globe. This goes on outwith the purview of existing government. If international business is distinct from other business and states are irrelevant[2] then what is international business? We feel that leaders within it must see it as global not international business.

In a globalizing world effective governance has to be exercised transnationally. This is especially so for the intellectual property that information and knowledge represents. It clearly can be and is. How this is possible, and how such governance is to evolve as current trends continue and intensify, is a principal focus of this work. But from the arguments put forward so far, proper governance cannot function in this area. To see how it might we need to explore two issues so that we can more clearly identify signs of the emergence of a new paradigm. We therefore look at:

(1) The basis by which effective governance can be exercised
(2) The particular significance of information and knowledge as products.

The value of knowledge is embedded in enterprises and through their stakeholders in society. In a globalizing world the growth of new institutions of governance and the creation, dissemination and use of knowledge are recursively inter-linked in a co-evolutionary process. The first enables the second, and the second provides a reason for the first. Each is a necessary but not sufficient condition for the other.

## Knowledge and governance in a globalizing world

### Knowledge

Knowledge has to be created, made available, effectively distributed and used for global connectivity it sustains to release the energy needed to drive the global economy.[3] Clearly, such energy is already being explosively released. However, the process of doing so seems to remain relatively well ordered despite the fact that we and others[4] suggest it is ripping asunder traditional geo-political boundaries. The paradox is that in doing this it generates a huge need for structural change in the political, economic and institutional overhead of the global society.

There are clearly forces at work here which are successfully replacing the cohesion provided within the old geo-political boundaries they are now destroying. The value being created using the information and knowledge on the existing global web of connectivity is so large it cannot be ignored. We would predict that this connectivity will accelerate even more over the coming decades. This leads to a need to reassess the framework within which international business is conducted. Traditionally states and enterprises approached strategy by viewing international business effectiveness as similar to, but reaching beyond, effectiveness on the national stage. They now have to see things in global terms and in particular in the context of global system development; they cannot control things in their traditional ways and cannot interpret what is going on using traditional inherited concepts. While much has be written with the globalization label attached to it, not so much has been said about the dynamic forces creating globalization.[5] These are evolutionary in nature and need to be seen as such. One will not be able to extrapolate on a phenomenon-by-phenomenon basis into the future, so it becomes critical to look at the complex of co-evolving phenomena.

To develop the understanding necessary to cope with this transformation, we need a new synthesis that includes the role socio-political organisations and institutions play in providing support systems for enterprise – especially if the information and knowledge industries are to flourish. The questions this synthesis allows us to address effectively are:

- How are the required new institutions for this global order to be created?
- How can institutions help enterprises thrive?
- What destroys them?

Some[6] thinkers have taken a step in this direction. They have analysed the importance to international business of an enterprise's domestic environment. However as we noted before, most treat the socio-political context as a given and a constant. It is then placed at one remove from the dynamics of working markets. This distancing is now too difficult to defend.

If one wishes to understand an emerging environment such as that of the knowledge industry, one has to understand the process by which this socio-political context changes in relation to enterprise. Our viewpoint, of seeing the socio-political institutional environment as co-evolving with the enterprises it supports, leads us to take the idea of 'embeddedness' further. A traditional nation's effective governance systems, and its associated inter-national competitiveness[7] are dependent on its polities' and societies' capacity to evolve useful institutions. These have to be the guardians of their communal interest in the value-creation process that enterprise provides. These efforts set boundaries to what is acceptable behaviour for individuals and enterprise. In stating this we merely extend the works of others[8] who have shown the evolutionary significance of the interaction of the interest of society and the polity in creating an atmosphere conducive to enterprise.

## Governance

Events since 1980, generated by the force of the information revolution, have stimulated much new thought on the processes by which effective governance[9], control, regulation and direction can be given to enterprise. Global forces have created a new competitive environment for enterprise; in this emerging system the leaders in any national business system have to provide a supportive context for their domestic enterprise that can sustain its trans-national viability.

They, the political and institutional leaders, have to help this happen at a time when the traditional boundaries of the state have been blown asunder by the emergence of a global system of enterprise. This makes it extremely difficult for any national institution to police its domestic market. This is before we even think of policing the global one. There would appear to be a need for support to be given to the evolution of new global institutions. These would enshrine the guardianship enterprise always requires to operate effectively. This protects an enterprise's interest in the resources it requires to operate and/or deliver to others, which as we have seen is particularly difficult in the case of knowledge, either as a resource or product. The role of such global institutions is to create a process to establish and sustain propriety over it. This raises the issue of how to pursue 'national competitiveness' and we find a need to consider three perspectives traditionally perceived – particularly for tangible rather than intangible products – when pursuing this:

(1) That of the enterprise itself
(2) That of the industry that it is a part of
(3) That of the political context both of these inhabit.[10]

We thus need to examine things from an enterprise, a socio-industrial and a political perspective. The challenge that now arises is that enterprise rarely sits within the framework provided by any one state or industry.

And as we have suggested, this is especially so for the knowledge industry. The frontiers that provide the socio-industrial context normally seen as providing the framework within which an industry has to operate are not easily evident.

If we are to understand the processes that are now driving the socio-economic wellbeing of the planet we need to be able to see things globally and relate them to all three of the above perspectives. For each, we need to understand cause and effect at the global level. It is through understanding these that decision-makers can see how the co-evolutionary processes that drive the joint development of institutions and enterprises operate, and so assist the process. One therefore has to compare the impact on enterprise of different approaches to exerting ownership – *propriety* – and then the rights of ownership – *governance*.

Because this is especially important, and most difficult to achieve, with information and knowledge and because the exploitation of these resources by enterprise is the key to better performance in the now emergent global business system, particular attention is due to the problem in this context. We hypothesize that the process by which different approaches may emerge and then evolve derives from the experience of all stakeholders. It is therefore important that the leadership within enterprise engages them all.

In all instances, what powers an enterprise must be sufficient to sustain the viability of itself and the system on which it depends. The institutional framework that needs to be constructed to achieve this has to be consistent with individual and communal interest.

We intend to provide a partial solution to all this by proposing a shift in perspective. We wish to suggest a new schema for categorizing the institutional context a business system needs for enterprise to operate. To do this requires us to consider governance from a comparative point of view. We will consider ways we might do this here, and in Chapter 3 will start constructing a model of the process that we can use subsequently to think about where society and enterprise needs to go in this emerging global world.

## Comparative corporate governance

In management research the systems and institutions of corporate governance have attracted much recent attention. Corporate governance has been defined as 'the relationship among a firm's shareholders, its board of directors, and its senior managers' (Roe 1994, 1). Since different societies adopt their own unique approach to corporate governance a new, society-neutral basis for comparing business systems is necessary. Any study of business systems needs to take governance into account in terms of the broader social, cultural and political pressures that bring a particular approach into being. The institutional framework for a particular system lies at the heart of the relationship between business and government.[11] Comparative governance pays due respect to the importance of distinct social and political institutions for each national business system's capacity to achieve satisfactory corporate governance.[12]

Much work on comparative governance sees things from a stockholder's perspective,[13] e.g. it compares stocks traded as commodities by impersonal professional dealers with stocks traded by groups of insiders with shared knowledge peculiar to themselves unbeknown to the wider public. The former is typical of the stock markets of the US and the UK. The latter is consistent with the communitarian and communal tradition of cross-shareholding, by banks or other financial conglomerates, typical in Germany and Japan. The former sets out to operate on the basis of common, public knowledge. The latter works on the basis of the asymmetric information held by their principal stockholders, the government and company officials. Fundamental to the former are impersonal legal contracts based on clarity about propriety and ownership. This is intended to provide equitable protection to a widely dispersed body of stockholders.[14] In contrast in communitarian/communal systems equity is most often owned by a few major financial institutions. Governance is exercised on the basis of informal, relationship-based exchanges of information and understandings. This approach is typical of many continental European and Far Eastern countries.[15]

The contrast between these two categories is reflected in their polities.[16] In the US and UK, the legislature represents the myriad interests of individual citizens and wields power at arm's length from the executive. In Europe and the Far East, legislatures are often weak, allowing the executive to be strong in pursuing national interest.

Each of these must be seen on its own terms. The Anglo-Saxon, individualist, shareholder-focused approach of the US has been, and continues to be, relatively successful into the twenty-first century;[17] however for much of the twentieth century the communal systems in Japan and Germany seemed to perform better. The near-simultaneous success of these different systems raises important issues for the study of comparative governance. It also brings us back to the question of how diversity can be viable in a globalizing world. An answer in this area could perhaps provide a clue to identifying the most effective approach for newly evolving systems.

Should the newly evolving system emulate that driven by the short-term dynamics of efficient stock markets, with equitably distributed, if not perfect, information? Should it look to the apparently stable dynamics of bank-financed systems where decisions are made on the basis of detailed personal knowledge of the business and its key players? The replacement of the German and Japanese successes of the 1980s and early 1990s by slow growth or even decline in the early twenty-first century, and the resilient renewed energy for growth in the US and the UK in the later 1990s[18] has ensured that the debate on the relative merits of these two systems has not closed.

In what follows we have two major immediate objectives:

(1) The first is to use the above thinking to compare and contrast the differing approaches to governance existing in national business systems. We will do this using the idea of 'political embeddedness'[19] and the issues raised by it for understanding the co-evolution of institutions and enterprises.[20] We seek to extend to comparative business systems the earlier work[21] which has shed light on the importance of the socio-political and environmental dimensions. It is simple enough to develop a means to categorize countries in the way we suggest. The approach proposed permits the clarification of ideas from these two systems which are most useful in understanding the evolution of emerging or transforming economies.

(2) The second is to understand how it is possible for distinct systems to appear to achieve success at similar times. Many of the emerging economies of the world, especially in Asia and Eastern Europe, are developing and refining the nature of the governance system they use.[22] The Asian economic and business crisis that began in 1997 has not had a large spillover to the West. What, then, is the relationship between performance (growth), conduct (reaction to change) and structure (approach to governance) in distinct but interacting business systems? How have these various factors evolved in particular socio-political contexts?

The above are all important issues for the leadership of enterprises and society to address, and to assist them in doing so we next intend to analyse the broad social, economic and political trends that allows one to categorize countries' business systems. We wish to use this as a basis for considering the likely consequences of adopting a particular approach in a context or creating a new one.

# 3

# Enterprise and the State: Individualist versus Communal Interest

## Introduction

Precisely because there is no global state the role of the state is an issue in our current age of global emergence. As mentioned in Chapter 2, there has always been an intense debate on the role the state can play in encouraging enterprise and development, especially where it involves international business and sources of wealth beyond the bounds of the state itself. An issue for decision-makers here has always been[1] whether the state can or cannot be effective in supporting the international global competitiveness of its domestic enterprise.

Much evidence suggests that when states disengage, enterprise succeeds – see the US in the twentieth century and the UK in the nineteenth. If this is so, the absence of a global state may well be irrelevant to enterprise. However, the twentieth century also shows examples where the state did play a major role: Japan and South Korea, or Central and Eastern Europe.

Given previous arguments, one should not be surprised that differing institutional approaches produce equally impressive results. However many argue that global competitiveness strips away government's capacity to enhance the competitiveness of its domestic enterprises relative to others.[2]

Empirical evidence suggests that states do have an impact on business success and competitiveness – the impact can be negative (e.g. the socialist experiment in Central and Eastern Europe), or positive (the current high growth of South Korea). We suggest that the presumption of some impact is the basis for studying business in an international context in a manner distinct from in a national one.

Clarifying the distinction between international business as it was, and how we wish to develop it, we observe that international business focuses on enterprise operating across national borders, and the impact of the regulatory policies of national governments and social institutions. If one argued that the national context of enterprise was irrelevant, one would eliminate the international component of international business.[3] Some of the factors transforming the global market are directly influenced by the prescriptions of governments – e.g. the deregulation of economic and business activity, the reduction or elimination of protectionism and treaties creating trading blocs. A key issue here must be how far should such interventions go, and how effective can they be.

## The issues

According to Stopford and Strange (1993), the competing forces in the global political economy operate in three ways:

(1) Governments compete for their nation's share of global value
(2) Domestically there is competition between a state and the enterprise within it
(3) Global networks of enterprises compete with one another.

At the government level there has been a shift from international competitiveness to international co-operation. This has resulted in a spate of bilateral and multilateral treaties creating trading blocs (e.g. NAFTA, Mercosur). Their formation seems driven by a wish to maximize the returns from intergovernment activity. This leads to the creation of trans-national institutions (e.g. the European Commission, or OPEC). In some cases this is seen by some as leading to the evolution of supranational government (e.g. the European Union). A consequence is that such co-operation erodes the autonomy of the nation state to act purely in the interest of its domestic enterprise.

The nature of the second interaction is changing fast and qualitatively. Until the late 1970s, multinationals were ideologically seen as capitalistic predators maximizing their own gain at the expense of nations and peoples. There has been a clear shift in attitude since, multinationals are now considered vital to domestic development that can promote internal industrial growth and exports. The phenomenal state-supported growth of the Southeast Asian economies and, within their ambit, the role played by multinationals, both domestic and foreign, has been crucial.

The third set of interactions is now proving the most exciting. Network companies in the information and knowledge industries are driving the huge energy-releasing change that provides the power driving the dynamics of the new global society. This, above all else, is undermining the power of the nation state and the larger enterprises.

While global reach is crucial for enterprise, it is not necessarily being achieved only by large monolithic enterprises. It is often being achieved by large networks of small to medium-sized enterprises (SMEs), perhaps orchestrated by a global brand leader but not necessarily always hierarchically managed by it (e.g. Benetton, McDonald's, CocaCola). These brands do have a global presence, but it is achieved by outsourcing to networks of franchisees on the retail side and a myriad of small suppliers on the production and concept side.

Finally the emerging global political economy is clearly influenced by the interactions between all of the above whether co-operative or competitive. The outcome from each influences all others dependent on the balance of power between the actors, states or enterprises. The fundamental point is that any change in one interaction affects all others. At the moment it is fuelling explosive global growth that is blowing apart mankind's legacy of boundary-setting nations and enterprises.

Thinking on international business borrows heavily from that on international trade.[4] It tends to neglect thinking on development and growth. The debate about the role of the state lies at the heart of the development debate. Until the end of the twentieth century this was ideologically fired. At one extreme were the advocates of the 'minimalist' state; at the other were those advocating socialist state planning. This debate was predicated on the idea that markets always fail to provide the answers needed for enterprise to truly flourish.

Earlier thought argued that comprehensive state planning was needed. Experience demonstrated that this created as many problems as were solved by it, and has led to an expectation of state failure as a counterpoint to market failure. Many now see 'state failure' as an impediment to development. In addition, the practical collapse of the experiments in state socialism in Central and Eastern Europe undermined the practical credibility of a rational ideological basis for intervention. It also destroyed confidence in its efficacy, even if thought desirable. This has led to a re-birth of confidence in the free market now that the deficiencies of rational planning have become manifest. However, a move back from faith in the emergence of communal man through socialism should not necessarily be seen as a reason to revert to the view that rational individualist man necessarily can solve the problem – markets can fail as frequently as states. Our judgement is a need to abandon both these extreme models and rediscover what we will call 'evolutionary man in a self-conscious guise'.

Such criticism has to be balanced against the phenomenal economic growth (and subsequent collapse) experienced by those in East and Southeast Asia. Arguably much of this was achieved by massive state interventions. The South Korean economy was deliberately and systematically stimulated and cajoled by government. Selected firms were given substantial assistance leveraged by soft loans conditional on taking direction on their investment policy, especially for import substitution, and South Korea subsequently had impressive growth rates. It was a poor Japanese colony in 1946, ravaged by war in the 1950s and became a member of the OECD twenty-five years later.[5] Similarly, since the 1980s China has achieved rapid growth using a number of different planning policies though not aspiring to minimalist government.[6]

## World Bank

The World Bank has heavily influenced past views on the role of the state. Its initial focus was on the alleviation of poverty. This was to counter communism and its associated now defunct socialist experiment. The policy was based on the belief that state macroeconomic policy, the subsidization of the R&D required to establish a knowledge base and capital replacement as occurred in North America and Western Europe after the Second World War, could have a significant impact on the growth of wealth and its distribution. It was believed that a similar policy would help alleviate unemployment and poverty in the underdeveloped world, and so prevent future conflict. By the 1980s the consensus on this had ended and many Western industrialized countries had abandoned macroeconomy intervention.

This later period saw the emergence of successful radical neo-liberal governments committed to downsizing the state and cutting its role even in delivery whenever outsourcing to the private sector was a possibility. The World Bank followed this trend. Poverty alleviation was demoted and a structural adjustment policy (SAP) took its place. However, this change was difficult to reconcile with the miraculous industrialization being achieved in East Asia. The Bank tried to depict the East Asian experience as normal capitalist development. It clearly was not.

By 1993, a Japanese government-funded study had influenced thinking on this to such an extent that a major World Bank publication was eventually forced to concede that government intervention played a key part in East Asian economic success.[7] But even in this and later reports, the role of the state was still taken as only sometimes relevant. The state was never seen as central. It was not until *The World Development Report – 1997:The State in a Changing World* (World Bank 1997) that the Bank fully conceded a role for the state. This report premised that the state was not simply an important determinant of national economic welfare, but that 'its capability, defined as the ability to undertake and promote collective actions effectively, must be increased'. The Bank now accepts the state can assist enterprise and accelerate growth.

Thus the debate on development in the last twenty-five years saw first the entrenchment of the superiority of the market culture before an eventual recognition of the potential for the state to enhance a nation's socio-economic effectiveness. This throws up a range of options for the state's roles in the development of banks, capital markets and other institutions. The state's role in evolving, co-jointly with enterprise, the institutions bounding the behaviour of enterprise within its jurisdiction is now accepted as essential to development and growth.

## An historical case study: emergent collectivities and international business

Consider one of the most dramatic shifts in socio-economic history, the expansion of commerce in Western Europe in the late medieval period. Until the eleventh century, trade was a static local affair. It took place mostly within the bounds of settlements in which a feudal lord could guarantee good order.

Within a century, this had changed. Glass was traded from Cologne to Paris. Leather and ironware travelled from Florence to Bari. Wool was sold from England to the Low Countries and traded back as fabric. Oriental spices and Maghrebian corn were imported by Genoese and London merchants. Between 1050 and 1200 the numbers in the merchant class reputedly rose from a handful to some hundreds of thousands. This new class transcended feudal borders, both national and international, much as the Internet and global enterprise is doing today. The processes lead to the internationalization of trade. The communication then made possible by the new merchant class foreshadowed the unfolding of global transition now observable.

What had happened? To understand the process of emergence at that time, we need to start by sketching the institutional environment before change took place. Under feudalism, the economic structure of Western Europe was based on conditional grants of tenure in return for specific services. Feudal lords granted the use of land, secured by military means, to villagers and freemen in return for labour and military services. They in turn legitimized their rule by undertaking military services for their overlords. A hierarchy was created with a king at its head. He represented the interests of the community seen as a whole. The king in a way held the nation in trust for the community, protecting it with levies of troops and equipment raised from the feudal obligations of his subordinates, and they in turn provided the social institutions needed for local trade based on agriculture.

In this system, the granting of monopoly rights was an important means of raising revenue. The local feudal lord claimed the monopoly for processing harvested goods. These rights were sold for a fee to millers, bakers and wine producers. These charges were justified as payment for the security the feudal overlord provided with his military capacity. For non-agricultural goods, property rights were vested in locally situated trade-based guilds. These enjoyed local conditional monopoly privileges in return for taxes paid to the local feudal lord. Peasants and the landed aristocracy were often explicitly forbidden to trade. Merchants operated as isolated travelling salesmen in a locale.

This environment is one of high legitimacy.[8] Commercial actors knew their place in an elaborate pyramidal scheme of conditional privileges. These were all transgressed by an emerging class of international merchants, often drawn from a scattering throughout the civilizing world of persecuted ethnic or religious groups, for example the Jews. These groups had familiar or religious connections that stretched from feudal nation to feudal nation. These provided a cultural web of connectivity across the whole of the known world. Others interested in trading at a distance could use this; they could plug into this network assured by experience of its integrity. As we shall see the merchants themselves policed it in a rough and ready, but effective way. This was the twelfth century's equivalent of the Internet. It was as slow as the wind or literally the horsepower that connected it up. But it did work, and it was reliable. The merchants running it generally operated using the wealth they could generate through directly financing the king's activities in return for national as opposed to local monopoly privileges. This finance freed the king from dependency on his feudal subordinates. He could raise a standing army and use it independent of any need for feudal levies of troops. His feudal subordinates clearly did not object to being freed from their obligation to provide troops and many of them obtained money from the merchant class and gave that to the king in lieu of their feudal obligations.

The result was a win–win game with huge positive feedback from the wealth generated. This led to an explosion in trade, independent thinking and wealth. In the end this led to the Renaissance and later evolved into the Industrial Revolution. It blew away tradition embedded in local feudal socio-political boundaries and instigated an institutional crisis that led to the system of national governments, financed by monetary taxes on enterprise and consumption, in which we are embedded today.

The pioneering traders of the late medieval period could be exposed to three types of unpredictability and risk:

(1) *Natural uncertainties*: There was no reliable way to mitigate the natural hazards of travel and harvest due to acts of God.
(2) *Institutional uncertainties*: The local feudal regime could make arbitrary changes to monopoly rights, the required specifications of goods, rates of taxes, etc.
(3) *Market uncertainties*: Between national and, increasingly international, merchants, the same merchant–agent–client relations might occur once only. In this there is a temptation to cheat on one-off transactions, since agreements and contracts across national and institutional borders were unenforceable.

These uncertainties provided the means by which groups could deviate from the established boundaries set for behaviour and exploit the huge added value available from national and international exchange. This could mitigate a failure, say, of a crop in one area, by exchange with another. There was an institutional vacuum, and it was filled in three ways:

(1) *Natural uncertainty* was ameliorated by spreading risks through the invention of insurance, shareholding among groups of traders in international trading projects – in effect the setting up of embryonic joint stock companies – and by the shortage in one country being mitigated by trade with an other.
(2) *Institutional uncertainty* was dealt with by central government. The king, for a fee, granted trading and other monopolies direct to the towns set up by the new merchant class. This made them independent of arbitrary local feudal lords and any lack of clarity in their administration of them. The state provided secondary law[9] in the form of judicial power to enforce developing primary commercial

law, and gave regulatory oversight to the guilds set up by artisans. This was the beginning of the rule of law where the social institution of the courts could not arbitarily alter the rules to suit their convenience. They had the king's authority to adjudicate, not his power to alter. This led in turn to the creation of individual property connected by impersonal trade and it replaced the communally connected system of feudal ownership.[10] Up until then the institution of private property was not strictly necessary for society to operate.

(3) *Market uncertainties* were dealt with by creating new social mechanisms in international trade. These filled what was an institutional vacuum. They created socially embedded institutional devices to control entry to trade, and regulate it. This was done through trade coalitions, merchant guilds, networks of foreign subsidiaries, trade fairs, centralized record-keeping, private judiciary and trading sanctions. These were all aimed at ensuring that exchange relations were more widely accountable. This was orchestrated by ensuring that trade was between people accredited with a carefully constructed social identity built on a reputation of a particular artisanal group, town or ethnic group for integrity in trade.[11]

A graphic illustration of this emergent institutional environment's capacity to reduce uncertainty was the case of a London merchant called Lucas. In 1292 he was accused of having secretly left the trade-fair in Lynn without paying £31 for goods acquired. He refused to appear before the fair's judiciary. Such merchant courts were constituted by elected law merchants (i.e. legal non-professionals). They spoke justice summarily and did so without taking account of the niceties of local law. Severe sanctions in dealings were placed on traders who went outside their jurisdiction by appealing to church or other courts. In Lucas' case, collective liability was applied. Foreign merchants refused to trade with London until the outstanding bill had been settled.[12]

The closed network of the medieval guilds has often been presented as socially inefficient cartels or as a response to moral hazard.[13] We tend to agree with the latter interpretation. The main point is that they provide an illustration of how institutional change evolves to support the emergence of new enterprise, driven by the possibility of exploiting the huge economic potential of international trade for lowering local uncertainties of the kind we have discussed. Guilds effected trade, and they evolved to socially embed emergent trade in a supporting infrastructure of what became primary law.[14]

## International business and society

If there is a place for informal social action even in emergent individualist-orientated situations there is a role for the state in helping formalize it. This implies we need a means of analysing the dynamics of a co-evolving relationship between enterprise and its socio-political context.

It is increasingly evident that an appreciation of the particular political, cultural and socio-institutional context set for business is essential to understanding how enterprise too can be effective in distinct environments.[15] We need a socio-economic ecology that allows us to analyse the interaction between enterprise and its supporting institutions.

Traditional reductionist thinking is not of much use when the interactivity between systems is as high as it is here. The system of trade observed is based on a devolved highly interconnected web of relationships across a network of communication and distribution spanning the globe. Reducing a network to its constituent parts and studying these independently is of no value to understanding the dynamics of the network working as a whole. Knowledge of the impact of price on sales volume – if other things were not to change – is not enough. Crucially, understanding is needed regarding the complex dynamics of cause and effect within the highly integrated information- and knowledge-based networks of activity enabling global trade.

To understand this scene of emergence, we need to be capable of going beyond the geo-political boundaries set by traditional nation states.[16] We posit that the latter are to the global economy what the local feudal lords were to the domestic socio-economic environment at the end of the feudal period:

> political behavior does not develop in a vacuum; it is conditioned by firm, industry and environmental factors – particularly those found in the non-market environment that includes government. (Boddewyn and Brewer 1994, p. 121)

Enterprise, society and government co-evolve, and their interactivity by analogy with nature invariably leads to the rich diversity observable in natural eco-systems like the tropical rainforest. The dynamic interaction between evolving and mutually reliant, but not totally dependent, systems leads to the evolution of different solutions in different circumstances.

This can occur in contexts which initially may appear very similar. Small initial differences in circumstance or timings can have a huge impact over time in any system supplied with significant positive change reinforcing feedback. This kind of feedback is of the essence in emergence. It is both caused by it and causes it. It is fuelled by the huge returns that can be gained from the new opportunities that social evolution makes possible – national and international trade in commodities and products in the late medieval period, and knowledge and its energy-releasing power today.

In both cases the result is a period of extremely rapid growth modulated initially by a few informal social institutions and only later by some more formal political ones. The outcome in a particular place and time is dependent on a unique sequence of historical actions and reactions. Small deviations in sequencing and timing in a fast-emerging context can produce accelerating differentiation between one, apparently similar, context and another.

It is important for any potential leaders in this process to observe that the political system reacts in response to both organizational supplication and its own fiscal interests, to create formal institutional order. It does this by setting up a legal framework for corporate governance. With this fiscal framework, enterprise acts to further the interests of its most active stakeholders, the state's fiscal ambitions being but one. In doing this, the government seeks legitimacy by providing formal sanction for the useful stabilizing institutions that evolve to support the interest of an enterprise's stakeholders, be they trading partners, financiers, owners, workers, etc.

In repeated plays of the abstract deterministic games of socio-economic evolution used in traditional analysis, a stable distribution of potential outcomes is contrived. This unrealistically suggests an unobservable unique best solution. In the real game of evolution, in the real world, only one particular play is permitted by nature in each unique geopolitical context. This is one draw from the theoretically infinite distribution of possibilities. Diversity between contexts is then inevitable. The solution that evolves in each context will not even be the best possible. It will simply be the one that emerged.

Without the pressures of internationalization it is possible for exceedingly inefficient solutions to be sustained for a significant time (for example, Stalinist socialism) or for a very long time (aboriginal Australasia). With globalization such socio-economically weaker solutions may not survive. This is not the same as saying that those that survive are the best. One can say only that they are those that survived. The set of survivable strategies is so very large that one has to expect distinct and diverse structures and forms to emerge from similar initial contexts.

It must always be kept in mind that evolution is not like Newtonian science: there are no unique first-best solutions to a problem, applicable for all time, only one that suffices for the moment.

Against this background, one has to accept the idea that there may be a multiplicity of equally effective business system types. This is due simply to the fact that all institutions and enterprises have a multiplicity of stakeholders. Different socio-political systems permit different enabling stakeholders to exercise differing degrees of control – for example, in Germany by law workers are represented on corporate boards. Such local differences provide a partial explanation for the number of distinct but equally successful types of business system that exist. Each copes with a different political regime created by the interplay of power, authority and responsibility between different stakeholders, and often with different sequencing in each society.

For example models[17] have been produced to examine the corporate and social performance consequent on the different approaches to social control possible with many active stakeholders. Such models have tried to go beyond the traditional narrow, efficient, capital market, shareholder-driven approach to business and economic success:

> In America, for instance, shareholders have a comparatively big say in the running of the enterprise they own; workers . . . have much less influence. In many European countries, shareholders have less say and workers more . . . in Japan managers have been let alone to run their companies as they see fit – namely for the benefit of employees and of allied companies, as much as for shareholders. (Donaldson and Preston 1995, quoting *The Economist* 1993, p. 52)

## Corporate governance again

Corporate governance needs to be seen in a broader context than that normally used. It needs to take account of the political process.[18] For example, the relative weaknesses of banks in the US was due to a political determination to sustain local control of individual state banking. It did so with laws prohibiting the inter-state concentration of banks. The relatively small local institutions that then emerged could not have financed corporate America; this had to be financed by the impersonal stock market system of Wall Street, which acted to concentrate the finance of individuals and local banks in a manner very different to that found in other, more communal, societies. In these systems this role is fulfilled by banks with a national infrastructure and owing much and owed much from considerable past patronage by the state. It should be noted that the globalization of banking is permitting powerful concentrations of capital in US-owned offshore enterprises, including banks.[19]

This tendency for such subtle local differences in initial conditions to be amplified by the positive feedback of emergence can be brought home by looking at the very different financing structure that has evolved in Canada. Banks there play a much more important role than they do in the US. They play a role akin to that observable in communal Japan, or communitarian Germany. Banks in Canada are not restricted to a province and many are derivatives of the monopoly granted by the state to the Hudson's Bay Company.[20]

Evidence exists[21] that the high success achieved by the US business system may not be due to evolutionary superiority over other systems. It could be that the particular sequence of historical socio-political events it faced in its context produced a good result. However, this does not preclude a different approach being as, or more, successful in a similar context: in Australasia marsupials, effectively occupy most of the ecological niches that elsewhere in the world are occupied by mammals.

However more importantly, given much recent effort at socio-economic engineering in, for example, Eastern Europe, one might be brave enough to suggest that transplanting the US business system into such a context is very likely to be inappropriate and totally ineffective. Because the tropical rain forest is a diverse highly effective exploiter of the equatorial region of the world does not mean that transplanting it to the northern temperate zone will work. One might surmise that attempting to transplant a highly effective business system into an analogously inappropriate context would not work either.

Corporate governance and ownership has to be seen as part of a broader set of socio-economic relationships. Each will be fundamental to the particular means used to organize enterprise. Within each society this will be done using its own unique separately evolved business system.[22] From this perspective, one type of business system is not better or worse than any other, it is only appropriate to its context. It will invariably be different from any other. Each business type is uniquely integral to its particular geo-political context, and this is what we mean by 'political embeddedness'.[23] In other words:

> By political embeddedness, we refer to the manner in which economic institutions and decisions are shaped by a struggle for power that involves economic actors and non-market institutions. (Zubkin and DiMaggio 1990, p. 20)

## Stakeholders

The high value that can be added by the successful exploitation of knowledge creates a totally new set of socio-economic evolutionary circumstances. We must expect the emergence of new global, probably unforeseen, types of both enterprises and institutions. These will be driven by the interest of the new socio-economic stakeholders of the new order to extend the bounds of their propriety and accrete value to themselves.[24]

There has been significant increased interest[25] in this notion of stakeholders, since Freeman's (1984) seminal book, *Strategic Management: A Stakeholder Approach*. Because of the diversity of stakeholder/firm interests and interactions, one has to take a pragmatic view when defining stakeholders. If one does this, one is left with the dilemma of understanding the mechanisms by which each particular stakeholder's interests can be voiced and made manifest in terms of effective enterprise performance, as seen from their particular perspective.[26] This then raises a secondary – some might say the primary – issue: the practicality of getting consistency between a social and a particular stakeholder's desired view of appropriate enterprise performance.[27]

This takes for granted that stakeholders have the capacity to measure the performance of the enterprise they have an interest in. It is not at all clear how all stakeholders can discern or value even tangible assets. However, some key assets are necessarily intangible and sometimes invisible; this implies that they are sometimes difficult to discern, and at times difficult to assert propriety over. It is fundamental to our view that as measurement is costly credibility must play a key role in determining the structures and form adopted by both enterprises and their supporting institutions.[28]

As previously indicated, these issues are particularly acute in the information and knowledge industries that are currently driving the evolutionary pace. The inherent intangibility of their product and service understanding and perception makes this inevitable.[29] The current co-evolution of these industries with their supporting institutional systems of governance is central to the current process of social evolution.[30] This area of enterprise is ubiquitous within the global economy, it is central to its very being. The generic utility of knowledge and its codification as information is integral to the web of relationships building an emergent global system.

Most activity in these knowledge industries is outside any political or social oversight or the ambit of the geo-political boundaries defined for existing nation states or enterprises. Industrial and national boundaries are being inter-penetrated by the web of contacts currently being created. This is happening at an ever-accelerating rate. It is generating change and innovation simultaneously throughout the globe and creating the complex and volatile global business environment social and enterprise leadership faces today.

## Stakeholders in knowledge and information

Most business stakeholders play a strong role in the creation, use and exploitation of knowledge. Each in practice and probably legally has legitimacy in any claim they might make for propriety over it.

(1) *Shareholders* finance it
(2) *Employees* experience and study to create it
(3) *Suppliers* contribute to it and increasingly have a significant share in it as enterprises outsource much non-core activity
(4) *Customers* purchase it, add value to it by the degree to which they are able to comprehend it and so innovate using it; they are also concerned that new developments may make that which they have just purchased worthless in due course – e.g. a slow, low-capacity computer cannot run the most up-to-date software
(5) *Government and taxpayers* contribute hugely to its creation through education, training and research budgets.

The above all feel some propriety in the knowledge products created by an enterprise. It would therefore be surprising if they did not want to exercise some control to protect this propriety. To do this, socially acceptable governance structures are likely to evolve.

The processes of knowledge creation, acquisition and dissemination that these stakeholders wish to mine for the huge value it releases are costly to acquire, and the following questions arise:

(1) Who are the suppliers?
(2) Is the person supplying it credible?
(3) Are the concepts as innovative and useful as any others in the market?
(4) Do I understand enough for a good return or will I need learning?
(5) Is the person I am going to buy from reliable in their initial provision?
(6) How soon can I expect what I learn to be superseded?
(7) Does the product or service come with after-sales support?

A practical answer to each of the above can be arrived at, but only after a significant investment of time and money. The answers are not free but are vital to ascertaining the value of any knowledge that might be purchased.

Institutions and enterprises co-evolve to modulate the relationships between them. For a better understanding, we will now examine this in a wider context:

Currently we have strong legacy national institutions. These could act either to constrain or underpin consequent change. It is very important for those providing leadership to understand how they can enable empowering change. Institutions have a pronounced effect on the behaviour of enterprises, especially on enterprises that have as yet not become truly global. We will study the impact of these national institutions first.

Global competition has to be seen in relation to the domestic institutions that still impact on the strategic behaviour of enterprise. A nation's culture, its legal and regulatory environment, its relationships between business and government, the role adopted by its own financial institutions and the differences between its corporate governance system and those operating abroad all impact on an enterprise's structure, its behaviour and its performance.

The importance of the national business environment to the international effectiveness of enterprise is a major topic of interest.[31] Especially if one wishes to understand the competitive strategies enterprise can adopt in approaching the global economy, one cannot ignore the domestic environment. In many parts of Asia, it is not financial markets or institutions but government ministries that are the principal stakeholders. In that role, they have an interest in monitoring corporate performance and controlling financial allocation. In continental Europe, in countries such as Germany and Switzerland, the banks are principal stakeholders in enterprise. Hence, they too wish to monitor corporate performance and investment decisions on a regular basis, including those occurring abroad. They can be, and frequently are, prescriptive about such investments.

An aspirant-global organization's behaviour and strategy, especially on investment decisions such as market entry, diversification, innovation and product development can be significantly constrained by the limits set for it by domestic institutions. At the same time these institutions can provide local sources of artificial competitive advantage which may be difficult to transfer outside the boundaries of existing political authority. If we are truly globalizing, this will leave such enterprises at a severe disadvantage.

# 4

# Institutions, Organizations and Enterprise: Their Co-Evolution

## Introduction

Before addressing the essential issue of corporate governance in the information age we will explain how the co-evolutionary dynamics of the relationship between institutions and enterprise play out. We will construct a model of the process, taking care not to confuse – as is often done – institutions with organizations. We distinguish the two and see institutions as the rules of the system, for example the rule of law,[1] and organizations as supporting the institutions, for example the high courts of justice which are created by so-called 'secondary laws'.

In looking at institutions as rules we distinguish between two types of rules: formal codified ones (the law, etc.) and informal understood ones (social conventions). The former typify Anglo-Saxon countries such as the US, the UK, Australia and Canada. Informal institutions are fundamental in communal societies such as Japan.[2] European countries, particularly northern Europe (Germany, Scandinavia) have a communitarian business system, which is closer to the communal system. However, in all systems both formal and informal institutions are significant. No matter which one dominates, all support, constrain and bind the viability of enterprise in today's global economy.

## Organizations and institutions

Our categorization of organizations is based on the roles each kind of institution and its supporting organizations play in the system. On this logic,[3] there are four types of organization:

(1) *Political*, e.g. political parties, government legislatures, city councils. These evolve to empower, design, then construct and enforce the boundaries that govern social structures, behaviour and performance – they are the source of secondary law.[4]
(2) *Social*, e.g. churches, sporting groups, interest groups. These evolve to use delegated authority to determine who is willing to relate to whom and how the groups that accrete out of society can work together to pursue some non-political mutual beneficial purpose. Social organizations work to both limit and expand human horizons given the underlying rules and mores each grouping chooses to adopt, so are a key source of 'primary law'.[5]
(3) *Educational*, e.g. research institutes, universities, vocational training centres. These evolve to catalyse human evolution using the authority they have to provide in-depth knowledge about the physical, economic, socio-political and existential environments. All the evidence is that they provide much of the knowledge base that catalyses our capacity to fuel the process of emergence.
(4) *Economic*, e.g. co-operatives, stock markets, banks, trade unions, enterprises. These evolve to exercise the responsibility given to them by their stakeholders to exploit the environment in the interests of their survival, evolution and growth. They provide the engine that powers the evolution of society. It is generally the discovery of a new source of economic potential that leads to the explosive growth that drives emergence.

Organizations are made up of people and knowledge, either codified or not. The people in a business system find themselves in one or more of these categories of organization, and commit to their rules. At the same time they also participate in generating new rules for the wider co-evolving system. The key repository of their organization's rules is found in their knowledge of that history, conscious or not.

Organizations enable the social accretions of the common interest in achieving a norm of acceptable stabilizing behaviour. This enables order to develop in what might otherwise be chaotic growth. Eventually this leads to the setting up of concrete formalized boundaries that can be sustained in normal times. Each individual is driven by their own set of beliefs and meaning. All have to work within a social framework of informal and formal institutions created as a business system unfolds.

The significance of the national business system for the behaviour of enterprises is evident,[6] but institutions and organizations are hardly ever distinguished. Understanding the interaction between institutions and enterprise enables a better understanding of the process through which both formal and informal institutions evolve. In pursuing this, we wish to understand the processes leading to success or failure in each business system.

Why are certain formal institutions, such as common or statute law, essential to success in Anglo-Saxon countries but not necessarily sufficient elsewhere? Jeffrey Sachs' 'cold turkey' advice, 'no state support or finance for anything other than the basics duties of the state', worked for the Polish business system. There is little confidence that it has worked or will work in Russia,[7] just as one would not expect to be able to transplant a tropical rainforest in Siberia. In both cases, one needs to take into account the governance of the business system seen as a whole, and within it the dynamic interaction between both formal and informal institutions and all types of organizations, especially enterprise.

Let us now examine the four categories of organization and examine in particular how their behaviour is modulated by, and in turn modulates, a nation's institutions and enterprises – the political, economic, social and, crucially, the one for catalysing knowledge, educational organizations.

*Political organizations* have as their principal focus the acquisition and use of power. 'Power' we take as the capacity to determine ends, hopefully social ones. Power enables one to formally bound social constructions and behaviour. Power in this sense is the source of secondary law[8] designed to enable primary laws to be altered. One can cede power to others, for instance in courts of appeal, or have it taken from one by revolution.

Crucial to our line of thought are the means a society evolves to modulate its use and to effect its transfer in socially advantageous way – revolution, democratic elections, selling (normally called corruption), etc. If one has complete power one has an absolute right to exploit and dispose of it as one wishes. If used badly, power can be very damaging, so societies try to limit and constrain its use. In a democracy one is given it for only a limited period of time. At the end of this period one has to be willing to relinquish it. If one's fellow citizens do not feel one has used it well, it will be assigned to others.

Power allows one to control the ends to be achieved and retain any benefits that accrue from its use. Political organizations seek access to power. If they attain it they can determine the ambit of the law. In doing this they can state how it can be used to define purposes and ends for themselves and for others. It can thus be used to set a limit, a boundary, to the control they themselves or others can use. It is socially useful, as it can be used to compel acceptance of communally beneficial results and the raising of finance through taxes and borrowing, to enable them.

*Social organizations* are allowed 'authority' by those with power. With this, they determine how things are to be done whether in organizations such as football clubs or social institutions such as prisons, government offices, or NGOs. They, together with educational organizations, are crucial to the development of our argument.

By defining how things are to be done within their ambit social organizations are local accretions of people who, by giving themselves an identity as a member of that organization, enable those outside to be able to anticipate how they will behave while operating within this ambit. For outsiders, that means decreased uncertainty about group members' values and behaviours. This produces cohesion in society conducive to enterprise, especially during times of very rapid, explosive or chaotic growth: 'He is a Christian', 'she is a golfer', 'they are civil servants', etc.

All this is vital to exchange. Social organizations provide a mechanism by which individuals and enterprises become embedded in a role that a society recognizes. This encourages stability. The authority they have permits them to determine means of usage not the ends to be achieved. In doing this, any benefits accruing as a result of their own efforts belong to them. However a social organization cannot dispose of itself. A prison cannot decide to sell itself, nor can a tennis club or a government office.

Those with the requisite power protect their power to determine ends by establishing a governance structure over social organizations – reports to be submitted, inspections to occur, etc. Social organizations in determining how, can and do enforce rules of behaviour. However this is restricted to the ambit allocated to them by those with power. Generally people are not compelled to enter a social organization: they do so for the advantages it brings.

If they do not play by a social organization's rules those within it are liable to exclusion and lose the benefits it brings. This does not seem a particularly onerous sanction for those in developed socio-economic systems. However, for people in traditional societies exclusion may mean death. In aboriginal societies undoubtedly, and even in quite sophisticated modern societies, social exclusion can be the difference between life and death. When one is hale and hearty there may be no problem for oneself or one's immediate family, but in the absence of social security and public provision of health care a serious illness or the loss of gainful employment can quickly turn a secure situation into a very insecure one, not just for oneself but for one's immediate family. In such a context, without the support of one's extended family or social group, illness or loss of the capacity to work is potentially fatal. There are very good evolutionary reasons why as human beings we have a very deep fear of rejection and have very powerful emotions underpinning our wish to retain the hard-won acceptance of others through what we call love.

*Educational organizations* are also social organizations. But they have a special role in emergence and development. They are crucial to the construction of the processes generating the energy to drive the current evolution of globalization – i.e. information and knowledge – either through research or by teaching: educational organizations seek to create, codify and disseminate knowledge.

In doing this they generally seek endorsement from those with appropriate 'authority'. And, in turn, they themselves generate authority through a reputation for knowing particular things in more depth than others. They might seek to determine the best way to design a golf club so as to increase its hitting power, the best means to design a new electronic machine, or the best means to run a state or its business system.

*Economic organizations* are limited to the exercise of 'responsibility'. They work to ends defined by their stakeholders, using the means those stakeholders are willing to make available to achieve the ends they specify. They produce the means for organizing the physical, intellectual and spiritual resources required to produce the energy the whole system requires to sustain itself and drive the development of society. Economic organizations can determine who, where, and when, but do not own the fruits of their endeavours nor any right to dispose of the resources they deploy. However, as the measurement of commitment or performance is often problematic we find that a great deal of autonomy can exist even within such an organization.

These organizations can control the means and circumstances by which responsibility is used, but all the benefits from its use are distributed in their entirety to their principal stakeholders: shareholders, financiers, employees and the community. The energy released by economic institutions, enterprises, powers the engine driving the whole system. Enterprises that act in a socially desirable manner will tend to accrete energy to themselves. Those that do not will lose it.

Figure 4.1 is a conceptualization of the model set out above. Enterprises compete in an environment, which includes various non-market, non-economic, determinants of value such as the community, the media, etc.

*Figure 4.1* Business systems: organizations and institutions (adapted from North 1990)

By varying the size and influence of each type of institution within society one can generate the rich variety of outcomes observable in a real-world national business system. A country's competitiveness can be attributed to the effectiveness of the interaction between enterprise and the institutions these four types of organizations support.[9]

Understanding the interactivity between formal and informal institutions, and the four types of organization that support them, determines the potential for success of enterprise within any business system, and the power it can generate to move society forward. At the root of this are the different means by which institutions and organizations impact on the way knowledge is created, sustained, exploited and used in enterprise.

In individualist business systems, such as the Anglo-Saxon one, there is a relatively weak connection between the four types of organization and the institutions each supports. A clear division of labour is established by hierarchy. This starts by those in power delegating authority to social and educational organizations, who in turn allocate responsibility to economic organizations.

The depersonalization of the resulting decision process means that enterprises have to rely on formal rather than informal institutions to protect their propriety and interest more generally. In such a system, one does not trust the other party to a transaction, one trusts the system that polices its integrity. Impersonal dealings are the order of the day. This is typical of stock markets. It is also reflected in the clear separation that exists between the US Federal Reserve System and the political process.[10]

If one were working as an employee in a business, or for the state in an economic organization, this would define one's public persona. This would be strictly separate from the private activities that one might enjoy in a social enterprise like a club or church. In fact if one crossed any of the boundaries between the distinct organizations in which one was a member this would be symptomatic of a failure in propriety. It could result in a persecution for fraud, insider dealing or corruption.

In the communal business system, crossing these boundaries is standard practice. Here the norm is considerable local interchanges of knowledge between all types of organization and enterprise. In such societies informal institutions dominate formal ones. Insider dealing, helping friends from one's own social organization and exploiting asymmetries in information between buyer and seller are the way business is done. Figure 4.2 shows the relatively strong linkages among enterprises and institutions in communal systems, and the relatively weak linkages within the individualist business systems.

In communal business system countries informal institutions are the stronger. It seems that the emerging economies of Eastern Europe may adopt the communitarian European system.[11] This is not surprising, given both their history and their EU aspirations. The current membership of the EU is largely communitarian, leaning towards the communal model. It is interesting to note that the emerging economies of South America

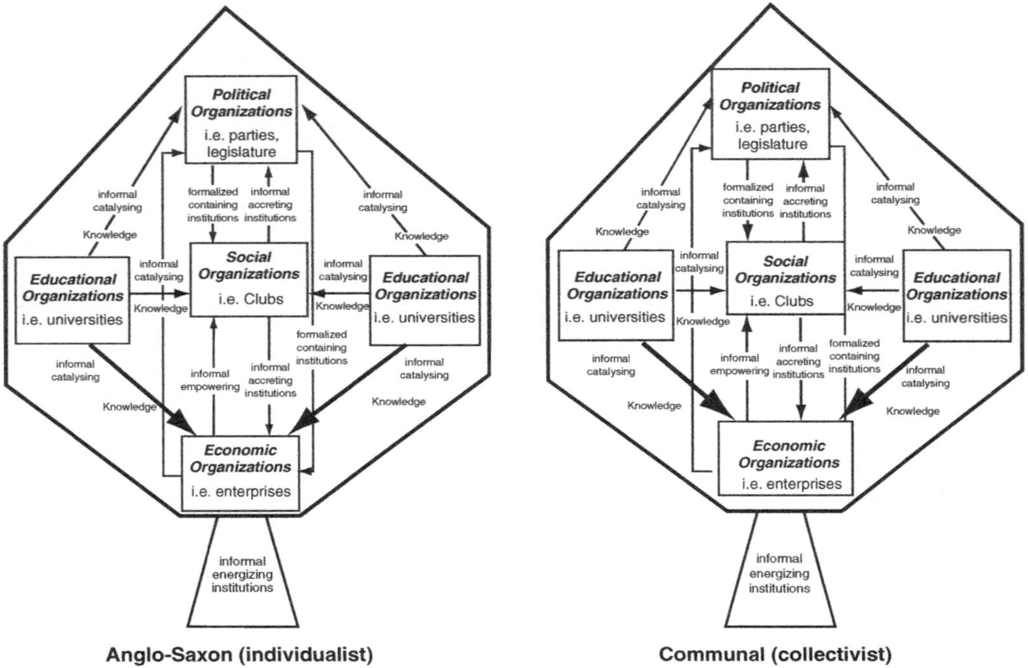


*Figure 4.2* Comparing business systems: the societal development rocket

are superficially attempting to adopt the more formal system of the US. In practice, this is modulated by their non-Anglo-Saxon European origins, but the more formal US approach is nevertheless evident in their approach to law. One country, Argentina, until recently, deliberately put itself under the rules set by the US Federal Reserve, by tying its currency one to one with the US dollar.

All the above systems have had their problems. Many argue that the Anglo-Saxon system is too short-term, driven by the needs of uninvolved stockholders whose sole interest is results now. If your enterprise does not supply these, there are others who will. This limits the finance available for much necessary but costly long-term strategic investment.

In communal systems, where banks and other large financial institutions or even the state can be deeply involved, their commitment is to the longer-term strategic investment needed for development. The Japanese *Keiretsu*, aided by the state, did this with memory chips and effectively stole the business from US enterprises that had a shorter-term view. However, long-term commitment has its price in terms of lost flexibility.

In communal systems in the 1990s, the move from a bull to a bear market had a traumatic impact on the community of interest supporting that system. It is easy to be all for one and one for all when markets are rising; you can help someone else share in a gain made larger by partnership. All gains from such co-operation accelerate growth. When the market matures and so levels out, things change; one person's gain is another's loss. when its markets fall it is survival pure and simple. My survival may depend on offloading a major loss on someone else. This is not amenable to sustaining a community of interest.

The fastest-growing parts of the global economy were the emerging economies of the Far East and the dot.com enterprises. All these are in the global web. Both these geo-political and industrial areas are facing a huge downturn in business, write-downs in capital and growing unemployment. Much of their employees' past 'income' may now be worthless share options. In such a context it is extremely difficult to retain a feeling for communal values. In emergent economies where future growth looked a good prospect relative to low beginnings, expectations have been dashed. The expectation of success has not been crushed, it simply has not occurred yet.

The economies of the Anglo-Saxon societies (the US, UK, Canada and Australia) are driven by the short-term needs of their stock markets. Their uniquely powerful stakeholder, the shareholder, likes a diversified portfolio of stock. S/he rarely commits to any one enterprise.[12] Future returns and the cost of investments do not look attractive when one can buy a better return by switching to another stock. Although the stock market undergoes a certain amount of government regulation and supervision, it is generally seen as an efficient institution. If left naturally it regulates itself through market forces[13] and when capital markets are competitive, and so efficient, there is likely to be less need for the official regulation and supervision required for other economic enterprises.

However, one consequence of these desirable ends is a short-term perspective. This Anglo-Saxon stock market phenomenon limits the capacity of US and UK companies to make profitable long-term investments. Such restrictions do not apply to their Japanese, German, Italian or Korean rivals.[14] In consequence the latter appear on the market place with the very latest technology, lean production methods and well-educated experienced managers.

In the bull market of the 1980s and early 1990s, decision makers in Anglo-Saxon impersonal stock market-financed enterprises found the competitive environment tough. This led many to rethink the values of this business system and its appropriateness in the global network of co-operative webs of commercial activity competing in the late twentieth and early twenty first centuries. The systems adopted by such communal webs of contact operate much like the Japanese *Keiretsu.*[15]

These co-operative networks have been very successful indeed. They introduced lean production, outsourcing to a community of co-operative suppliers using just in time (JIT), each had *Kan Ban* pull stock control in production, etc. All this and much more had been created and exploited to devastating competitive effect by the Far Eastern communal/familial business system.[16] However, the resilience of the Anglo-Saxon systems subsequently became evident. They were not destroyed by these results; they absorbed the manufacturing and distribution lessons and then came back competitively.

Without the competitive pain from the Far East they did not act; with it, they did so successfully. What is more, they appear to have coped far more robustly than their Far Eastern competitors when faced with a downturn. Many Anglo-Saxon, commercially successful, enterprises have been the financial and managerial saviours of their Far Eastern competitors, for example Ford at Mazda, etc. This matters, as many of these systems depend on international communications and distribution systems to support 24/7 working.

Enterprises in the Anglo-Saxon business system adopted the form and some of the substance of the communal systems. The latter are deeply rooted in trust, created by demonstrable commitment sustained over long periods of time. The stakeholders in such a system work continuously to generate and maintain that trust. 'Jobs for life' means workers have no fear of machines replacing their jobs. A close personal relationship between the CEO and his banker sustains the bank's commitment to future returns despite short-term losses; the mutual posting of staff between customer and supplier ensures trust between customer and supplier in JIT working. To reach high performance in the communal system, one sets up a system of trust requiring all to share knowledge unquestioningly. All know from experience that the fruits of its use will be communally shared. Such local sharing of knowledge between stakeholders is either not legitimate, considered insider dealing, or simply not well advised in the Anglo-Saxon individualist system.

The individualist system is deeply rooted in a market-driven view of business strategy: size and economies of scale are everything. If marketing did not grow market share then acquisition could. A take-over, especially a leveraged buy-out, was one means of avoiding any need for long-term marketing or even capacity investment. With the monopoly power market dominance provided, the theory went that one could cut back on cost in the amalgamated organization and push up price. This would obviate the need to supplicate one's financiers and stockholders to commit more resources for longer.

Stockholders liked this approach. In most instances it appeared to be a win–win game. Those selling shares saw them gain value, and if the merger was perceived as a success so did buyers. Apparently everyone could be a winner. Of course that was not always the reality. Such financial engineering produced a new enterprise. This could survive in the short term however all one had done was to re-finance the existing capital stock of the merged enterprises. One had not made any longer-term real investments in methods, plant or machinery. The consequence could be a loss in international competitive advantage.

## The emerging market business systems

An increasing amount of international business goes on in emergent markets. The states in this category may evolve into one of the other major business systems. They may not. They may even be, as we suggest above, at the leading edge of a new emergent system. For the moment, we will treat them as a third system defined simply by exclusion – i.e. everything associated with success not in the previous two categories of mature systems, and not remaining in the dormant heritage system.

In analysing this group, let us first consider the major characteristics of its member countries:

(1) A history of being able to achieve very high economic growth rates
(2) High uncertainty and turbulence, caused by rapid change
(3) An infrastructure delivering distributive, communication and financial services
(4) A high overlap within and between institutions and organizations
(5) A relatively weak legal and social system for the enforcement of arm's-length contracts
(6) A drag on enterprise from a legacy of personal and business relationships.

These characteristics are, where applicable, largely shared with the emerging industries that lead development in all three business system. The easily observable macro forces of emergence are thus a reflection of the underlying forces which are being effected at the less visible micro level. Not surprisingly, and significantly, information and knowledge-based industries are a prime example. The characteristics are symptomatic of emergence in any context. It is the first three characteristics above all else that set the successfully emergent states apart from the heritage system from which they are emerging. One finds the last three characteristics in any mature heritage system in stasis.

The 'emerging' economies, especially those in Asia and Eastern Europe, are of vital importance to anyone interested in the future global economy. These economies have rapidly developing enterprises and supporting institutions. The rapidity of the change involved destroys their heritage of containing boundaries and breaks asunder traditional social accretions of cohesiveness. This all looks, and is, chaotic. It is therefore useful to develop understanding of the interactions between institutions and enterprise that produce constructive not destructive consequences. It was well illustrated in the 1997 economic crisis that hit the emerging markets in Asia. Emerging economies had to deal with far higher levels of uncertainty than did the more mature systems. They had few, if any, mature institutions and no reliable legal structures. This amplified their turbulence and put them apart from the mature systems already described.

These circumstances are those we saw in the Middle Ages case study in Chapter 3. As we suggest in Figure 4.3 enterprises in emerging economies have no formal or informal national institutions providing a framework supportive of newly emergent enterprise. They also have

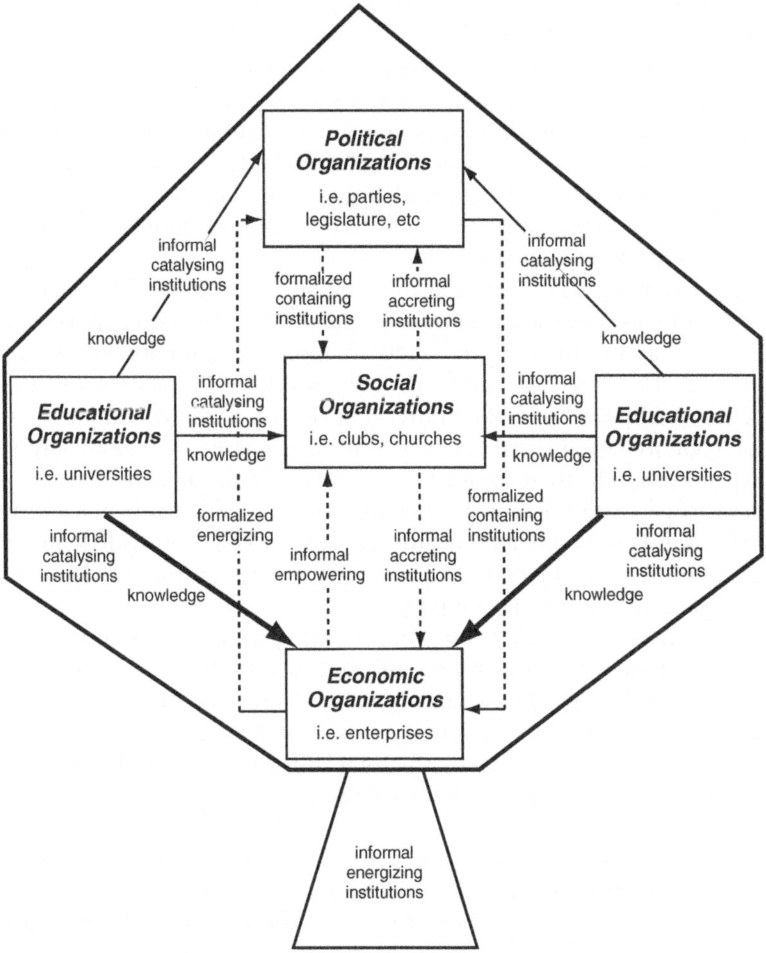


*Figure 4.3* Comparing business systems: the emerging economies

to exist with a legacy of institutions, such as the feudal system in our case study. This will impede their growth. In some cases, it may even prevent emergence. The supportive systems that do exist initially within their boundaries tend to be local to an area or ethnic group. These are often outside the reach of any national regulatory authority. The prospect for such economies is not good. However, given the right circumstances they can emerge into the wider economic environment of their time.

In emerging economies the regulation of exchange by either law or community is problematic. First their laws are generally inappropriate to new enterprise. The law suffers from much uncertainty on both the predictability of judicial decisions and the time required for it then to be delivered. Secondly, difficulties in communication outside a restricted locale are likely to stop emergence in its tracks. However, emergence is extremely unlikely to be stopped if good title can be established in production and the supporting infrastructure of distribution, communication and finance is good.

In most emerging market contexts, informal, especially family-supported, credit and insurance arrangements are the norm. One's personal security is one's family; there are no social or political commitments to an individual outside that ambit. Such an institution is very robust, it is delineated by one's blood and that is unequivocal: family will be there for your welfare in hard times. However, similarly and reasonably it expects you to be there for it when you have good times; your successes have to be shared. You will generally have got to where you are with help from your family and in turn they expect you to provide help for them in the form of jobs, money handouts or other patronage when you have success and they need support.

The effective marginal tax rate on the enterprising to support this can be more than 100 per cent and, unlike taxes, is almost impossible to avoid. You often live in the same home as the tax collectors. With such a prospect, the incentive to enterprise is virtually non-existent. Emigration, voluntary or enforced by the total collapse of the local economy, is the only way out. It may be the only means of saving enterprise in such a context.

There may be no social security worth bothering about when you get to a country like the US but you have only you (and if you get married your wife and your own children) to care for and that is it. This has huge advantages as compared to the familial burden immigrants leave behind in a traditional society.

## Achieving perspective: triangulation from our three business systems

The processes we have described in each of these three business systems suggest that the changes that bring about emergence depend on two related processes: one to do with enterprise and the second to do with institutions. Both are necessary for emergence.

The first is what Joseph Schumpeter has called 'creative destruction' (Schumpeter 1950 [1942]).[17] This results from the inventive and innovative competition between enterprises and requires them to continuously re-invent themselves or go out of business to be replaced by others nearer the leading edge of development. Competition produces the edge required to fuel the process of inventing and innovating new products. These inevitably destroy old market positions and create new ones.

The second comes from what we call, by analogy with astro-physics, a 'social wormhole' in the fabric of society. This permits one to discontinuously jump from connectivity in one society to connectivity in an otherwise unknown distant location. Historically, the network of contacts established between dispersed social, ethnic or religious groups created such wormholes. Such groups sustained connectivity with each other. This enabled distribution, communication and finance to be confidently effected between different nation states. In each state one could make a connection with someone from such a group: they would know you, and you them; they knew someone in the society with whom you wanted to trade. That individual would know someone in his local community who wished to trade with you, and they could vouchsafe for him to his colleague in your society. Such individuals would stand surety for the two principal transactors and charge a fee for the service.

The merchants of the eleventh century found such a route, a wormhole, by which the king could provide support for such access through Jewish merchants or Lombard bankers to a national, and through them an international, market, inaccessible using the traditional feudal structure. It made possible trade between cities in different nation states provided members of the appropriate Diaspora lived there. The king used his power over his feudal subordinates to award monopoly rights to towns and guilds; this permitted them to evolve the new institutions required to enable enterprise and trade to flourish between cities in different states.

We would argue that both these processes are necessary. One cannot be effective without the other. The first produces the pressure for explosive change; the latter provides the means to release the pressure of new enterprise to ensure that the critical mass can be generated that is necessary for self re-enforcing explosive, but controlled, growth to occur. Something akin to it may occur, but without the release provided by such wormholes it may be so explosively destructive it creates an institutional vacuum.

Without the competitive pressure from the potential birth and death of enterprises the incentive for evolutionary adaptation would not occur. Without wormholes in the social fabric of a legacy institutional infrastructure enterprise could be so constrained that it would either be stifled or be so explosively released that nothing constructive could emerge. Social constraints are essential, but so is socio-economic controlled pressure release. Without it, we would have commercial anarchy with no certainty in the propriety so necessary for enterprise to flourish. Without creative destruction, the pressure would never build up high enough for emergence to occur. Nothing will change if new ideas and sources of potential energy are not thereby generated. The creatively destructive energy thereby released will be of use only if institutions can be constructed quickly to support propriety in what is created by it. In the past, this was generally provided by the Diaspora of the kind we have described. Now it is provided by the fast-growing global communication network that in establishing itself is creating it.

The explosion in international trade in the pre-modern period can be seen as the co-evolution of institutions with enterprise. Institutional and technological forces cannot work independently of each other. However old constraining institutions need to be gently not explosively blown asunder, hence the value of structural wormholes in the pre-existing institutional fabric of society to help pressure build, up but also eventually to release it constructively.

Adding the emerging market business system to the two mature ones, the Anglo-Saxon individualist and the communal collectivist one, leads to three distinct perspectives from which to look at globalization. These three should be contrasted with the three traditional perspectives used by international business gurus: the existing success stories of the US, Europe and Japan (the 'triad'). But these three ignore one of the fundamentals of economic development pointed out a long time ago by Alexander Gershenkron (1962)[18]: late starters can copy their precursors but have to overcome their own legacy of institutions to do so. They have, in his terms, to overcome their own 'backwardness'. The more backward they are the greater is the absorptive challenge they face. They not only have to absorb the desired end state but evolve from where they are to it. This is not a trivial problem, yet most commentators still seem to ignore it. For that reason, trying to cajole developing countries, bribe them with soft loans or promises of debt forgiveness conditional on them emulating some existing ideal society (an idealized US for example), might be – or, rather, is – asking the impossible. We need to be able to guide our thinking about end states with a capacity to see starting points more clearly.

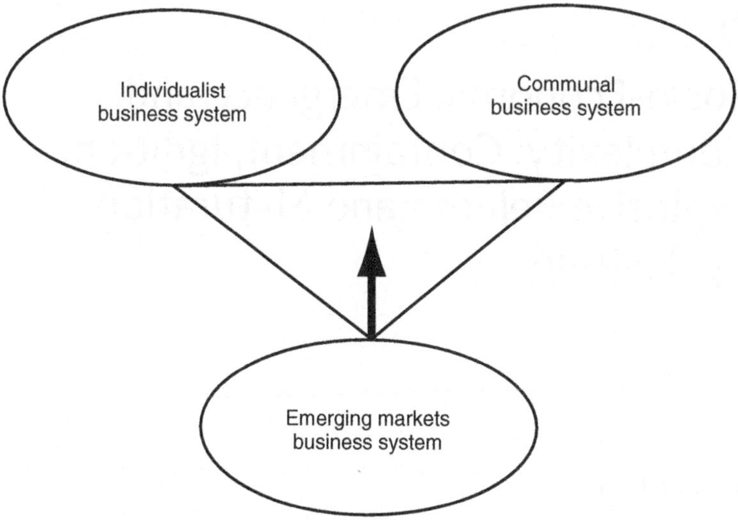


*Figure 4.4* The defining triad for our three business systems

This is why our approach is aimed at keeping all three perspectives we have set out in this chapter at the front of our minds. The way we can now look at the elements of the globalizing world is set out in Figure 4.4.

# 5

# Socio-Economic Emergence and Complexity: Containment, Ignition, Explosive Release and Maturation by Restraint

## Introduction

Having set up a model to assist understanding how business systems are constructed, we now wish to explore how emergence changes them. How do business systems that are settled into a fluctuating but basically stable state achieve a revitalizing impetus that drives changes that generate massive new value added? This is emergence. What fuels the instability that leads to such emergent activity? What enables the resulting explosive growth to be sustained? What brings the new system back to a new state of stable fluctuation at a higher level of organization? In other words: what are the processes in emergence that:

| | | |
|---|---|---|
| (1) | Create the opportunity? | New potential energy |
| (2) | Initiate it? | Initiating energy |
| (3) | Power it subsequently? | Kinetic energy |
| (4) | Bring it to an end? | Accreting energy tending to convert kinetic into potential energy. |

The processes involved are driven by the tension between the two fundamental forces at work: individualist enterprising and socially stabilizing ones. Enterprise is seen as adventurous and creative while social forces are of their essence communal, accommodating and ordering. Where the first dominate, one has anarchy not conducive to business. Where the second holds sway, enterprise halts and sterility reigns. To flourish, business needs a restraining, not containing, institutional guardianship.[1]

Case-specific factors explain the evolution of a context in which enterprise flourishes and so powers social transformation. In late medieval trade, it is suggested this was the expansion in the money economy. This enabled the merchants to be independent of the existing feudal system and able to finance the aristocracy including the king. Such merchants, for example the Jewish Diaspora, were independent of any particular nation state. This finance allowed kings to recruit standing armies independent of the troops communally levied from their feudal subordinates. Such armies increased the safety of trade routes. This encouraged more trade and generated further wealth. This fuelled even more of the self-re-enforcing explosive change typical of emergence. What spark ignited this explosion in trade? Why did this occur when it did? We ask this question because an incidental case of change does not cause emergence: for example, while the electric dynamo was invented in the 1880s it was forty years before electric power impacted significantly on industrial productivity. And in the fashion industry, the sartorial world is not transformed if someone revives a 1970s outfit. The explosive emergence of a 'new' fashion comes about only if a critical mass of trend-setters accepts the 'new' style.[2] Only then will the idea become *en vogue* and displace the existing style.

## The cycle of emergence

In emergence, the spark that ignites the forces that eventually lead to explosive change may remain as mysterious as the timing of a stock market crash, the fall of the Berlin Wall, the advent of the mini skirt or the appearance of the singularity that founded the universe.

What is observable is the build-up of pressure in an existing system. After this has achieved a critical level almost any spark will release the forces its existing institutional infrastructure strives to contain. What brings this pressure about is the identification then access by enterprise of some new source of potential empowering energy.

If ignition then occurs, the evolutionary process can shift from being in stable fluctuating equilibrium to explosive growth on a short time scale. This growth will quickly destroy the utility of any existing institutions attempting to contain it. The then liberated power of enterprise will exploit the newly identified potential in a self-re-enforcing cycle of growth and development. From the point of view of enterprise the joy of this is that, with a degree of due diligence, most commercial activity leads to a win–win game. That is the essence of positive feedback. For the resulting growth of new enterprise to be sustainable, it has to co-evolve at a rate similar to that of the formation of new order-supporting institutions. Society cannot generally move fast enough for this, so short-term enterprise has to create temporary stabilizing constructs. Enterprise creates the energy and means to power change but social institutions are needed to harness it so that enterprise can accrete the structure required to support the inter-enterprise exchange needed to create sustainable added value. In particular, knowledge is valuable only when it is exchanged or shared.

Initially existing institutions provide containing forces. These are designed to keep the old slowly evolving system in a stable dynamic equilibrium, homeostasis. However, when enterprise discovers a means to access new potential the consequences are profound. Think of:

- The wheel and manpower to move large local loads
- Horsepower to underpin national trade
- Wind-power to enable international trade
- Water carriage and power to create the scale that enabled the initiation of industrial-like production
- Fossil fuel and steam power to enable scheduled and therefore co-ordinated distribution of goods needed to create the scope required for capitalistic production[3]
- Electricity and electric power to cheapen the transmission of power to enable modernistic commercial industry
- Knowledge and the power of knowledge systems to efficiently co-ordinate all previous extractive, productive and creative forces to release the energy that is empowering global emergence.

Each of the above increased the pressure within its containing institutional boundaries until a critical point was reached at which explosive growth was initiated. If there is no social release valve for such pressure, the result is revolution. This may so destructively destroy existing institutions that in the anarchy then reigning enterprise cannot flourish. It should be noted also that human history suggests that each trip through this cycle, from emergence to stasis, has had a shorter and shorter length in each successive occurrence.

Enterprise finds the unpredictable chaos that results from emergence potentially lucrative but difficult to tolerate. If not barred by the polity, enterprise will act to bring order to the conduct of affairs, as did the merchants in the Lucas case in our earlier case study. They created their own courts of law and rules of behaviour, which is absolutely necessary if enterprise is to become a self-, and socially, sustaining activity. In a newly emergent environment successful enterprises will construct connectivity that through time will mature into the mutual trust and reliability of a new stabilizing embedding social order. This will provide the rules that support the social integrity required for enterprise to operate primary law.[4]

To ensure the reliability and regularity of that social order a further evolutionary step is simultaneously necessary. One needs to clarify continuously the boundaries, geo-politically and socially, within which primary law will operate. This is the business of secondary law.[5] This is required to deal with those who refuse to accept understood social mores and constraints, such as Lucas in the case study. In the end, one needs a polity to emerge with the power to enforce compliance on those who exceed the bounds of socially acceptable behaviour. Enterprises require stability. They need confidence in the consequences of the exchanges they enter into with others and in the propriety they feel they have gained as a consequence. To guarantee this, institutions of social guardianship have to co-evolve with the power to formalize, enforce and change the rules of the system – secondary law.

So, paradoxically, while enterprise always seeks to liberate itself from containing forces to access new potential it is also among the first wishing to re-establish restraining institutions to co-evolve with it in a self-re-enforcing manner in its new emergent context.

## In the beginning is containment

An example of a containing institution is social and individual welfare in many parts of Asia and Africa. There, welfare is not provided by the state or enterprise. It is supplied by the extended family or 'non-market' organizations such as the mosque, synagogue or church.[6] In some parts of the world where poverty is high the extended family is seriously debilitating to enterprise. As soon as any enterprise bears fruit relations appear expecting jobs, handouts, debt relief, health care and education. This has to be supported and carried out. Those with enterprise know that the wheel of fortune can easily turn. In time they may be the ones who will need help from the same extended family. This creates a huge marginal tax burden on any enterprise; in many poorer societies, it almost halts enterprise completely.

In Japan, enterprise itself has formalized this and taken on board the social welfare of its employees. In the extended economic upturn of the international bull market that Japan experienced in the latter half of the twentieth century, this was no problem. However, it has caused major problems in the economic downturn of a bear market that East Asia has had to face in the early twenty first century. Japanese enterprise is unlikely to be able to continue shouldering the human welfare responsibilities of their employees; in some instances, they may even have to fire them rather than guaranteeing them jobs for life.

One might surmise that there is likely to be a push for a more individualist-like arm's-length legalistic contracting mode of doing business, distinct from that typical of the communal systems. To an extent, this is happening as many of the most troubled East Asian corporations are being taken over by corporations from the more robust and resilient Anglo-Saxon business systems, e.g. Ford and Mazda, though one should be clear that individualist systems are not exempt from similar problems. Corporate America has a huge overhang of debilitating health care insurance to finance. As medical costs have soared and economic growth has stuttered this is causing enterprise increasing problems. It is also true that support is being given from the more mature communitarian systems of Europe, e.g. by France's Renault to Nissan.

The layers of social embeddedness characteristic of the communal business system exist also in the individualist business system. However, such embeddedness is at its most debilitating in many of the economies in the emergent business system. There the legacy system of social welfare found in much of Asia, all of Africa and some of Southern and Central America is proving very difficult to change quickly. Next to their fiscal burdens these countries carry the socio-economic friction that arises from their lack of an effective means to finance the creation of enterprise, the lack of a reliable communication infrastructure capable of supporting the co-ordination of their activities once started, and often a total absence of any means of distributing the resources it needs and produces to and from the enterprise. To the extent that systems to support any of these exist, they tend to be local rather than national. Such systems are of little value in amassing the finance required for the simplest growing enterprise, let alone one aspiring to national or global markets.

One solution to the restrictions such social institutions impose on enterprise is to use the power of the state to enforce change. The effectiveness of this strategy can perhaps be explored best by reference to the now emerging market economies of Central and Eastern Europe. Their emergence is from a former state socialist system in which an attempt was made to overcome the problems described using the polity 'dictatorship of the proletariat' as the tools. Apart from in the former

Yugoslav Republic, rationalist socialist ideology was used to give the state power to provide finance, communications and distribution and to underwrite the social welfare provided to employees by all production units. Their recent history is saturated with collectivists, or absolutists, who set out to control their productive capacity in this way.

Unfortunately the directors of this process were human and even when rational the human mind is collectively incapable of encompassing the dynamics of complexity.[7] And when rational planning goes wrong, it goes uniformly and expensively wrong. When it gets it 'right' it tends to create a monoculture that can leave sterility elsewhere – the cotton fields of Kazakhstan and the Aral Sea being two of many examples. A solution in one place ignores a need elsewhere and any protestations are overridden in the pursuit of the greater social good. Central socialist planning was simply not able to tap into the richness of knowledge and knowledge, especially of the 'knowing' that exists in each human being's local circumstance of time, place and situation.[8] Central planning loses all of this and in addition provides huge counterincentives to enterprise, which it effectively forbids. This is not helpful.

The result is stagnation or the inert enforced growth of a monoculture sustainable only by continuous effort by a central authority, which has to work ever harder to keep up with the problems it has created in the first place. This occurs despite the best efforts of natural evolution to pollute it with the randomly distributed weeds of enterprise.

So if one were to assert that by suppressing individualism through socialist planning communalism would naturally replace it as a result of the enforced absence of capitalistic enterprise, the evidence would contradict one. Instead of the emergence of communal trust and commitment under socialist planning, it succeeded instead in producing a system in which trust was almost invisible. Locally, in the familial sense this may not have been the case, and to the extent trust thrived elsewhere it was as a means of overcoming the gross inadequacies of socialist rationalist planning in the communal interest. This was communal failure in contrast to market failure.

These countries' experiences of enforced collectivism and the arbitrary non-predictable corrupt treatment by 'them', whoever they may have been, in the end resulted in a pervasive, if not universal, reaction against third-party social institutions. This carried forward into their new experience with capitalism, especially in banking. The latter has a dreadful recent history of failure. The result is that individualism, and individual rights against the state and other social institutions, are now firmly on several national legislative agendas, despite the fact that many of these countries have virtually no means of establishing an effective means of enforcing the rule of law.

## Initiation

In such circumstances, it is hard to envisage any hope for enterprise. The 'rule of law' or the acceptance of some other kind of social norm is a pre-requisite for success. This requires a high degree of certainty on the conduct and regulation of commercial affairs[9] which does not exist in many of the above countries. However, one should never despair of the capacity of evolutionary forces to produce good out of evil. These forces are in all respects far more robust and reliable than the mind of rational man, operating individually or collectively. History tells us they are very capable of turning what looks like defeat into a glorious victory.

For example, the lawlessness of the American Wild West, or America in general, towards the end of the nineteenth century was notorious. It may be that the American social acceptance of the idea that the rule of law is essential for individual liberty was as much due to this as it was to the Founding Fathers' effort to incorporate that idea politically into the US Constitution. Interestingly, the latter was written as a consequence of the Founding Fathers' own and their successors' direct bitter experience of the abuse of power by state and social diktat in the nations from which they had escaped or been evicted. Nearly all the citizens of the US are themselves immigrants or the children of the wave after wave of emigrants escaping from the tyranny of states, the failure of other states' business systems and occasionally the vicissitudes of the natural environment. This may in part explain the naïve faith the citizens of the US seem to have placed in legally enforceable contracts. The newly forming 'Wild East' and hopefully the still to emerge 'Wild South' may in the end evolve to a point similarly replete with popular support for legally enforceable contracts.

What is exciting is that the distribution, finance and communications technology now connecting up the rest of the world is already having a massive impact on these potentially emerging markets. Firstly a mobile-phone network is cheaper, easier to install and intrinsically more reliable than traditional phone systems. As a consequence emerging economies often have better digital telephone access than many advanced countries such as the US – the US especially carries a huge legacy of old analogue and even older cable telephony. It goes without saying that the Internet café is now ubiquitous, enabling connection almost anywhere on the planet for very small sums of money.

On distribution, the needs of enterprise in the mature business systems are such that they required and have constructed trunk and even local distribution networks into emerging economies. DHL, UPS, Federal Express, etc. are all globally ubiquitous and operate out of all such countries' capitals at the very least; 72-hr delivery is probably now possible between any two points on the planet. Flowers are air freighted from East Africa to Amsterdam on a daily basis. Thanks to Dutch enterprise you can now buy fresh cut flowers from East Africa in distant parts of Europe and Central Asia within 48 hours.

The local transport system (for people) that enterprise has constructed in some of these countries is awe-inspiring. One of the authors travelled the 40 km from the high street in Kampala to the front door of his hotel in Entebbe by public privately owned transport in 40 minutes, including the 5-minute wait for a suitable minibus in Kampala and the immediate transfer from the mini-bus to the pillion seat on a small moped in Entebbe. The cost of this journey was $1 US.

On finance, provided one has the required underlying assets or reliable cash flow it is possible, no matter what one's nationality, to get a credit card. It is unequivocally possible to use it virtually anywhere where enterprise is close to or past the ignition point required for emergence.

Some of the economies that may possibly be emerging – China, India, Indonesia and the Philippines – have the largest potential customer base on this planet. Their populations are poor in cash terms. However, the value adding product, knowledge (the focus of this book), has extremely low marginal production and distribution costs. Another copy of Windows 2000 has a vanishingly small cost, especially if the same disk is used to install many copies. This is precisely what happens in much of the world. No after-sales support, no upgrades but still functional on a third-hand desktop powered by an old Intel micro-processor.

Part of the globalization process is the emergence of such new markets. Many products these days fall into this category. Their development costs are huge; however, if these are written off against first-generation sales in rich countries and the technology then moves on there should be no problem about second-generation hardware and software from secondary markets coming back to the primary market. Sales in poor countries will not result in resale back to the rich ones, as they will want only the latest well-supported technology. This business opportunity is such that some enterprises in rich countries are already actively pursuing such business themselves, rather than leaving it to third parties.[10]

## Restraint

In this whole process, the link between change in the opportunities facing enterprise and collective action is particularly important. For a new but effective industry to appear enterprise in it must have developed a product, and a critical number of customers sufficient to be credible with suppliers and financiers. Without these, production cannot go forward. One thus needs a credible idea and customer base to attract support from potential backers to cover the delay from concept to market.

The opportunity for initiating change is greatest where creative individuals pursue enterprise unimpeded. However, as already indicated, this can be the route to anarchy, but this will not generally be the case as the processes involved in mobilizing resources is so lengthy, costly and risky that it is unachievable on short time scales without the support of some kind of collective action. Finance is rarely given easily to an entirely new enterprise in an entirely new field.

However, if a number of potentially competitive enterprises face each other competitively with a similar product but co-operate to market themselves as an industry, more may be possible faster. Their mutual recognition may give each enough credence to get the support required to proceed. In the late medieval period, such credence was given by merchant guilds. They could and did impose standards of trading on their members. This provided the collective social capital required for credence. Others outside their craft then used guild membership as a guide to the risks involved in financing a guild member. The processes by which such social capital can accrue social institutional legitimacy is vital to understanding emergence.

Social capital is any institution that recognizes mutual acquaintance and recognizes a function for each individual within the network of relationships so defined.[11] A key institution is *reputation control.* The reputation of a town or a particular guild or a particular social group is social capital it can use to enable its members to succeed. In the medieval merchant network, this enabled them to grow their business nationally and internationally. Some[12] choose to call this a 'governance structure' rather than 'social capital'. The governance approach generally implies some access to power to generate the primary law required to enforce it. The social capital[13] approach, on the other hand, stresses the voluntary alteration and exploitation of network structure by individuals and enterprises to create opportunities. In the institutional vacuum typical of emergence,[14] a collective is hard to find. In the modern setting, appropriate to the emergence of a global society, weakness appears in two areas. Each requires the empowered collective action of a polity, as the incentive for a voluntary social approach is limited. The two are: support for knowledge creation and an institutional infrastructure:[15]

- **Knowledge-creation and knowledge:** In pursuing new technologies everyone wants to be aware of the latest research and to inform and influence developments regarding technical standards and compatibility. The process of technological emergence is facilitated if all are prepared to participate in activities such as conferences and technical committees.[16] Yet each enterprise would benefit most if it had access to its competitors' thinking without giving access to its own. Useful collective action may then not happen.
- **Institutional infrastructure:** During emergence, no established code of conduct exists. Institutional mechanisms are needed to monitor, then signal, an enterprise's reputation while it is in its infancy. Each enterprise benefits from the reliability of others of the same ilk in dealings with others. Collective action is needed to initiate structures to certify and police this. This is beneficial to all. Each enterprise can get advantage in using the social capital accruing from such work, yet act in a manner opposed to it.[17]

Change requires collective action but collective institutions have embedded in them an incentive for opportunistic individual behaviour, free-riding, that undermines their effectiveness. This is the pressure in emergence that leads to the creation or acceptance of a supportive polity. The polity is invested with the power to direct appropriate behaviour. Pre-commitment to the new and as yet unclear social norms of a potential trading partner is unattractive if not downright stupid. However without it socially, and individually, lucrative investments may not be made in people or cultures that cannot support strong and appropriate socio-political institutions.

It is clear that when enterprises are struggling with such uncertainty communal inaction and regulatory uncertainty are maximal. The power of a polity, the state, is then required. It can give formal legitimacy to the educational or social organizations that provide the support enterprise requires. Medieval merchants financed the king and he used his feudal power to put the merchants beyond the reach of containing and constraining feudal institutions. On the contrary, emergent enterprise, given its lack of coherence and size, may be viewed with such suspicion that investment in it by any stakeholder will be more often problematic.

## The return to stasis

We now turn to a final question. What happens after the traumas of industry creation are passed and a new field of enterprise is established?[18] It has been argued[19] that the early experience of an industry is imprinted on its future behaviour. We agree that history matters. Behaviour becomes embedded in each enterprise and is co-evolved with its institutional basis of support, and this relationship is carried forward increasingly.[20] This is not surprising. In emergence, co-evolution is self-re-enforcing for institutions as well as enterprise.

First, enterprises realise early on in an emergent context that they are playing in a win–win game. They thus gain from co-operation, not competition. It gives them credence with potential stakeholders. Most studies presume such that groupings are simply there. They do not attempt to explain their evolution to that point.[21] As we have seen, a group of co-operative competing enterprises has a useful source of social capital. Those negotiating and dealing with them can approach each in a similar manner. However this sameness leaves little room for adaptation to change – although, with maturity of enterprises and institutions, this may no longer seem important.[22]

In our late medieval case study, from such early co-operative activity emerged merchant guilds as social then politico-legal institutions. The autonomy these fought for led to the regulated foundation and growth of cities. However, this meant that towns that did not achieve such status found it difficult to grow given the jealousy of existing cities and the states supporting them. Success breeds success and exclusivity that has to be accommodated – but as the towns that cannot then grow do not lose anything and actually may gain a greater variety of goods from the cities that do grow it is a win–win not a win–lose game even for them. Institutions that emerge to support enterprise in this process are then captured by the existing successful enterprise and used to suppress competitive activity by others. Institutions therefore generally start as the instruments of enterprise but in the end slowly but surely restrain the process of emergence until a point is reached where the opposing powers of the energy generated by enterprise are overcome. We then slip into a constrained and contained state of homeostasis.

The key to our synthesis is thus not so much how enterprise flourishes as how in doing so it creates the 'embeddedness', both social and political, that in the end will contain its further unfettered expansion. This is of course only until a new source of potential is revealed to encourage it to reach beyond the bounds it has set itself in. The co-evolutionary processes described lead to the construction of the embedding infrastructure necessary for enterprise to flourish. In the end, these mature into a guardianship supporting honest stable enterprise, inimical to new enterprise.

Our two extreme poles of business system, the individualist and communal systems, place different emphasis on the relative importance of formal and informal institutions, and their overall interconnectivity with successful enterprise. However, that interconnectivity does exist. This means that a very complex set of national objectives can be orchestrated by these systems, whether consciously in the communal case or unconsciously by the 'invisible hand' in the individualist case.

If this is to produce an effective business system, such orchestration has to evolve within the bounds of the emerging markets of Asia, Eastern Europe and South America. Many countries have tried to emulate the two existing systems combining elements of each, but institutional and organizational backwardness makes this difficult:

> it is the mixture of formal rules, informal norms and enforcement characteristics that shapes economic performance. While the rules may be changed overnight, the informal norms usually change only gradually . . . The implication is that transferring the formal political and economic rules of successful Western market economies to third-world and Eastern European economies is not a sufficient condition for good performance. (North 1994, p. 366)

## What can go wrong

There has always been interest in the kinds of institutions and supporting organizational structures that can assist the process of emergence. Too often the approach is to try naïvely to transplant successful institutions from mature business systems into emerging ones. The importance of understanding the fundamental differences between these emerging societies and more mature ones leads one to inquire into the relevance of non-market, non-standard customs and practices in effecting business transactions in such contexts.[23]

For us, such interest is fundamental. We do not want merely to understand the attributes of success, but the pathways by which it can be achieved. Huge wasted effort has gone into transplanting organizations and institutions form mature systems into emerging ones. Almost without exception in Africa, South America and Asia they have quickly become totally moribund.[24] The successful parts of Asia are those where they have found their own pathway, it has not been imposed upon them. In Chapter 6 we will explore ways in which it is possible to establish effective propriety in the interest of stakeholders who would otherwise not become engaged in the process.

There is no guarantee that a successful national business system, whether individualist or communal, can be transferred successfully to other parts of the world. The experiences described suggest that it cannot. The economic crisis of 1997 in various Asian countries such as Indonesia, Thailand, South Korea and Malaysia showed the difficulties such countries experience in absorbing the lessons of others. Without an evolutionary matured institutional structure, formal or informal, into which these lessons can be embedded, difficulties will be inevitable.

As we have argued, the relative ratio of formal, legal mechanisms, to informal, societal norms, varies enormously between systems. Trust is essential in all cases. Recent experience is such that, to a large extent, trust has been destroyed. In any emerging economy the credibility of some types of institution and enterprise has been eroded, limiting the capacity of emergent forces to break free of existing institutional limitations: we refer, for example, to the pyramid banking scandal in Albania.[25] It does not really matter whether the Asian economic crisis that began in 1997 was due to an insufficient level of institutions to support effective exchange, or simply to the fundamental difficulties of adjusting to globalization. The result has been to dent confidence in these countries' emerging institutions and enterprises.

In South Korea, the economic crisis can be attributed to the difficulties of an insufficiently mature banking sector. This misallocated funds to inefficient, government-supported corporations. In other Asian countries, such as Malaysia, the difficulties can be attributed to a newly established stock market whose shortcomings were shown up by excessive amounts of foreign investment relative to the size of the domestic economy.

The complexities of national business systems, as shown in Figures 4.2 and 4.3 (pp. 50, 55), suggest that the realities of the Asian economic crisis, as it affected emerging economies, arose out of the lack of maturity in the relationship between 'institutions', formal and informal, and their defining 'organizations'. Organizations, whether political, social, educational or economic, in such a context cannot communicate sufficiently well to allow them to foresee such crises and avoid their worst effects. Mature business systems, on the other hand, have weathered a significant number of business cycles.

Both institutions and their supporting organizations need to have a maturity of trust and an ability to communicate effectively that ensures that the dramatic changes going on in their political and economic context do not unbalance them and undermine what has begun to grow. Communal growth and the win–win scenario of the bull market are far easier to deal with communally than the win–lose scenario inevitable in the decline of the bear market. The relationship between institutions and organizations needs to be seen holistically if one is to appreciate the complexities required to achieve successful economic performance.[26] The traditional view has tended to generalise naïvely from the successes of mature economies, and to apply these generalizations to new and emerging ones in an inappropriate – or, more frequently, a badly timed – manner.[27]

The rest of this book sets out to give substance to the idea that any emerging system requires potential stakeholders to have certainty substituted for uncertainty, order for turbulence and trust for mendacity. We believe this is possible in the global business system now emerging. Chapter 6 explores this.

*This page intentionally left blank*

# Part II

# Analysis

*This page intentionally left blank*

# 6
# Markets, Individual Interest and Social Governance

## Introduction

Emergent systems[1] face major challenges. To take advantage of the business opportunities available they need a well-ordered institutional environment; enterprise requires this. Generally they cannot provide this themselves and thus third-party intervention is required. The states in this category have nevertheless all had phenomenal economic growth, high rates of population expansion and ever-increasing numbers of globally successful enterprises – Embraer Aircraft for Brazil, Proton cars for Malaya, Samsung electronics for Korea and, further back in time, a company like Toyota for Japan.

In good times, they get keen attention from investors and multinationals. The former seek very high rates of return from what is initially a relatively small investment. The latter seek economical outsourced supply. However, emerging nations' means of doing business – legal systems, public policy and consumers – differ considerably from those found in mature business systems. Those transacting with them seem to face major difficulties in ensuring that the results they hope for are achieved.[2] They are, or emergence would not be the phenomenon of interest that it is.

To aid our subsequent discussion we now summarize discussions to date in Table 6.1. This shows the chief characteristics of the emergent and the two mature business system, the individualist and communal. In this chapter, we offer a conceptual framework for analysing the response of enterprise to the challenge posed by the contractual and social uncertainty endemic to emergence.[3] We set out to articulate the means by which stakeholders – investors, suppliers, partners, customers, state, etc. – maintain appropriate propriety when the institutional

*Table 6.1* Three major systems of governance and business

| Type of business system | Key characteristics |
|---|---|
| Individualist | Strong legal system with reliance on contracts between autonomous individual enterprises; strong commitment to free markets and trade; culture supportive of creativity, invention and enterprise; clear demarcating boundaries set between the state, financial markets, banking, industries and other social institutions; stable returns and high resilience in the face of change up or down – freedom to act within strong clear limits or boundaries formally set by the state. |
| Communal | Weak formal legal system with reliance on personal relationships rather than contracts; individual has strong social obligations; strong commitment to trade and commerce using protected or directed markets; culture supportive of conformity, innovation and strong leadership; the state, financial markets, banking and industry intertwined; stable returns and very high growth in the bull market but the bear market hard to handle – strong social accretions of power and influence constrain enterprise to a limited set of socially acceptable behaviour. |
| Emerging | No reliable legal system or relationships except very localized ones; individuals isolated apart from immediate family who often hold a lien over any wealth they can generate; little commitment to the market and trade; the markets that do exist are highly volatile and unreliable and often corrupted; culture not supportive of any change or enterprise that disrupts the status quo *ex ante*; the state, financial markets, banking and industry either collectively or separately hardly exist in a cohesive way; all this brings high levels of discouraging unpredictability which amplifies uncertainty and magnifies risk leading to very high but erratic returns – no strong formal boundaries and no significant social accretions of informal control modulating growth and development. |

frameworks, formal and informal, normally used to achieve this either do not exit or are no longer reliable.

Here we explore solutions to this dilemma by considering what systems of governance can be established given that transacting can have very high opportunity costs. In emerging environments, these costs of opportunities foregone can be considerable: bad debts, the delivery of goods of inferior quality, etc. The costs of establishing the integrity and *bona fides* of those with whom one intends to deal can be very high: in some cases, it may be so high that potentially lucrative trade does not occur.

The cost of doing business, transacting, varies across societies. On average one would expect societies with lower transactions costs to be more viable and so prosper more than those where these costs are higher. The structure of governance and enterprise each has available to address these issues varies. Truly emergent systems are particularly interesting. They have no legacy of governance as we define it.

## Institutional scaffolding

The emergent business system works, we propose, because such a system is supported by a temporary scaffolding of techniques supportive of the longer-term construction of the institutions needed to support enterprise. One such technique is 'counter-trade'. This can ensure reciprocal commitments which will be honoured in the absence of any informal social or formal legal enforcement mechanisms.[4] We would argue that if it were not for this, emergence, once ignited, could not be sustained.

In emergence there is an institutional vacuum, created by explosive socio-economic development. In principle, this makes enterprise difficult to sustain. It is our contention that competitive self-seeking behaviour is even less sustainable in emerging economies than in mature ones. The temptation to renege on any co-operative arrangements set up to police exchange is also high, given the huge potential pay-offs from cheating and the virtual impossibility of monitoring performance and/or enforcing agreements. In more advanced systems co-operative trade is supported by the socially accreted characteristics of reciprocity, trust and forbearance. The existing social embeddedness limits opportunism.

The latter has to be seen in sharp contrast to what happens when we rely on formal contractual exchange.[5] Here, trade may be more aggressively individualist and competitive. The results required are achieved through the formal processes that evolve to provide a 'politically embedded' context for exchange. In parts of modern society personal acquisitiveness is not modulated by social norms and sanctions but by the state's use of its power to sanction bad behaviour.

In emergent economies neither of the above routes to a supportive environment for effective enterprise is available. Yet such societies can grow very rapidly. One cannot rely on social or judicial sanction to constrain bad behaviour. What can one rely on? How can, and is, enterprise facilitated in such a context?

## Governance in emergent networked contexts

A key feature of the emerging wider global economy is the proliferation within it of international joint ventures, alliances and the interconnection of value chains in loose networks. The fact that these have much in common with constructs that have been observed to emerge in Japan has heightened interest in Japanese industrial organization. Since the Second World War, the organization of Japanese industry has been deliberately constructed on the basis of groupings of such loose connectivity,[6] *Keiretsu*.

Looking at this system enables one to reflect on how similar methods may work within the networks of more informal commercial relationships that now span the globe.[7] As we have discussed, one would expect transaction costs in such a system to be so high that little trade would occur, but the reverse is true – because both market and non-market-based knowledge exchange, whether within or between enterprises, is crucial for the choice and design of processes leading to efficient governance of those involved in transactions.[8]

Transition or emerging economies and industries are currently undergoing massive economic transformation. Many are still changing rapidly in all socio-economic dimensions. Many radical solutions have been proffered to overcome the difficulties they have, first in igniting and then sustaining the rapid economic development they wish to generate so as to participate fully in the global economy – for instance: privatization, prescribed investment, directed international trading.

However, without the right historical context in which to embed these ideas it is unlikely that transplanting techniques directly from other business systems will work. Those that attempt such transplants should be given as much credence as we would give an ignorant immigrant who, on observing that as all wealthy people drove around in expensive cars, thought that he could become wealthy by using his savings to buy one himself.

In this chapter we develop[9] a typology for exchange and stakeholder governance that can work during emergence. Our analysis suggests that in emerging economies counter-trade arrangements may be made effective where exchange based on trust or contract cannot. We have already seen that one way that trade can be supported, when the institutions necessary to support markets are absent, is through counter-trade. This type of trade has the advantage that each transaction can be constructed to be self-enforcing. It provides a strong basis from which to establish effective co-operation. It buys the time needed to allow trust to grow. To do all this entails a high price, but hopefully only in the short term. This can be paid, and is paid, in the highly volatile, unpredictable but potentially lucrative business environments typical of emergence.

As we will show, counter-trade appropriately configured can create mutual, irrevocable commitments with significant mutual upside benefits and very tough downside penalties.[10] This is structurally much like what is achievable by taking and giving hostages to fortune: I will marry my daughter to your first son if you marry your daughter to my first son to guarantee our mutual goodwill. With such hostages at stake any weaknesses of contract or mutuality of trust can be overcome, even in highly unpredictable environments. This is an expensive way to transact. The returns have to be very high indeed to justify the costs involved.

Such mutual hostage taking and giving is a means to provide the support exchange required in volatile emergent environments[11] and provides one answer to the dilemma posed by institutionally void business systems. Such institutional deserts are the inevitable consequence of explosive socio-economic growth, meaning that legacy institutions and organizations are destroyed, wiping out all the old certainties in advance of the creation of new ones. Traditionally, counter-trade is explained as a response to a shortage in foreign exchange; we argue that it is better seen as an institutional construction that can remedy deficiencies in the structure of governance during emergence. It enables transactions to take place in circumstances where at first sight transactions of any sort would seem impossible.[12]

## The significance of measurement and enforcement costs

The costs of transacting must affect the viability of different styles of enterprise. As much of the value created today is in 'knowing' then how can it, being partly intangible, be traded? The argument has been that it is not.[13] As no contract can be written for it, 'knowing' is nurtured as a core activity within a large single enterprise and its managerial hierarchy controls its output. The income to support its production comes from the products made available by the use of knowledge.[14] This cannot tenably explain much knowledge exchange, which is huge and often does not take place within the ambit of one legal entity. This approach is also deficient unless one can make the cost of measurement and enforcement used by an enterprise's hierarchy explicit. One needs this to ensure that the value wrapped up in the 'knowing' of employees adds value commensurate with their costs.[15]

Management requires measurements as much as the market does. To be truly effective, it needs to be able to compare the cost of an activity to the value it generates. The enforcement costs incurred to ensure that the value transacted for with employees is also delivered need to be recognized, too. Such costs are especially important in international business settings, where multiple legal jurisdictions and cultures amplify rather than attenuate the complexity and unpredictability faced by all transactors, whether within or without an enterprise.

## Measurement

Contractual arrangements have to take account of the need to reduce sorting, searching and measurement costs. This is particularly so when the perceived value of the product may vary substantially from unit to unit. To illustrate, let us consider two cases: that of trade in movies on first release and that in uncut diamonds. The methods used in these cases show that transactors can gain by *not* measuring and comparing value received against cost on a single transaction. It is only sensible to do so over an agreed series of transactions. The way this works is that the buyer agrees to purchase on trust and unseen a batch of movies or a series of parcels of diamonds of a given prior agreed weight. However, the system works only if evident value is added over that series. The first exhibitor of a movie may lose on some movies but hopefully makes sufficient profit on the successful ones to more than compensate for the losses incurred on others. The diamond merchant who buys parcels of diamonds by carat weight must make sufficient of the really good stones he occasionally finds to cover the cost of the bad stones he has to process and/or sell on.

Either party in such a case may still be tempted to insist on value measurement.[16] In the examples quoted, this will lead to higher costs for both parties. In the film case how does one pre-contract a price based on how much the public will like the film and therefore how many will turn up and pay the ticket price? The system and research needed for answering this question to the satisfaction of both parties would be very expensive. Similarly a system that tried to price every diamond prior to cutting would be expensive. A really large very beautiful stone may easily shatter on the workbench. These higher costs could be recovered only from the final customer. In a truly competitive market where others transact more economically, one would find the consumer unwilling to pay.

The temptation to insist on prior valuation can be reduced by inducing credible commitments between the parties to an exchange.[17] The film distributor agrees to show a sequence of movies from a supplier; a diamond buyer agrees to buy weighed parcels of stones unseen. Deliberately maintaining, or even increasing, the already high measurement costs would probably assist this process. This increase in the knowledge asymmetry between the transacting parties makes it more worthwhile for the buyer to trust the long-term integrity of the supplier. Strategies such as these reduce the time and effort spent in measurement and pricing. This produces gains for both parties over a sequence of transactions.

## Enforcement costs

In considering the next type of cost, that of enforcement,[18] one can contrast institutionalized social trust as in the communal business systems – for example, in Japan – with legalistic contracting ones as in the individualist business system, common to the US and UK. In the latter case contracts reduce enforcement costs by stipulating the terms of trade in advance and by arranging for third parties to undertake any necessary enforcement.

The alternative in communal systems is for a reputation for 'fair trading' to be maintained by the threat of a social, not legal, sanction. Social sanctions may appear more expensive to establish initially, but are more robust than a system that relies on the passing of laws. These may then exist but be unenforceable. The social sanction approach is more time-consuming and expensive to set up but provides a basis for confidence that performance to agreement will be enforced. It also promotes the co-operative attitudes required to create networks or the cluster of relationships needed to establish enforceable if implicit contracts.[19]

This kind of evolved context can be exploited to far greater advantage than is represented by the accumulation of transactions that go on within it. The non-contractual elements of business relationships, such as a sense of trust and goodwill, can then produce such huge pay-offs that any threat of their loss can effectively deter the taking of any possible easy short-term pay-offs from the pursuit of self-interest. This does away with any need to have recourse even to the threat of litigation.[20]

## Hostages to fortune

But the two approaches to enforcement described do not address the cost of transacting during emergence. Neither trust nor contract can be relied upon then. However, if the parties to a transaction mutually exchange a valuable hostage co-operation is guaranteed independent of any reliable institutional underpinnings. If default is perceived as having occurred by either party the hostages can be taken irrevocably. This is a very powerful incentive to compliance. Note it is not necessarily the actuality of default that matters but a trading partner's perception that it has occurred that triggers the forfeiture of the hostage. Where no other means can be relied upon, as is the case in emergence, this may be the only means available to ignite the initial series of trades required to institute explosive growth:

> [T]he ancients exchanged hostages, drank wine from the same glass to demonstrate the absence of poison, met in public places to inhibit the massacre of one by the other, and even deliberately exchanged spies to facilitate transmittal of authentic knowledge...in a lawless world that provides no recourse to damage suits for breach of unwritten contracts, hostages may be the only device for partners to strike a bargain. (Schelling 1960, p. 72)

This approach can safeguard a sequence of transactions in unpredictable and so uncertain circumstances. The parties construct a situation in which both will lose heavily if they do not co-operate, and gain significantly if they do. Note that the same hostage can be used over and over again to cover a series of transactions, much the same as the contracts did between movie distributors and producers and between diamond merchants and diamond producers. If the dynamic of a series of transactions is completed in good faith, then trust may become so well embedded that the hostages may no longer be required.

Social institutions evolve to accrete order and reduce uncertainty. In doing this they promote economic and social exchange as cooperative processes.[21] Establishing co-operation is difficult if the game is only played once. Knowledge about the other actors is limited and extremely costly to obtain and/or unreliable. If there are a large number of actors involved in a potential exchange, the costs are prohibitive. In emerging and transition economies the initial trades required to ignite development are like this. This magnifies the level of uncertainty and complexity that must be overcome to initiate emergence. The old order is being eroded and the new will not be sufficiently established. In such circumstances, socio-economic or political analogues of hostage taking can work.

Emerging markets are those characterized by such unpredictable socio-political environments where neither trust nor contract can be relied on.[22] Certain types of counter-trade, such as buy-backs, offsets and counter-purchase produce are usefully analogous to hostage taking. They can insert sufficient obligatory reciprocity into a deal to build the confidence required to reduce transaction costs.[23]

## Three business systems, three institutions: contracts, trust and hostages

It is important to consider the means used to monitor and control exchange once initiated. Here we show that the method used helps explain the rationale behind alternative governance structures.

The choice is:

(1) Vertical integration by managerial hierarchy in a single enterprise
(2) Horizontal integration over a network of long-term relationships[24]
(3) Horizontal or vertical market relationships.

In any transaction the parties involved need to protect themselves from 'self-seeking with guile'. Such 'opportunism', meaning the 'threat of one party ceasing to trade so as to appropriate a greater share of the surplus after specific investments have been made'[25] is inimical to the growth of the connectivity required for network-based growth whether to be achieved through social reciprocal exchange or commercial trading, and can be reduced depending on relative enforcement costs. These are determined by evolutionary experience by one of three alternatives:

(1) Contracts
(2) An established reputation in which a partner in exchange can place trust
(3) Obligations enforced by one of the forms of hostaging already described.

At one extreme are explicit legal contracts enforceable by a third party provided by the polity, in the middle are commitments undertaken within a defined social context and at the other extreme obligations enforced bilaterally by some mutually agreed hostage to fortune provided by one or both contracting parties. Some – for example, many in the US – overemphasize the role litigation, laws and regulations can play in value-generating transactions. There, this approach is invariably relied on in preference to institutionalized trust.[26] On the other hand, there are societies where reputation and trust are crucial to all economic transactions and social responsibility holds sway over reliance on the possibility of judicial action – e.g. at one time in Japan there were only 100 lawyers in the whole country. In such societies inter-enterprise transactions are fully embedded in social institutions.

Such practice recognizes that, in addition to the specific transactions supported, relational networks are expected at other times to provide value and social assistance, especially during a crisis.[27] However, as we discussed in Chapter 5, in any prolonged crisis, such as has occurred in the Far East since the late 1990s, such loyalty may not be sustainable if one is ultimately faced with the choice between survival or abandonment. Here the impersonal individualist business system has an evolutionary advantage. In such systems, one has no responsibility for a duty of care to suppliers, customers, staff or shareholders beyond that explicitly contracted for. This allows one to make the survival decision easily with no damage to reputation or self-image. This, as we have seen, is not at all easy in the communal business system.

On the other hand, the communal business system can still operate in circumstances where an individualist market-based system may fail. In communal transactions there may be no immediate consideration given in exchange. Such reciprocity may be very appropriate for trading knowledge, given the problems inherent in trying to contract for all its unknowable and non-measurable dimensions at the time it is communicated.

However, none of this is academic if the social relationships essential to trade do not exist and have to be constructed at the time and then maintained independent of any contractual enforcement system maintained by a polity or social pressure. This is the case in the emergent business system. Enterprises in the emergent system have to deal with market uncertainties either by internalising them, as do multinationals, or by setting up a network of 'reliable' local personal contacts.[28] Thus in all instances transactions, and the institutional and enterprise configurations supporting them, are influenced by the trust that can or cannot be established in their particular circumstance.

Enterprises and the institutions supporting them, when faced with environmental uncertainty and complexity, evolve whatever combination of hierarchy and socially enforced governance structure is cost-effective and appropriate to modulating their exchange activity. At one end of the spectrum they can capitalize on an existing level of political or social trust, or at the other set out to develop trust specific to their new partner and a specific transaction with him.

One way of setting up trust by the latter route is by making a credible non-refutable commitment. One or both parties invest in contract-specific assets that visibly and actually commit them to a sequence of deals with a specific partner.[29] Such assets are their hostages to fortune.

In the individualist business system, these do not have to be specifically set up. They are implicit in the enforceable liquidated damages that cover premature contract termination; these are automatic to any deal in this context. This means each party can finesse, at virtually no direct cost to themselves, the trust-building element of credible commitment. However to finance the political and social institution involved they may well be taxed by the polity creating and supporting this service.[30]

In the communal world there could be no question of termination – 'my word is my bond'. This is socially conceivable only if arrived at by mutual agreement; both parties have to have confidence in its validity.

In counter-trade transaction-specific safeguards are constructed for each transaction. If this is possible, then credible commitment can be signalled in bilateral trade.[31] In such circumstances, the contractual arrangements are designed so that the compensation or punishment for a breach of agreement is safeguarded by the internal properties of the deal. This is analogous to an exchange of hostages. Illustrative of this are the deals which used to be set up by the exporting arm of Central and Eastern European governments. Because of the uncertainty of their markets and institutional environments due to the unpredictable, often arbitrary manner in which government officials apply their law, it was impossible to have recourse to exchange mechanisms based on contract law or institutionalized trust:

> [M]any of the gains from trade cannot, however, be attained through spot transactions. They require legal and governmental institutions that guarantee, among other things, individual right to impartial enforcement of contracts and property... the order in Soviet-type societies came from administration – from official discretion – rather than from the rule of law. Olson (1992, p. 72)

Such capricious use of political power discourages parties from trying to form long-term business relationships. It leaves recourse to legal enforcement worthless. In this sense, emerging business systems such as those of Eastern Europe might be characterized as having an unstable mix of the remnants of the old regime and of newly liberalized markets.[32] They thus lack both the formal, legal aspects of the individualist business system and the informal institutions and non-market processes of the communal system.

## Counter-trade

Counter-trade is a distinct type of organizational response to a lack of legal or social institutions. It can be differentiated from other type of bilateral exchange based on political or social capital. It relies on an analogue of hostage taking to reduce trading risks. Traditional explanations rely on threats to future contracts or a firm's reputation as sufficient to explain the continued prevalence of counter-trade. We believe, with others, that they are not.[33]

A particular form of counter-trade is a joint venture agreement in which two parties each provide some input to a production process. The goods produced are allocated to each in a pre-arranged fixed proportion. Clearly this involves the exchange of metaphorical hostages, namely the value wrapped up in the goods or services supplied initially, usually machinery, and are paid for out of the sale of the output from the imported machinery. This kind of deal works best where the product concerned has no market whatsoever in the country where the manufacturing activity is carried out. There is then a very strong hostage to fortune for both sides. One has lost effective control of their asset used in production but the other has production they cannot sell without the assistance of their machinery supplier.

Given the increasing role of emergent markets in the world economy it is therefore not surprising to find that buy-back is the fastest-growing form of international counter-trade.[34] It is currently estimated at some 20 per cent of all such trade. Another kind of counter trade, production-sharing agreements, can also be categorized as a type of hostage-based exchange. The output of a jointly financed production facility is shared between the parties. Indonesia, for example, receives accurate knowledge from oil exploration and development companies, by paying them with a proportion of the oil produced from any deposits they find and develop. IKEA's practice of providing machinery in exchange for price discounts on output is another example. While similar to buy-back the latter is not actually an example of buy-back, as the compensation is in cash discounts not output.

Although offsets and counter-purchase may be seen as having no hostage element, this is not strictly true as they generally have some hostage to fortune embedded in the deal. Both parties set things up so that they have something to lose if they break their agreement. This provides a strong incentive for mutual commitment to be maintained. Offsets are commonly used in defence industry purchases, or civilian aircraft contracts. They are characterized by the imposition of performance conditions on the seller of the good or service.

Through an ancillary transaction these allow the buyer to recoup, or offset, some of his capital costs. Whether the offsets are direct or indirect, the purchaser, generally a state, is likely to sustain reciprocity beyond that associated with normal market exchange.[35] If it were to renege on the deal it would severely damage its own interest in technology transfer, foreign market access and the domestic political leverage a government can achieve by distributing the economic and social largesse so generated.

Counter-purchase is a commitment to buy a certain quantity, or receive a percentage of the sale price, of goods to be received from the importer's country as payment for the goods originally exported. The goods received may be from a third party in the originally importing country. It has been suggested[36] that this is undertaken because the link between the first and subsequent transactions creates a bond between the parties. Counter-purchase is frequently used when there is a need to exchange high-quality technology and the seller's incentive to cheat on quality is great, and/or perhaps the buyer's creditworthiness is low. In terms of the hostage mechanism, it is important to note that Western firms may be tempted to under-supply quality. They can then blame the adverse circumstances in developing countries for the resulting unsatisfactory performance.

Table 6.2 summarizes our typology for the governance of transactions.

## Integrating governance and control

We have now looked at how the stakeholders in exchange act as players in any of the three institutional frameworks we have distinguished. They evolve to effect a proper system of governance sustaining their propriety in the results of trade. This is driven by the cost of transacting using a rationale based on the idea of counter-trade.[37] Its utility in emergence is significant.

Such hostage-type arrangements are in fact a portable institution. This is capable of being set up even in the most difficult circumstances to assist the initiation of transactions. It thereby aids the development of a climate conducive to continuing trust-building socio-economic exchange. Hostage-based exchange is manifested in certain types of

*Table 6.2* Enforcement mechanisms

| | |
|---|---|
| Contract | Requires mature, stable business environments where reliance can be placed on the bounds set to behaviour by political institutions for the rule of law. Contract-based exchange is essentially one-off with an efficient competitive market providing the systemic and contextual stability necessary for the governance of transactions. The archetypal type of exchange in individualist business systems such as those of the US or UK. However, it requires a capacity to be very specific about what is traded – if this is not possible, market failure results and, even in the individualist business system, relational hierarchies must then emerge, in the form of enterprises. |
| Trust | Requires mature, stable business environments where reliance can be placed on the socially enforced integrity of others. The archetypal type of exchange in communal societies such as Japan (North 1990; Olson 1992). Does not require high specificity for the value exchanged but does require large investment in trust building measures, social and practical, to sustain the social hierarchy it creates. It is therefore *a priori* more expensive than the market but arguably in a bull market context where trust is easy to sustain produces higher quality more cheaply than the market. Co-operative inter-organizational networks based on social relationships are a natural consequence. Where contractual uncertainty would exist on individual transactions over a sequence of transactions some faith can be built on the return that may be earned from the reciprocal exchange that is the essence of this system. |
| Hostage (counter-trade) | Does not require a mature stable business environment. The archetypical means of doing business in emerging markets. Effective when measurement and enforcement costs are difficult to ascertain. Reciprocal trade arrangements create artificial bonds and dependencies that ensure compliance with the transactions outcome as perceived by the other party. This requires a very expensive initial commitment of a valuable hostage, but the same hostage can be used repeatedly to produce economies of scale conducive to a continuing trading relationship. |

counter-trade, e.g. buy-backs, offsets and counter-purchase. These can be seen as instilling reciprocity and mutual commitment. This reduces the prohibitive transaction costs which are a consequence of the issue of identity – the subject of Chapter 7. One needs to know with whom one is dealing in such problematic circumstances. What is their reputation?

Do they have satisfied customers? Do others speak well of them? Is their business registered or certificated in some way by the state or others? A transactor's identity so described is inevitably weak during emergence:[38] his business may have been created only shortly before he starts to deal with you.

The kind of approach to the problems of transacting during emergence we have described here is one way of overcoming the identity problem and as such can better explain the persistence of international counter-trade than, for example, a local shortage of Forex. We see it as providing institution-building scaffolding. This helps overcome the uncertainty inevitable in emergence when explosive development has undermined the utility of existing social and political institutions.[39] The artificially created hostage-in-exchange counter-trade provides is effective in enforcing trading agreements in the interregnum between the ignition of emergence and the evolution of institutions appropriate to the new environment. We also see measurement and enforcement costs as having a significant[40] role to play in exchange and why identity, bureaucratic, social or bilateral, is essential to co-operative exchange.

Transaction cost considerations can be very useful in helping one understand the processes of emergence, especially those leading to the formation of institutions supportive of enterprise. While political identity and contracts facilitate market transactions, trust is crucial to the formation and sustainability of co-operative relationships.[41] Where neither contracts nor trust provide a viable institutional means of enforcement, hostages impose mutual commitment in a workable fashion conducive to the formation of a trusting network. Contracts, trust, and hostages can all be seen as alternative means to affect exchange. They represent sequential evolution with a dynamic driven by, or that needs to affect, measurement and enforcement costs.

This framework for analysing the response of enterprise to contractual uncertainty has several implications. With high levels of unpredictability, the advantage of pure markets in co-ordinating economic transactions is weak.[42] We therefore have to consider the emerging complexity and diversity of the globalizing economy. Our analysis of types of exchange hinges on issues with wider implications for the future of the global economy.[43] The configuration of institutions and enterprises was seen as brought about by different transaction cost conditions, and by the socio-political foundations of a transactor's identity, or lack of it.

Thus, in the globalizing context now prevalent, the players in international business need to take their thinking away from the level at which transactions occur and raise it to the broader question of how they can nurture enterprise and institutional co-evolution in an emergent context. This may be difficult, as exchange always requires an identity for each transactor. We will now give some consideration as to how these issues may be overcome in the particular circumstance of knowledge, seen as a distinct value adding resource.

# 7
# Knowledge Exchange: The Role of Identity and Trusts

## Introduction

Fundamental to success in today's global market is an enterprise's ability to create, use, exchange and exploit knowledge. The value of knowledge is inextricably intertwined with the credence of a specific and identifiable supplier and buyer. Knowledge of a supplying enterprise's 'identity' is basic to evaluating its market offering. Identity is not sufficient in itself; it has to incorporate trust. Only with trust can one be sure of delivery. External confirmation of this helps – if others consider a supplier worthy then credence can be given to its claims to credibility.

One has to remember that a key feature of knowledge is that it is inalienable – that is its value cannot be separated from who either sold or bought it. The identity of the purchaser is fundamental to its value. Knowledge is valuable only if it can be used. The capacity of the purchaser to absorb and use knowledge is crucial to this. Identity – who is offering to whom – is thus doubly significant in knowledge exchange.

When acknowledging this, one has to be aware of its implication for the cost of transacting. These costs can be high, yet are vital to net added value.[1] In addition to the cost of assessing the value of the knowledge offered, these costs include assessing the credence and trustworthiness of the supplier and one's own capacity to absorb what is offered and the means of policing delivery. This re-doubles the significance of identity to value. If trust regulates exchange generally then in knowledge exchange it is of its essence.

Once one moves away from the abstract models of perfect freely distributed knowledge and frictionless exchange that economists use, one finds an imperfect reality.[2] As we have seen, exchange is embedded in a web of social investments in institutions, personal contacts and relationships.[3] This social capital[4] is especially important in knowledge exchange. Here the value of a particular exchange is always uncertain and inextricably interwined with identity. Both at the time of purchase and in subsequent use it is very difficult to assess the quality and value of knowledge independently of the capacity of its seller.

In this chapter we explore the interaction between identity, trust and value in knowledge exchange. Central to this is the idea that knowledge exchange has to be a co-operative not competitive activity. Two strands of thought come together: first, knowledge exchange absorbs time and money.[5] Second, such costs depend on both the seller's and buyer's identities.

## Identity

As identity matters, it is important how business systems choose to deal with it.

### Anonymous individualist exchange

In the individualist contractually dominated environments, one needs at a minimum the social security number or registered name of a seller. This identity is needed so that the legal system can find them and bring them to justice if necessary – where they may be sued if they have failed to deliver to contract or criminally prosecuted if dishonest. Such a 'bureaucratic identity' is provided at some cost by the state. It is financed out of general taxation. In a stable system, this produces huge economies of scale as its costs are spread over the whole population. A huge number of transactions are then supported and most of them do not require recourse to the judicial system. The cost per transaction is then trivial. It can be ignored in any analysis, and is.

Figure 7.1 models this system of anonymous exchange. This is what can result when exchange is well embedded in a system of secondary law making, courts and law enforcement. The assumption is that the value of the product and the consideration given in exchange for it are tangible and self-evident to all. What is exchanged has become known as a commodity. There are no uncertainties and value measurement costs are zero. Under such assumptions, there is no need for the actors to know or trust each other. A social identity is redundant. A bureaucratic identity, a social security number or company registration is sufficient to define the relationship needed to transact.

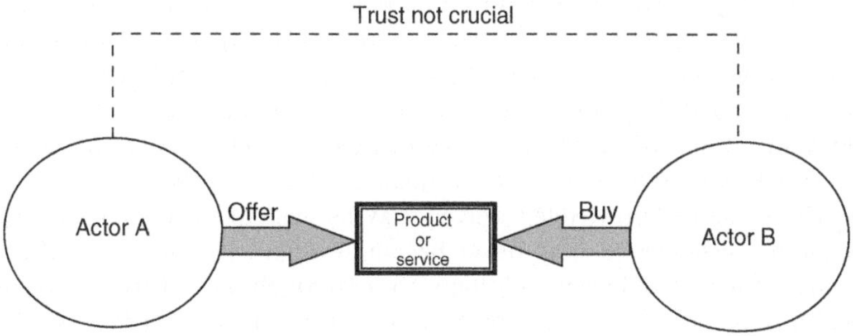


*Figure 7.1* Anonymous exchange: the individualist business system in the limit

## Personalized social exchange

In communal, relationship-dominated societies, one needs a lot more than the above. One has to discover, at some cost, the trustworthiness of the transactor's associates and antecedents. One must be confident that those that transgress that group's code of ethics will be socially sanctioned. We call this a 'social identity'. The costs in time and money of establishing such an identity are borne by the individual concerned and the social group to which h/she is identified as belonging. The economies of scale here are less than for bureaucratic identity as a smaller sub-group of society bears all the costs and the volume of transactions that each such social sub-group supports is significantly smaller.

This is closer to imperfect reality. The measurement costs of value as they relates to supplier and purchaser are fundamental to exchange.[6] These costs could be impossibly high in parts of the knowledge industry, and this is where the intangibility of content, extent and a detailed identity for the supplier and buyer are essential. Traditionally this has been used to justify keeping exchange within the hierarchy of an enterprise.[7] Within its bounds, one has social exchange; this adds value within the enterprise which can be used to produce products. These can then be traded to generate the value required to support the enterprise's stakeholders. The identity of the enterprise's internal transactors is important, but being inside the enterprise this is a matter for management not market exchange.

However, in the modern age the latter approach will not work. There is a need to network, to trade knowledge globally beyond the bounds of any single enterprise. In such networks each enterprise focuses on its own core competence and as knowledge is the key value adding ingredient it has to be exchanged. The uncertain nature of its content, extent and value at the time of exchange leaves serious identity-dependent issues to be addressed. Knowledge exchange is totally dependent on the intellectual capacity and integrity of both the supplier and the purchaser. Exchange then has to be based on a co-operative relationship in which the identity of each transactor is fundamental to value received.

The value of knowledge received may be evident only after its use. In some instances, it may never become evident. Its value may then remain a matter of belief, and there is a need for absolute 'trust' between the transactors. At a minimum, this must be until that worth becomes sufficiently evident to justify its cost to the buyer. Another question then arises. The buyer may find a way to use the knowledge acquired in a manner that increases its value beyond that it had on receipt. Does he or the seller own the intellectual property now newly available for exploitation from the original idea? In such a case, 'trust' is vital to the initial exchange and subsequent exploitation. An incentive then exists for 'trust' to be sustained indefinitely in a mutually re-enforcing conspiracy to validate the value of the purchase. This is typical of the systems operated by elite universities or top business schools, their old graduates give employment to their new graduates, and so on. The line these take is that 'they must be good as they went to the same school as me. I know it was good because it got me where I am today. My enterprise has certified this by funding their chair in international business. This was of course set up by me and my fellow graduates in the enterprise'.

Thus in co-operative exchange the focus shifts from the product or service to the identity of the people and enterprises transacting. In the limit, the product or service is hardly distinguishable from the identities of the transactors: their respective quality and status, and the continuing trust each displays in the other. This process becomes more one of collaboration than trade. Figure 7.2 provides an abstract model of such a structure for exchange.

This is embryonic 'social embeddedness' leading to a social identity for each of the actors and a relationship between them where the existence or otherwise of 'trust' is crucial, both to make exchange possible and to police its subsequent exploitation.

## Personalized bilateral exchange

In the emerging market hostage-based societies there is in a sense no need to know the other transactor's personal or social identity. One has only to be certain that the hostage to fortune offered is far more valuable

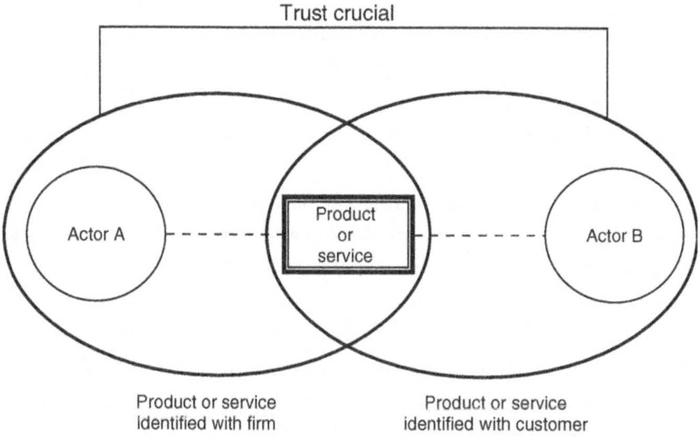


*Figure 7.2* Identified, trust-based exchange: the foundation of the communal business system

to the transactor than the outcome of any particular transaction or sequence of transactions the hostage assures. We will call this a 'bilateral identity', where all of its costs have to be borne by the transactors themselves. They cannot be spread across society as a whole or in part. In one sense, this is the apogee of individual rather than communal responsibility.

As is typical in emergence, there is no political or social embeddedness. The parties to the transaction have to invest themselves in an external guarantee of the continuing integrity of their dealings, by providing each other with a hostage to each of their fortunes. The hostage chosen has to be so valuable that to relinquish control of it would be unacceptable to the giver. A slight advance in sophistication can be considered here. If each party can identify an external party of unimpeachable integrity acceptable to both they can ask them to be their stakeholder. This third party then holds the hostages to fortune put up by each. If either transactor fails to deliver in the opinion of this third party his hostage to fortune is forfeit to the other. Such third parties who do not participate directly in the exchange and derive no direct benefit from it can be very useful. They themselves may be enterprises. As they have no direct interest in the value to be exchanged their views as to value and the trust to be placed in the parties involved have a degree of objectivity of use to all.

In the nineteenth century, accepting houses provided this service. The hostage to fortune they facilitated the use of was the 90-day bill of exchange. The buyer certified on the bill his acceptance of the debt; his banker would then get an Accepting House to sign the bill as an external guarantor of the buyer's *bona fides*. If the goods were not delivered in the 90 days, payment could be withheld. If they were, and the buyer did not effect payment, then the accepting house, having 'accepted' the bill, had to pay.

Model 7.3 completes the grammar of exchange: Figure 7.1 showed anonymous individualist-style exchange and is first-person exchange, 'I'. Figure 7.2 showed social communal-style exchange and is second-person exchange, 'you'. Figure 7.3 shows the embryonic system of scaffolding, external to the transactors, that can be used to support emergent exchange and this is in effect third-person exchange. This is embryonic 'embeddeness'. However, it has to be integral rather than external to each specific exchange or sequence of exchanges.

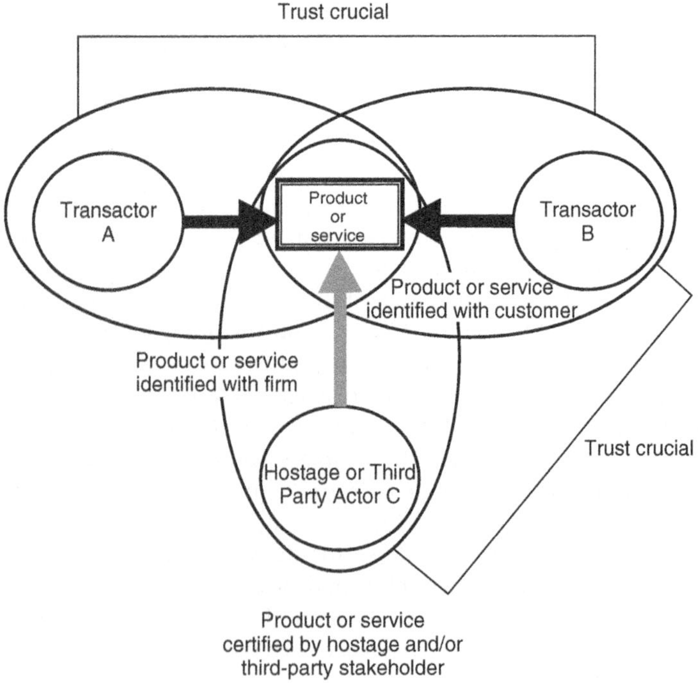


*Figure 7.3* Identified and certified trust-based exchange: the scaffolding for an emergent business system

## The forces at work

If we are to fully comprehend the nature of the three enforcement and exchange mechanisms of trust, contract and hostage, it is clear that the issue of identity needs further exploration. We wish to understand the significance of the identity to the process in each of our three business systems. We follow through an earlier argument that this depends crucially on the processing costs of transactions. In this context, these are measurement and enforcement costs.

The extent to which the transacting parties need to use shared values, as revealed by their identity – bureaucratic, social or bilateral – is a key factor in distinguishing between our three business systems. We will now consider the factors influencing the choice and design of the processes in each so that we may understand the circumstances in which trust, contract and hostage exchange have their respective strengths.

### Anonymous exchange, the individualist business system and bureaucratic identity

The individualist system effectively uses the classic market contract. This is most effective when product value measurement and enforcement costs are low. A stable slowly evolving society with a strong, politically supported independent, legal system is required for this type of exchange to work well. This is paid for out of communal funds and supports every single transaction in society. The unit cost per transaction is then very low indeed. For all this to be possible, there has to be little uncertainty about product quality and no difficulty in measuring its value and content. It is then sufficient for identity to be on record with the state. In such a case, the frictionless market will co-ordinate the trade between anonymous transactors, because both parties are assured that *in extremis* the communally funded judicial system will enforce the contract.

In such a system a sequence of contract-based transactions can form a basis from which future trust-based exchange can occur, and such trust can form the basis of relational contracting that can in the end enable the transactors concerned to work to mutual advantage to share and exploit any tacit knowledge each may have access to.[8]

The progression described from anonymous market exchange, to trust-based exchange, to a willingness to share tacit knowledge, is important. It is what is needed to abstract value out of an intangible like knowledge. It can permit effective transactions to go on between parties in what becomes a co-operative common cause but where the value of any specific exchange between them is unclear.

## Personalized exchange, the communal business system and social identity

In the communal system, enforcement costs per transaction are always higher for the transactors than under the individualist system. To establish the trust required for trade to be possible the transactors have to invest time and resources in cultivating a social identity. This can be through the membership of a club or religious institution or by being a member of the alumni association of a particular school or university, etc. The process of gaining acceptance by such groups can be costly for new members. In addition, there are collective or social enforcement costs. These spring from the social sanctions that have to be imposed if trust is breached.[9] These costs are hopefully only potential ones, but they are occasionally incurred – namely, and only, if there is a need to sanction opportunistic behaviour.

While a social identity is more expensive for an individual to set up than a bureaucratic one, it can be used over all the transactions an individual is involved in. Therefore overall the cost per transaction can be quite low. It is also true that trust-based social exchange can be established more quickly with this approach. This type of exchange facilitates the transactor's capacity to finesse measurement costs transaction by transaction. In this, it is similar to the De Beers' cartel way of selling diamonds.[10] In either case, there is no need to measure or even check the product being purchased each time. You can be confident that over time you get a good deal. One can thus avoid writing a prohibitively expensive individualist-style contingent contract to cover the full range of possible outcomes subsequent to purchase.

To establish trust-based exchange requires a social identity, and this has to be built into the individualist system. Here it is the starting point, though taking some time to establish robustly. It works because social institutions rely on an exclusivity principle[11] that greatly assists the establishment of an identity and being clear about what that means in reliability and other terms. Social institutions impose beliefs and norms on their members; transactors can generally take these personal characteristics as a given. This is very helpful in getting into, and developing, exchange relationships such that in the end one can trade intangibles with some confidence that one will not be cheated.

However, to become embedded in any social group requires the time to nurture trust. In the limiting case of a closely-knit clan[12] transactors are born into this and share a strong familial identity underpinned by ethnicity and religion. Each of these has its own clear norms for behaviour that can be applied with confidence to any individual from that group seen as a whole.

However, negotiating parties with less strong social identities may still be able to co-operate effectively. They can use tacit understanding to do so. They can make communication possible from their implicit knowledge of shared social practices. The business of transacting in such a context involves a side co-ordination game. Harvard academic Tom Schelling explained this in terms of what he called 'focal points'.[13] These involve some well-understood rules or norms and provide excellent clues and signals as to what a member of that group might do in given circumstances. In unfamiliar situations, these can and are used to co-ordinate a social group's expectation of each of its members. The stronger the shared values between the transactors, and the easier it is to identify a group member socially, the easier and cheaper it is to affect co-operative behaviour. This can be so even when the product or service dealt in would normally be associated with high transaction costs.

Social identity can be especially important in international business settings. There, the transacting parties confront each other transnationally. They come from very different cultures each with their own conventions, values, norms and behaviour standards. Knowing the social identity of a transacting partner makes it possible, especially in a communal business systems, to know the likelihood of the other party fulfilling both their obligations and commitments to your expectation.[14] Generally in a communal system not being able to situate a potential partner socially seriously impedes one's capacity to do business with them. In such societies, any uncertainty concerning identity quickly translates into exclusion from business.

It is this context that highlights the advantages of an international Diaspora of people from a particular, easily recognisable, background. In each society in which members of such groups live they make contact with a significant number of local people outside their social group. As we have seen earlier, those people in each society can then use the members of such a Diaspora as a communication channel between their countries.

Even when the value of an exchange has been ascertained to the satisfaction of both parties, the problems of knowledge limitations, communication distortion and differences in interpretations of what has been said or written never disappear. Under such circumstances, social identity as a signal helps to determine the boundaries of an enterprise, its authority, and its likely behaviour and attitude to any opportunism that might then ensue. This lowers both communication and co-ordination costs.

The same purpose is served in individualist systems by brand names, warranties, international quality standard certificates and objective third-party expert validation – all these provide an identity with the same purpose. This reduces the costs per transaction. If such guarantees exist, over time buyers may become happy with self-certification by the seller.[15] Especially if there is real synergy between them, the parties have then got to the point where they can co-operate to mutual advantage in exploiting the potential wrapped up in their respective knowledge bases.

## Hostage based exchange, the emergent business system and bilateral identity

In an emergent context, the identity of a potential partner is not always known, and even if it is, measurement and enforcement costs may be so high that trade is near-impossible. A bureaucratic or social identity can be very difficult to establish in such circumstances, due to the political, social or market volatility and institutional instability.

Before a transaction, or sequence of transactions, has been instigated many things may happen. The polity may change import and export laws, or officials may arbitrarily change them. For example, a previously valuable export can be made valueless if a state official prohibits its export. Situations vary depending on macroeconomic stability, on government intervention, on the type of product and on the identity of each transactor.

However, a hostage set up by counter-trade[16] compels the parties to provide identity, to the subjective satisfaction of the other parties involved in exchange. Here measurement and enforcement costs before purchase are not an issue, because if after purchase the subjective value of what is received is not as expected, then the hostage will be taken. No time or effort is needed to further identify the transacting partner or discover the robustness of that business system's commercial law. One needs only to be certain that the hostage provided is more valuable than any gains possible from reneging on the deal.

Thinking in transaction cost terms suggests that institutions emerge as a means to reduce transaction costs, and exchange will not take place if such institutions are non-existent. With counter-trade the reciprocity of hostage taking provides a transportable institution, directly linked to each transaction. This obviates the need for a social or political identity. In consequence, exchange can occur where it otherwise would not.

Although the hostage mechanism may seem crude and primitive, and inherently inferior to trust and contracts, it does offer a prospect for initiating exchange even in the dire socio-economic contexts typical of emergence. This is true of African, some Asian and many emerging business systems in Eastern Europe. A conversion to trust or contract-based exchanges evolves later. If after a sequence of transactions the benefits to both parties are sufficient to encourage them to continue to exchange, hostage or no hostage, and the institutions have evolved to provide them with first a social then a bureaucratic identity, then the hostages can be returned.[17] Thus, if the identity of the transacting parties can eventually be established, exchange shifts naturally to a trust basis, which can at a later date become formalized by an enforceable contract.

However, if the transactions have become embedded in a polity, and the polity acts to build external transactors' trust in the robustness and integrity of the institutions it co-evolves to support trade, it is possible for the shift to take place directly to a basis in contract law. This was the situation in South Korea, but it is very hard for a state to achieve if it is politically volatile. It is hard even for a democracy if governments change regularly. Each of these may have very different policies on issues of concern to enterprise; without a bureaucratic identity guaranteed by the state the measurement and enforcement costs before trade starts can be very high. They will be too high unless the value added from the transaction occuring is high enough to make the risk worth taking, even if there is the prospect of a failure in trust. We would hypothesize that, in some instances in the globalizing economy, deals based on knowledge exchange often fall into this category.

Table 7.1 summarizes the results of our reasoning in this section.

*Table 7.1* Types of exchange and identity

| Exchange mechanisms | Measurement costs | Enforcement costs | Identity of parties |
|---|---|---|---|
| Contract | Low and objective | Low | Bureaucratic politically embedded |
| Trust | High and subjective | High | Social socially embedded |
| Hostage (international counter-trade) | Low and subjective | Generally high, but uncertain | Bilateral hostage embedded |

## The co-evolutionary dynamics of identity

Those within an industry tend to share views, values and perspectives, producing a system of shared beliefs.[18] This provides an industrial identity for the enterprises within it.[19] Those considering transacting with an industry are well advised to see whom within it the others treat as belonging to it. By adopting a principle of exclusivity those within an industry identify themselves to those outside their 'club'. Membership communicates a set of values to which members adhere.

Transactors rely on such an exclusivity principle to provide a useful identity. They use industrial membership as others might use nationality, ethnic background, age, income or social status. Such exclusivity helps overcome uncertainty as to value, especially in emergent industries, for example 'knowledge'-based industry. However, this kind of basis is also common in mature industries. In that case it is very reliable, with well-developed historical norms, values and standards. In a mature industry, the definition of value is more certain, and the identity – and so the trust needed in one's exchange partner – is less important. But exclusivity adds value in and of itself. It permits the purchasers to signal worth. Here as always, the value in exchange of the product narrowly defined – i.e. without the seller's identity – is very different from its value in use. However, with exclusivity as a caveat and the product broadly defined to include the seller's identity, its value in use can be greater than its value in exchange.

In newer or emerging industries, such as knowledge, where value and quality are intangible and norms, values and standards have not, nor ever can, become fully established, none of this can apply. This is so while at the same time an enterprise's most valuable asset is its embedded knowledge.[20] This is especially true of its tacit knowledge; the very existence of such an intangible is difficult to establish and this is independent of any ability to measure its worth. In such cases, if this value needs to be traded – as, for example, goodwill on the sale of the business, one is left with nothing other than the choices made by others. This could be the size of its customer base or some such other external cue – e.g. if traded, its share value. These provide a guide to worth as subjectively assessed by third parties.

Let us now consider cost and context together. Given our previous arguments, one must not presume these costs are fixed. It is the enterprises' endeavours to lower transaction costs that drive co-evolution. Enterprises finding transactions costly under a particular regime will seek to modify that regime to their mutual advantage.[21] Such social co-evolution is what has led to the social embeddedness that marks out the communal business system and the political embeddedness indicative of the individualist business system.

In the communal system, significant social investment is required to establish and maintain the relationships and contacts this system requires. The social capital so constructed is in the working of the social institutions this system draws on to deliver performance.

The individualist system of anonymous exchange operates with minimal transaction costs at the social level of the enterprise, but has to sustain considerable political institutional cost in setting up and sustaining the legal systems in which its type of exchange is embedded. Which of these is in use in a particular context depends crucially on the stage in the evolution of the relative cost of transacting that is driving it.[22]

To accept that relative cost determines the institutional structure in operation is neat, although not analytically helpful in the dynamic setting within which we wish to operate. It ignores the need for the cost of transacting to be visible so as to incentivize necessary socio-economic change. If these costs are not visible there may not be change. There will then be no dynamic to drive the co-evolution of enterprises and institutions. The comparative measurement of value against cost affects the value in exchange received in different contexts. This is especially so with knowledge, whose value is not necessarily evident even after purchase.

However, 'exchange' as we have seen, can be maintained in the absence of any legal sanction as normally understood.[23] Social exchange can occur without any politically embedded sanctions. Women are masters of this kind of exchange: in the sorority of mothers, rides to school, shopping hints, judgements on the quality of this or that professional are all part of the social exchange that shapes their lives: knowledge is freely contributed to the sorority's social capital; no detailed reckoning is kept of a particular member's balance.

This does not describe the process of value in exchange for a consideration that is the basis of contract in the individualist system of anonymous exchange. It is an investment in social capital that the sorority jointly constructs. All can draw on this as needed; there is no excessive concern for each participant's balance at any point in time. This sorority exchange is akin to Keynes' view of savings – i.e. something put aside now with an unarticulated expectation that it will be spent at some unspecified future date for some unspecified purpose. Helping a neighbour repair his car, or organizing a round of golf with some buddies from work, are comparable examples. A history of experience in shared values and in constructing local social norms plays an important role in policing such trust-based social exchange.[24]

This is a form of co-operative exchange. As we shall see, it is particularly useful in trading knowledge. It is essential in making choices to do with

(1) Creating new understanding of technological choice
(2) As a means to share risk
(3) As a means to penetrate a new market with a partner already situated in it
(4) As a means to achieve savings from skills complementary with those of a partner.[25]

## The value of knowledge

Given the high risks involved in trading knowledge, simplicity in stating desired ends belies the difficulty in achieving them when dealing with the exchange of an intangible like knowledge.[26] Understanding the processes by which one might assess the use value of knowledge is essential if one wishes to analyse emergence in the knowledge age where knowledge itself is the core resource.[27] A modern enterprise's competitive edge hangs crucially on being able to do so sensibly.

Given the high uncertainty as to the content of knowledge and the consequently high cost of attempting to measure it, its exchange has to be based on the trust one has in the integrity and intellectual competence of identifiable individuals. Any view of exchange that sees knowledge as a product cannot therefore be based on individualist anonymous exchange. This requires an externally well-defined product available to all in an explicit easily measured volume.

Knowledge is peculiar to each pair of transactors. It is imperfectly specifiable. Its value is inextricably tied to the credibility of its seller linked to the intellectual absorptive capacity of its buyer. These linkages between buyer and seller mean that there is a very important role in knowledge exchange for external intermediaries. These can credibly measure and then 'certify' a provider's worth and so the value of his offering to the market.

As the value of knowledge can be known only after its effective use, the identity and credibility of both supplier and user are crucial to its worth. And as knowledge is often tacit and uncodifiable, its value and quality may be difficult to ascertain even after it is traded. The cost of measurement and enforcement as a proportion of the whole is likely therefore to be significant.[28] Apart from that, its value can be assessed only over time. Its utility then crucially depends on the user's absorptive capacity.

To achieve absorption, a continuing mutually supportive relationship is needed between the supplier and user. How is this to be paid for? All this suggests the market for knowledge may best be mediated by informal social rather than formal political institutions.[29] A person's value as a partner or user of knowledge depends on their social identity.

Third parties that can assist others can add clear value in making this process of choice less costly. It goes without saying that in planning the purchase of access to knowledge, potential users depend heavily on 'external cues' – for example, the choices made by other evidently successful transactors. This means that external cues validate or certify who can be trusted and provide better indicators of the appropriateness of a choice than the cost of transacting for an advertised benefit. Intermediaries can and do specialize in collating and analysing such knowledge for others. By having a large client base they can make such knowledge available at low cost – e.g. the Standard & Poors and similar credit rating systems.

In order to construct the sustainable and strong trust required by such exchange knowing the identify of all transactors is crucial.[30] Transactors may use the same knowledge differently in different contexts;[31] in one way when working within an enterprise, and in another as a sub-contractor working for it through a network. There is a problem here for the individualist approach: anonymity is assumed in that system but identity is crucial to knowledge exchange.

Identity can be based on unalterable static characteristics such as ethnic backgrounds, kinship, religion, ties to certain communities, etc. None of these is variable. However it is possible to act to provide oneself with a meaningful identity. One would do it by one's choice of club, place of worship, educational establishment, qualifications received or CV of experience. A transactor's past record of successes or failures, based on their own efforts, motivations and capabilities, may be better indicators of their current utility as a source of knowledge than would unalterable ones such as their ethnic background, etc.

We do not only have the identity given us by the network of constraints creating and sustaining our own substantive relationships in kinship, authority, and intimacy but we can also be given one by those situated in another group. Those ethnic or religious Diaspora forming what we call 'structural wormholes' between societies can provide one with an identity useful for international exchange. By being connected in exchange with an individual in one's own society from such a group one can make connection, directly or indirectly, with an exchange partner in another society. Such connectivity provides a pathway from a node in one network to that in another of perceived embedding relationships, real or imagined.[32] It is no accident that Mediterranean Jews of the twelfth century or the Overseas Chinese community of today provide a useful linkage from one society to another that short-circuits any official channels.

Why are third-party relationships so significant in determining the value of knowledge? Surely value can be implied from the signals a provider makes to advertise his own competence?[33] Potential transactors do send out signals indicating their presence and the value they have on offer. However they can manipulate such 'signals' to put themselves in a good light. 'Indices'[34] of the type we have begun to describe created by third parties are far more credible. They are far harder to manipulate. They are validated, and generated, by external third parties.

Given the objectivity of indices and their general availability they also provide a strong incentive for transactors to behave in a manner consistent with achieving good ratings on them. For this reason, they can be used to underwrite any value that may be on offer. An important dimension of a potential transactor's value in exchange is the trust built with such intermediaries. These in turn see themselves as promulgating objective 'indices' of worth.

The trade press, stockbrokers, etc. specialize in such third-party intermediation. The third party's job is to indicate the value of a product or service to others by incurring the expense of measuring and or assessing it in an objectively researched manner that others trust. By doing this, and selling the results to a large client base, they spread the cost of such measurement economically over a large number of transactions. The structure this suggests is set out in Figure 7.3 (p. 98). Here the transactors rely on a third party of mutually agreed status and reliability to certify value and worth to each of parties to an exchange.

Such third parties play an important role by providing 'certification' as to worth, a very important function in the knowledge industry.[35] They also can provide affirmation to others of the appropriateness of any deal struck when the value of an actor's product or service is difficult to measure, as is the case with knowledge. In such a case, the market tends to shift away from reliance on internally generated cues as to value, the seller's 'signals' as to the quality of what he offers, to third-party generated 'indices' based on objectively researched knowledge. The fact that such external cues can be significant reinforces the importance of such indirect effects on market forces and competition.[36]

# 8
# The Emergence of a System of Dynamic Identity

## Introduction

In complex environments co-evolving emergent behaviour has a multiplicity of causes. Direct causal links between intentions, decisions and outcomes disappear. Long-term prediction is impossible.[1] The inherent uncertainty in complex environments is such that what evolves is not a process for forecasting followed by informed rational action, it is a process for learning and adaptation. Those who cannot adapt, fail. Those who do adapt become increasingly embedded with others who have also learned to adapt quickly. The most successful ones quickly fit co-operatively into whatever niche presents itself.[2] The resulting system is a variety of enterprises and institutions rich in size, focus and purpose. Survival comes not from rational choice between alternatives but as a result of choosing the right adaptive processes to enable one to fit in what ever happens: 'set[s] of heuristics, or rules of thumb, that perhaps can be explained (and perhaps justified) insofar as they economize on cognitive effort' (Orbell and Dawes 1991, p. 517).

There is extensive evidence that such outcomes are not driven by rational choice. They occur as a result of the market identifying the type of reaction that permits survival in the face of rapid change.[3] The successful enterprises are the ones flexible enough to respond swiftly to unforeseen events.[4] Such adaptability is humanity's evolutionary advantage, too. However, even there birth and death play a role as regularly the old, the least adaptable proportion of the population are replaced with the young, the most adaptable portion. The capacity the latter have to learn and use to adapt to whatever environment they choose to enter is mankind's evolutionary advantage. Effective enterprise has to evolve similar adaptive capacities if it wishes to limit the impact of unforeseen complexity on its viability. To achieve this, it needs to evolve (to be a bit like humanity) and be able to learn and adapt by constantly renewing itself.[5] Enterprises can do so by broadening the range of variation they can absorb while remaining viable and by establishing behaviour that sustains their cohesiveness despite the explosive torrent of disruptive forces of complexity characteristic of emergence.[6]

Thought of in this way, the dynamic evolutionary perspective capable of integrating the pursuit of self-interest is normally associated with the individualist system model and the social identity is seen as indicative of the communal business system model.[7] Often these different approaches are seen to be mutually exclusive: the first, self-interest-driven and dependent on bureaucratic identity, and the other, selflessly driven and dependent on a capacity to sustain[8] a social identity.

The self-interest paradigm views group behaviour, such as co-operation in exchange, as derived from the discovery of overlapping self-interests.[9] This is then manifest in a sense of public spirit, interdependence and complementarity. Identification is thus a process of rational choice[10] based on one's own interest: 'One actor has adopted, or taken up, the other's interest' (Coleman 1990b, p. 158).

The selfless paradigm sees humanity as imbued with a sense of collective responsibility that drives us to behave in the interest of the collective whole rather than just ourselves. It is undoubtedly true that the dynamic of a social identity drives us this way. We can use social capital because of our willingness to participate selflessly in constructing it.

Sustaining this in the face of the tension between self- and communal-interest is difficult.[11] Identification with a group, the industry, in the business world is much more complex than identification with a group characterized by a single feature such as gender or race.[12] In most cases the group that can be identified does not have a single, stable, externally recognizable feature. The boundaries between industries in a truly co-evolving environment have more of the attributes evident in ecology than in the economy as many economists envisage it. Identities are constantly re-formed to serve new purposes.[13] Therefore at all times there exist indiscernibly evolving socio-economic groups.[14] It is in understanding the dynamics of these that we learn to understand better socio-economic emergence and co-evolution. The members of a cohesive group have boundaries impenetrable by those outside the group. This gives the group form that enables others to identify its members as having characteristics that can be relied on and trusted.

In the emergence of a new industry or market, such boundaries may not yet have formed. However, in such an environment while the positive feedbacks derived from the exploitation of a new source of commercial energy are driving things apart, slowly but surely the counter-forces of negative stabilizing feedback are at work to accrete the cohesion and co-ordination required to affect enterprise in normal times. Unbending exclusivity has powerful advantages in stable situations but dynamic inclusiveness is what is needed in the rapidly changing environment of an emergent system.

As we have already seen, in international business the players in an enterprise operate in a dual environment. One is driven by the imperatives of sustaining trust within a network of constraining but empowering social relationships. The other is powered by oversight by third parties created by a polity, which formally defines the boundaries of acceptable behaviour and maintains a capacity to enforce respect for them. The first layer of this environment provides a social identity and the other a bureaucratic one.[15] This duality enables one to understand the process by which a transactor's identity is formed and leads to a process to signal it within the market[16] which 'demonstrate(s) to others the actor's intentions or abilities or some other characteristic about which the actor has private, unverifiable knowledge' (Milgrom and Roberts 1992, p. 212).

If one can tune into the process by which such signaling might be achieved, one can see how it might be possible for the distinction we discussed between outsiders and insiders to become blurred. It then becomes possible for enterprises to provide sufficient self-identification for third parties to provide the institutional certification required for social legitimacy and reliable identification.[17] The process by which this occurs is fundamental to how an enterprise is identified from within its population of origin[18] and empowered to effect favourable social results.

## Dynamic identity: the power of association

We have established that the diversity of stakeholder interests and the high costs of value measurement provide an incentive for the evolution of new institutions to modulate them. Enterprise is providing the power driving the system forward faster during emergence than it is possible for legacy, social or political institutions to cope with. One way an enterprise deals with this is itself to construct temporary institutional scaffolding to support exchange in the short run while new socio-political institutions are evolving. As we saw in Chapter 7, one effective means of doing so that improves on the basic hostage idea, is to have a trusted stakeholder as a third party to an exchange.

Such third-party enterprises can observe and note the 'associations' that enterprises form with customers and other enterprises. This knowledge provides others with objective indices indicative of an enterprise's perceived worth in terms of trust, reliability and usefulness to others. Such third-party enterprises can then sell this knowledge to those seeking to do business with the parties it has observed. Enterprise itself thus constructs from within itself[19] the means to situate other enterprises in an identified place in an as yet barely formed emergent context. Third-party certification by specialist enterprises will affect the value enterprise can access. The more such accreditation it receives the more value it can attract to itself and the easier it will be for it to receive such accreditation in the future and in turn, the more value it can create, and so on. This is a very powerful positive feedback loop. It reinforces valuable emergent activity. Over time, it leads to the accretion of self-identifying groups, an industry of certified effectively adapting enterprises, arising out of the chaos of emergence.

The maintenance of such an identity requires care. Exclusivity in one's dealings is fundamental. If one deals down from one's own level in the emerging socio-economic hierarchy one's standing will undermined. If one deals up then one's status is enhanced. Here is a dynamic driven by subjectively assessed value. It is constructed by enterprise itself, not by pre-existing socio-political institutions. Upward mobility is supported as it brings with it ever increasing self re-enforcing rewards. Downward mobility is discouraged as it increasingly lessens potential rewards. This means that value-enhancing network connectivity will be stimulated and valueless network connectivity will be terminated[20] in the end.

## Dynamic identity: the constructing enterprises

The group of enterprises and institutions that are themselves emerging to measure value and certify the worth of others can and does have a significant impact on the evolutionary dynamics of enterprise generally. Once we appreciate this, the importance of the infrastructure it creates for co-operative exchange will be clear.[21]

We need to make explicit the nature of the process by which the co-evolution described proceeds. There are a number of elements and a process that:

(1) Accumulates knowledge on an enterprise's customer base
(2) Accumulates knowledge on the innovativeness of its product line and brand reputations[22]

(3) Tracks the impact of an enterprise's associations on its worth
(4) Generates external commentaries, favourable reviews in business publications, etc. that build up others' perceptions of an enterprise's worth.

The enterprises and institutions used to achieve this are of course themselves part of the emerging knowledge industries, and will similarly be tracked themselves.

The consequence of such a system is self reinforcement. In a world where value and worth come from interconnectivity the processes described attribute worthiness to trusted association. Enterprises fulfilling the criteria will attract resources only when they act effectively in the interest of the connectivity they serve. They will lose resources when they do not. In a world where the principal source of new value is derived from knowledge and information, which are by their very nature communal property, self-interest and communal interest are as one.

We have returned to a pre-Renaissance world where individual ownership had little meaning. Any enterprise seeking to survive sustains its viability by increasing the level and significance of its connectivity. It can do this only if it is seen to make a contribution to communal capital worthy of the value it seeks to take, by the net of communities in which it seeks connectivity. By opening its own knowledge up to such social exchange while serving the communal interest it is serving itself, and so its stakeholders. Such communal self-serving connectivity, once established, forms an intangible global social asset that the process described will nurture and maintain.

The institutional framework that supports this result is of vital importance to the modern globalizing world. It is a self-organizing framework. It is created by enterprise for enterprise to provide an identity independent of any legitimizing state or pre-existing social group. The essence of the new global economy in the end is the increasing irrelevance of traditional nation states and legacy social structures. The world is already becoming transnational rather than international and the transformation that global emergence will bring about has only just begun.

The turbulence of today's increasingly uncertain socio-economic environment has increased the importance of such self-organizing processes. Their structure arises by directing resources to those areas where value is being created in the communal interest, and this is occurring independent of any cognitive pre-visioning or direction and control by self-interested states or social groups. This is the essence of the global network now being generated by the still-emerging knowledge industries. Those enterprises certifying and commenting on the performance of others form a pivotal part of this emergent industry.

## Dynamic identity: indices and certification

The externally generated cues the knowledge industry develops, also named 'indices', are the means used to direct and police the flow of resources to high-value adding areas of network connectivity. Indices have been defined as:

> statements or actions that carry some inherent evidence that the image projected is correct because they are believed to be inextricably linked to the actor's capabilities or intentions. (Jervis 1985, p. 26)

We can then construct a definition of dynamic identity as a compilation of a number of such indices. In total, these will help identify each enterprise's possession of the essential intangible assets, such as 'knowing', required to be successful in the global system now emerging. The dynamic identities that result are constructed on four bases. These underpin the production of the indices required to establish identity in this emerging environment:

(1) An enterprise's set of clients is suggestive of quality, because the position or status[23] of particular clients can promote or demote the enterprise's ranking.
(2) The enterprise's reputation for being innovative – developing new products or a dynamic corporate culture – is essential in the knowledge age.[24]
(3) An enterprise's networks, whether of collaborators or competitors, gives peer certification of its significance, an example would be top-ranked business schools as competitors yet holding executive programmes or conferences together.[25]
(4) Third-party comment using external sources of knowledge, such as Standard and Poors, the FTSE, DAX and other financial indices, consumer reports written up by other enterprises, and of course the trade press whose whole business is the knowledge required to produce saleable business magazines and commentaries. All these serve the function of institutional certification.

Dynamic identity is derivative of all of the above and can be defined as follows:

> **Dynamic identity**
>
> is the cumulative impact of the following four types of indices:
>
> (1) Client lists
> (2) Reputation for innovation
> (3) Network of partners and competitors
> (4) Third-party evaluations.

These four bases for indices define a firm's dynamic identity. In doing so they certify its quality and status and provide an organizational base from which to institutionalize performance measurement.

Any explanation of an enterprise's continuing success in exchange or dominance within its network of connectivity is encompassed by this concept of dynamic identity. It represents living network connectivity and strengthens or weakens an enterprise's assessed worth because its utility to the whole does not rise or fall just in relation to its individual acquisitiveness seen in isolation. It is based on a perspective derived from the views of all stakeholders interested in the governance of enterprise. It encompasses measures related to the responsiveness of the enterprise to a variety of external constituencies apart from customers: national governments throughout the world and all kinds of interest groups situated in other societies and other cultures throughout the world.[26] If the role it plays does not take these considerations into account, then it may lose what has become known 'as the license to operate'. Increasingly, one finds this is very carefully monitored by the new organizations and associated institutions now coming into being, such as non-government organizations (NGOs) such as Green Peace. These generate third-party institutional pressures for certification that encourage the accretion of enterprises that operate with due consideration of the wider global communal interest.[27]

Enterprise now needs to take account of this wider, increasingly global, stakeholder interest in its acceptability. Enterprises that choose to ignore such pressures may find themselves unable to operate. In this new world intrinsic social worthiness may become as important as the value of the knowledge it assists its global network to generate. Anonymous exchange is of little use in such a business environment. It is known visible exchanges that impact most on value. The system is driven by acquisitiveness, but in the knowledge-based age this has to be synonymous with communal rather than individualist interest. This 'visible hand' is as fundamental to the new age as the 'invisible hand' has been to the one it is surpassing.

## Dynamic identity: its visualization in emergence

We can construct a picture of the pivotal elements of this fast-emerging knowledge industry, devoted to certifying the worth of other enterprise as in Figure 8.1.[28] This summarizes what we have described and illustrates the process involved. It helps us visualize the pressures from stakeholders impinging on enterprise. These produce the identity needed to support the cohesion necessary for establishing value adding network co-ordination through exchange. It is through this that the viability of enterprise can be guaranteed in the complex social environment within which it now has to operate. This process drives the generation and then accrual of the social capital[29] required to make knowledge exchange viable. The processes are summarized in Figure 8.1 as they have far more subtlety

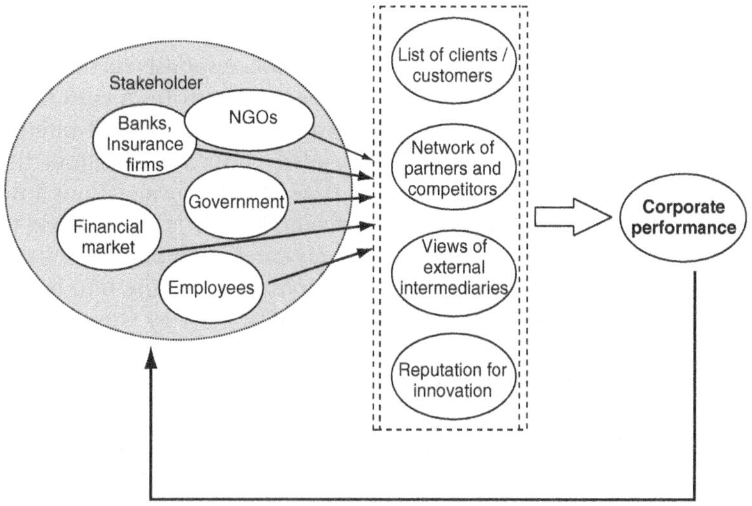


*Figure 8.1* Stakeholders and indices: indirect measurement

and complexity than it is possible to capture in any diagram, which can do no more than attempt to capture their essence.

What Figure 8.1 describes is a mechanism for tagging and identifying enterprises in a dynamic way. Instead of directly attempting to capture the complexity of an intangible like knowledge it satisfies the requirement from two perspectives and four points of view. These cover the processes generating knowledge (Reputation for innovation) and exploiting it (Network of partners and competitors, and the Views of external intermediaries) and their value-generating consequences in value acquired from others (List of clients/customers).

The first perspective is that of the resource-based view of the firm.[30] What processes does the enterprise possess for creating and producing what it offers in value? There is one direct index of this and two indirect ones that highlight it. The latter two also span the second perspective.

This second perspective is that of the market-based view of an enterprise's strategy.[31] The directly observable consequence of this is the enterprise's List of clients/customers. The two points of view that span both this and the enterprise's resource are views on its worth as seen by third parties (press, stock analysts, etc.) and associated second parties (Network of partners and collaborators).

All the above taken together encompass the totality of a self-reinforcing means of achieving the internal results that lead to the selection of network partners to reinforce the formation of knowledge-generating communities that add value to the wider community they serve.[32] We would contend that if stakeholders lack evidence on any of these tagging characteristics, enterprises and the products they proffer in the market become more problematic in value. In such a case, fewer resources will find their way to support them. Their capacity to participate in exchange will then be limited, and they may cease entirely.[33]

On the other hand, transactors in emergence who can identify themselves and others in terms of the four indices lock into a self-reinforcing system of advantage in which enterprises and their stakeholders can gain a clear multi-dimensional picture of the network in which they operate and of their position within it. It also makes clear to enterprise and their stakeholders where effort needs to be concentrated to achieve increasing and ultimately maximal returns from the potential being exploited. By generating the right connectivity, as perceived by the community in which and with which it operates, enterprise has huge self-reinforcing opportunities during emergence.[34] Beyond emergence at maturity, the same process generates a stable environment whose potential enterprise can milk for as long as a positive yield is available.

During emergence having the right strategy for adaptation in this complex environment can rapidly alter an actor's position in this schema. Rankings on the four types of indices are self reinforcing. They promote further network-generating relationships if and only if they serve the interests of the evolving whole. Equally, as time progresses, this process identifies those displaying a consistent capacity for delivery and reinforces their dominance.

An enterprise's dynamic identity is a metaphor for its quality and exchange potential in the global system, it is mediated by what is a new phenomenon in the evolution of this planet[35] – a developing culture of self-organizing enterprise operating independently of existing organizations, political or social, and the institutions they support.

Given the environmental uncertainty inevitable in an emergent situation, much choice and exchange has to be made on the basis of faith.[36] In this context, by 'faith' we mean the faith of the creators and users of networked knowledge. It means that what they are doing now is for the good of the communal whole. As such, it will attract support from it more than sufficient to sustain the effort required, and that support will come from the system as and when needed. This is a process of reciprocity, not exchange. There is no necessarily immediate coincidence between the process of contributing to the network or community and receiving value from it. This is of the essence of social, as opposed to individualist, capital, and the rewards that accrue to those helping to create it.

Stakeholders use these indices to generate a yardstick by which they can judge enterprises. They can be used to reproduce what is identified as valuable and so worth proliferating. Identity defined in this way is like a genetic code for each enterprise. Knowing it enables success to be propagated by adaptive self-organizing enterprise. This leads sequentially to:

(1) Hostaging
(2) The emergence of third-party stakeholders for the hostages proffered
(3) The emergence of enterprises independent of a local social or political context to take on the role of providing dynamic identity for others
(4) The emergence of a stable context with which to homeostatically sustain the successful.

This permits enterprises and stakeholders to indulge in the self-conscious evolution of the useful and successful. The existence of such a capacity to generate a 'dynamic identity' from within the body of enterprise is thus a very powerful property of the emerging global business system. It holds out the opportunity for the self-conscious growth and short-term continuing viability of enterprises capable of exploiting newly identified potential.

## Dynamic identity: its visualization in evolutionary dynamics

The rules of dynamic identity are based on already existing outcomes, the products of past stakeholder cognitive processes and on future outcomes: 'attraction via [iterative] gradient search, without the need for a map of the evolutionary landscape' (Macy 1997, p. 435).

This is to be contrasted with the extrapolative rational analytical approach typical of the efforts of strategists in the modern age. We illustrated this in Figure 8.1, with the introduction of a single-headed arrow facing towards 'Corporate performance' instead of double-headed ones picturing complex and indiscernible interaction. The picture is completed with the introduction of a feedback loop. This performs the process that in emergence seeks out the route to ever-increasing positive returns on all four dimensions (see Figure 8.2). This process is such that

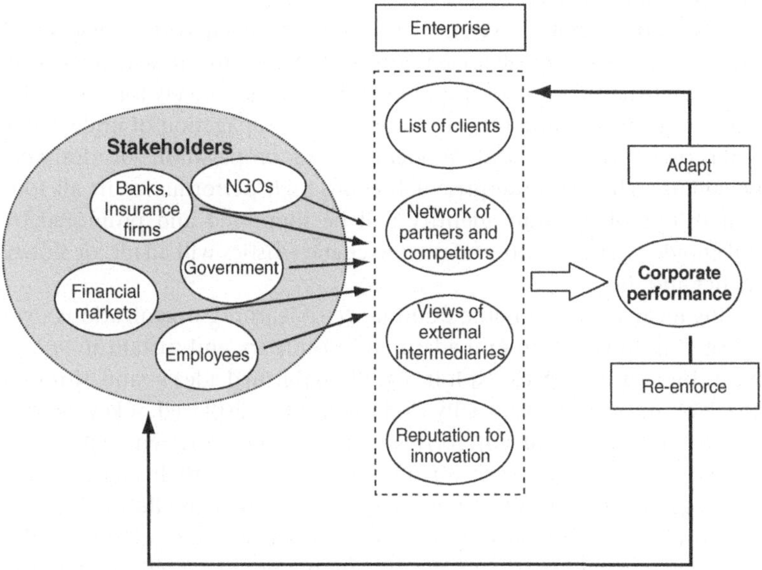


*Figure 8.2* The adaptive dynamic system

whenever a maximum is achieved it can sustain an effectively adaptive organization and so sustain homeostatic exploitation of any identified potential.

Each time the process goes round one loop, the schema as a sense-making mechanism creates cognitive structures in the stakeholders' minds that determine their attitudes and actions in the next round of co-evolutionary activity. These slowly establish the emergent then evolving future landscape of the global system. These path-dependent iterations generate a rich pattern of principles and rules that govern individual action and interactions to generate a wealth of possible outcomes all tolerant of significant large local variation and variety.[37] It is not conducive to the appearance of any organization or process that seeks domination over all others. This world is one of accommodation to the needs of others, not of conflict between them.

If unexpected undesirable outcomes emerge they are unlikely to be intolerably large at inception. Their effects will thus tend to be localized given the diverse environment into which they are introduced. So while they may be locally destructive they are unlikely to be generally so. In the knowledge and information age any lessons are quickly learned and propagated. For this reason alternatives will be expeditiously and iteratively explored to permit enterprise to steer away from such a source of potential negativity.

This highly adaptive system has an integrated capacity to assess and measure the identity of an enterprise dynamically. It will iteratively change all that it is uncomfortable with. This has effects for the evaluation of future performance. It punishes the propagation of undesirable enterprise behaviour and accelerates the propagation of desirable behaviour. Thus an enterprise achieving high performance in all four dimensions of dynamic identity will be supported and promoted by stakeholders. Those with undesirable characteristics will adapt, or slowly wither and die.

This means the inevitable dominance of learning organizations over those that do not learn and adapt and simply try and sustain their viability by continuing to exploit a well-established idea – and through a lack of innovation eventually find themselves displaced. A key characteristic of a successful enterprise in such an environment will be its capacity and willingness to abandon old ideas and their related value offerings and to introduce new ones. Old defunct intellectual capital will in the worst case absorb more value than can be created from the new. The inevitable consequence of hanging onto to it will then be the demise of such an enterprise.[38]

## Dynamic identity: the way forward

We have now shown the pivotal role played by those enterprises that provide institutional certification, external measurement of quality and assessment of value beyond general market knowledge. In a truly global stakeholder system the self-organizing enterprises in the knowledge industry that provide this service are the pivot around which enterprises, based on delivering value from intangibles such as knowledge of the 'knowing' kind,[39] can be nurtured in the interests of the emerging global community – unimpeded by their local legacy of institutions in the particular part of the globe in which they are situated.[40] Provided they satisfy the global need, value will flow in their direction in a manner that it is impossible for legacy organizations social or political to have cognizance of, or influence over. Self-organizing institutional certification by enterprise itself, in terms of 'dynamic identity', makes possible the huge changes now being observed in a manner that was never possible before.

Reputation and trust is something that enterprise can generate or destroy itself with. The external indices that are assembled by enterprise itself – list of clients; reputation for successful innovation; networks of partners or competitors; evaluation by external intermediaries – all free enterprise from the burden of past value systems, social or political.

Enterprise has thus to rely on enterprise and not on the authority of social, or the power of political, organizations. Patronage, political or social, is redundant in this system. However long-term relationships are and will be supported by this system of institutional certification. This provides a sustainable process of continually adapting indirect performance measurement. This supports the full engagement of all stakeholders and intrinsically favours the small, focused and adaptive over the large, unfocused and rigid. In this new environment, the hierarchical multinational corporation of the past is redundant.

The latter can participate in evolution only by a process of creative destruction. Such large, adaptive organizations do exist,[42] but they are not sustainable as monolithic hierarchical enterprises and to survive the successful ones have to outsource all but core activity to others. Recent experience suggests they are not generally safe places for stakeholders to engage their resources. All the pressure now, not least in the interests of shareholder value, is for large unfocused enterprises to de-capitalize themselves by outsourcing non-core activity and/or when that does not work to de-construct themselves. The framework for achieving this is a dynamic one. This seeks to uncover the rules, processes or principles for strategically placing enterprise in a position of quasi-stability in the face of unknown future outcomes. In doing this it enhances its survivability in the complex co-operatively competitive environments now being created by stakeholders using the fast-emerging information- and knowledge-based industries.[43]

Given the vital role of these latter industries in the globalization process, there is a need for everyone to develop understanding of the dynamics of the relationship between socio-economic and cultural diversity as it currently exists on the planet. Anonymous exchange can serve as a starting point for analysing competitive processes. However it is not competent to aid one in understanding the co-operative exchange processes essential to the survival of enterprise in the global system now emerging. This has to be increasingly accountable to stakeholders who refuse to be embedded in existing social and political structures. Such stakeholders actively seek effective governance over enterprise. The substance of this governance system is that it is evolving to limit the accretion of too much power at any point and so encourages diversity as essential to the wider communal interest.

We now need to understand the ongoing dynamics of the relationship between trust and identity: how they interact and influence the effectiveness of co-operative exchange in knowledge-based industries. In studying co-operative exchange one has to understand the ongoing reality of social structure and relationships that are evolving to aid this process. By definition, these cannot end at a particular, defined point of sale. Knowledge can be transferred only slowly. It generally requires ongoing communication between its creator and its user. The latter has to learn how to absorb and exploit it.

There is clearly a need to integrate thinking on collaboration and co-operation with that on competition and personal acquisitiveness. We have started to do that here.[44] The nature of trust and identity requires interdisciplinary thinking. This must encompass the role of complexity in management, economics, anthropology and socio-legal studies. In Chapter 9 we start to integrate our previous arguments so as to examine the co-operation that is required to ensure that real communication can occur in the rich, diverse and dense environment that is now evolving through global networking.

# 9

# Global Diversity, Psychic Distance and Communication Costs

## Introduction

Earlier, we noted the importance of identity to exchange, especially regarding the exchange of knowledge. Now we raise the issue of communication between identified individuals or enterprises. For communication, anonymity in exchange is not an option. Exchange requires mutual comprehension and will be more difficult when transactors are embedded in different cultures,[1] which is likely to occur in the global system. Different cultures have distinct mores and each culture uses its own historically evolved frame of reference for communication, to aid internal understanding. Generally speaking, this includes a language particular to this culture, and all this creates a barrier to communication between societies. This barrier is compounded when the product exchanged is knowledge.

Co-operation in knowledge exchange requires very high levels of trust and costly effort to understand the different perspectives of exchange partners. Such exchange is essential if the networks of connectivity required to create, exploit and sustain value from knowledge are to remain viable. In a globalizing world the co-operation required to operate the system needs to be reconciled with local interests and different communication styles.

The global business system requires connections to be established globally between nodes of locally accreted enterprise. These need to engage co-operatively to generate value from knowledge. For explosive growth to occur value, in the form of money and energy, needs to be attracted disproportionately to those nodes generating the most value. For this to be achieved such nodes need to be identifiable to others and the value of the knowledge generated understood by geographically and culturally dispersed stakeholders.

The importance of the processes of trust-building to negotiation and bargaining in such networks[2] cannot be understated. In the currently evolving global business system a framework is needed to aid thinking about the role major turbulence plays in its evolution. A litmus test of this is the ability of any explanation to reconcile, within the same frame of reference, the Asian, communal business systems, the 1997 economic and business crisis and the renewed success of the individualist business system.

Third-party institutions such as governments and NGOs are the embryonic basis of future co-evolved institutions and enterprise. We posit that the enterprises functioning in this area are at the leading edge of the new globalizing community and form the basis for a future embedding infrastructure for enterprise. Initially they themselves have to operate outside the guiding context of any legacy, social or political, infrastructure.

The communication agenda has to address the issues raised by these needs. For any system to be effective one needs to establish understanding between the various and different nations and cultures. This inevitably has to occur over what is called 'psychic distance'.[3] This arises from the differences each culture has evolved. Inevitably inter-enterprise global networks have to reach beyond their own cultural context to communicate with others. Psychic distance can be significant. With the very varied frames of reference each enterprise uses, one must expect misunderstanding in global communications to occur. The barriers to meaningful contact may be significant and could prevent the ignition needed to begin value adding collaboration.

Comment on the 1997 Asian crisis has been widespread[4] but not the understanding of its roots in non-economic, organizational and institutional factors. We believe the co-evolution of enterprise and its supporting institutions[5] is the key to understanding how the global system-to-be will sustain itself at maturity and respond to the discontinuities that will inevitably disturb its smooth progress.

As we established in Chapters 2 and 3, national business systems are both socially and politically embedded. Forces other than the market act upon enterprise. In Chapter 8 we saw how socio-political forces act to ensure that resources find their way to where the most social value is being added in the global network. Existing thinking on co-operation and exchange, especially from an international business perspective, does not always take into account the costs of communicating across 'psychic distance'. Such gaps in thinking and understanding are most apparent when exchange is within or with an emergent system.

Globalization and its significance to the knowledge industries is said to lead to competitive pressure that will lessen psychic distance. We noted this in Chapter 2; we saw there, and have illustrated since, that global competitiveness leads not to sameness but to institutional diversity. The ecological analogy suggests that this is to be expected during emergence. Newly sustainable cultural diversity is an inevitable enriching emergent feature of the new order. Competitive pressure will not reduce this to a monoculture. Monocultures are also rare in the natural world. It is only the 'rational' choices made by man that destroy diversity; natural competition leads to co-operative diversity, not uniformity. The new world order needs to be seen from such an evolutionary perspective if the processes creating it are to be understood. These lead to the norm of mutuality of interest and collaboration.

The business system now emerging is one that totally transcends the political boundaries of the nation state.[6] Its primary driver is the knowledge industry. This operates 24/7 around the globe using the Internet. The resulting cultural diversity of those collaborating raises 'psychic distance' as a potentially significant issue worthy of careful consideration which needs to be addressed effectively. It involves costs in transacting, namely the costs of inter-cultural communication.

Such costs are both direct and indirect. The direct business of translation is costly, especially when it has to encompass not merely language but socio-political context as well. Linguists prefer to use the word 'transposing' instead of 'translating' in such cases. Indirect costs exist in monitoring and enforcement – for example, those appropriate to assessing performance in one context may be inappropriate in another.

Our analysis to date has concentrated on the modulation of transaction costs. We now need to consider how such costs can be attenuated or amplified by the process of communication across psychic distance. The relevance of this for exchange, especially non-market exchange, is self-evident.[7] If exchange has to take place within and between enterprises, as is essential in the knowledge industry, cross-cultural communication costs could be significant.

## Communication as a cost

We, as well as others,[8] have suggested that institutions co-evolve with enterprise. The forces driving co-evolution are the pay-offs that come from reduced uncertainty in exchange. However in inter-cultural transactions pre-existing institutions set up to ameliorate local exchange uncertainty tend to increase global exchange uncertainty. Transactors in distinct cultures have different mores, values and laws governing exchange. It is not clear whether the processes prevalent in emergence compound or ameliorate such difficulties.

In emergent systems the institutions required for national co-ordination have yet to develop. This seems to imply more uncertainty. However, if a global identification system exists, this effect may be slight. If a global system of dynamic identity as described in Chapter 8 exists then with few if any local legacy institutions to contend with, a golden opportunity presents itself for an enterprise to self-organize. It can create a new global order in which to embed itself. This transcends anything existing locally and could effectively obviate the need for a global polity to evolve.

We may able to pass directly to global institutions in which local exchange is accommodated naturally. As a result of the emergence of a global business system we may thus find psychic distance being attenuated rather than amplified. This lessens the significance of the communication problems. At a technical level, this is evident in the spread of global communication links. Many poorer societies have no legacy telephone infrastructure; they therefore find it easy to go directly to a modern digitized telephone system. The most dramatic illustration of this phenomenon is in the growth of mobile phone usage in China.

The obvious solution when faced with large communication costs over large psychic distances is to avoid them. One simply cannot deal with enterprises situated at a large psychic distance from oneself. Many enterprises take this option. Their main means of accessing the pay-offs from international business is in collaboration with partners in business systems similar to their own. This strategy is frequently evident. It is exemplified by the fact that the UK and the US have consistently been the largest inward investors in each other's economies.[9] This avoids the issue; if a truly global system is to emerge, like the rain forest, it will have to exult in difference and so there must be processes lowering the communication costs of bridging psychic distance.

Psychic distance has two components, one derived from cultural[10] and the other from institutional differences. The latter emanates from the former. It is reflected in differences in law and administration.[11] These embedding institutions are what we now concentrate upon. We wish to develop a framework to aid understanding of how psychic distance can be overcome. The problem is acute for those in the individualistic business system. Enterprises here have a style based on anonymous exchange backed up by legal enforceability. This insists on transparency in any contract, which is awkward when one's partner is in a business system where personal contact is all, and asymmetry in knowledge is a major source of local value. From the perspective of the individualistic system, much of the familial and social trading that occurs in communal or emergent business systems is corrupt.

However, as we showed in Chapter 6 a sequence of transactions can be initiated using hostages to fortune, although in the longer term we also saw that such an approach could be expensive. Longer-term, some kind of cross-cultural accommodation is necessary between those exchanging with each other. Such an accommodation allows them to dismantle the expensive social scaffolding provided by hostages.

Here we want to understand the process by which this state can be achieved. There is a need to create a foundation for co-operation in the medium to longer term. This needs to be based on mutual understanding of the differences in belief, perception, images and values each holds. For example, Islam turns its back on lending at interest. Individualist business systems see the giving out of asymmetric knowledge to a local politician or official as potentially corrupt. Yet, exchange and communication have to take place.

## Global communication

If one accepts mutuality of understanding, rather than a commonality of view, as the end game, then one must accept psychic distance as endemic. It is not something to eliminate but something that global business has to overcome.[12] To achieve this, we must be able to explain how the varying characteristics of the business systems can be accommodated. It is also necessary to understand how enterprise can operate beyond the bounds set by existing political entities and still be enabled to set up the cross-cultural alliances need to make the emerging business system work.[13] To do so, our analysis needs to take account of all the dimensions along which a business system evolves to embed enterprise, be they political, sociological, legal, anthropological or economic.[14]

The differences that exist along these dimensions between business systems potentially limit the continuity of trans-national business co-operation. Often international bargains and co-operative projects terminate when their initial goals have been achieved; they often do not lead on to continuing exchange. If communication failure leads to a loss of actual or perceived control of jointly possessed resources, one has to expect any co-operative relationship to be weakened[15] and so lessen any tendency for globally dispersed enterprise to accrete together. The significance of psychic distance to the feasibility of such accretions must therefore be lessened if a global business system is actually to emerge. The power emergence releases rips asunder the old certainties provided by local legacy institutions. If globalization, the process, is a reality countervailing forces must be at work. It is they that bring the coherence needed to add new value in the new emerging order.

One un-adventurous way this may be achieved is for those operating within similar business systems to work together. This avoids some of the difficulties of working across large psychic distances. The similarity of the working context compensates for dissimilarities in the cultural one. This might have been the case in the past but does not seem to be the route followed now. It seems the gains from working globally are so great that the costs of working at greater psychic distances is no longer a deterrent to co-operation.

The most interesting angle on this is that in a creative context observable differences in culture add such huge value that the costs of communication across large psychic distances become relatively unimportant. It seems that it is possible to develop trust and understanding across large psychic distances when the rewards are great, where what is exchanged is insight and understanding, both of which are significantly enhanced by seeing things from multiple perspectives. Mutual tolerance between enterprises and people in diverse business systems is then heavily incentivized. The communication gap exists; its resolution is to find ways to exploit the value in difference, not seek to eliminate it.

As we have seen, well-identified national business systems already exist. These contain a legacy of institutions that need to either adapt or die to enable born-global enterprises to flourish. For this to occur a system has to evolve that easily permits the creative destruction of one enterprise[16] or institution to let newer ones flourish in every niche in the value chain. For the reasons indicated, the emergent global business system seems to have a trans-national culture tolerant of difference.

In Chapter 2 we argued that business systems could usefully be categorized by the emphasis they gave to the role of different stakeholders: their shareholders, the community, employees, suppliers, customers and government. There we considered two limiting cases: one in which one stakeholder, the shareholder, dominated all other – the individualist business system; and another in which all stakeholders influenced enterprise, with a more limited role for shareholders – the communal business system.[17] In stakeholder terms we thus had an individual shareholder's system, and a community of stakeholders' system.

The geopolitical division of the world to which these labels might be applied is already familiar to the reader. In countries such as the US and the UK, the business system is dominated by stock and financial markets, which provide one means to measure and assess worth, or shareholder value. In numerical terms, this boils down to a comparison of the dividend yield with the return on capital employed (ROCE), as measurable from this year's profit and loss account (PLA) and the balance sheet.

In contrast, in stakeholder systems, in countries such as Germany and Japan, enterprises are more communally organized. They are monitored in a manner reflecting this and involve significant collaboration between company officials, bankers, financiers, government and employees. These groups may be seen as using their mutual trust and personal understanding of each other and the business to support the business's way forward.[18]

Beside these two extreme cases, we discussed the emerging system as having ad hoc local stakeholder involvement. Only the state is in a position to be really influential nationally and then only in a very limited way, given the speed of emergent development.

How does the nature of emergence as it affects the utility of emerging economies provide a model for emergence generally, and global emergence in particular? It entails the destruction of existing geopolitical boundaries. The knowledge-based industries are arguably the leading sector[19] of this emerging form. They certainly offer the most dramatic manifestation of it, having products that are in part difficult to specify, measure, regulate, control and exchange – all of which has consequences for exercising propriety. One might surmise that the concept of propriety will change to accommodate this newly emergent form.

We have to recognize that emergent business systems appear to differ markedly from those in mature economies.[20] In its global form, the cultural diversity within the category is itself extreme, and some emerging markets themselves have internal cultural diversity. We defined the emergent business systems only in terms of what they are not compared to others. In dealing with them one faces a much higher rate of unpredictability than one would if dealing with enterprises in more mature systems. However, if an enterprise within them wishes to operate globally it has to plug into a node in the network situated in a mature economy even if it is simply to access the financial services necessary to transact internationally.

Cultural 'translation' or transposition is always needed from the periphery of an emerging system to a node in a mature one. There can then be easy onward transmission to another node in a mature system. A partner in exchange in another emergent system may be connected similarly. This involves two translations rather than four, yielding a 50 per cent saving in potential communication costs. One needs only one for trunk-line communication with local translation provided at either end of any communication link, epitomized by the growing use of 'English' as the language of global business.

Any analysis of emerging economies must consider what additional factors need to be taken into account to ensure comprehension so that the full nature of a transaction is translatable into the *lingua franca* of the trunk connection into a mature business environment. The same is true of the now-emerging global business system. Given high levels of unpredictability the traditional advantage of pure markets, their power to co-ordinate exchange partners, is considerably weakened[21] in the mercurial and harder to measure knowledge industries. This double dose of unpredictability and lack of susceptibility to measurement are the defining factors in assessing the psychic distance between emerging and mature business systems from both an enterprise and an institutional perspective.

## An example: Asia's emerging markets

In Figure 9.1 we show the stages of potential and relative emergence for Asia. We have superimposed on this our view of the position of the US. Immediately under each indicative stage we show emergent criteria. These are derived from the identity and embeddedness factors developed in Chapters 2 and 3.[22] As Figure 9.1 shows, we believe that Asia can be divided into at least four stages of emergence. Japan, which is in stage 4, is technically and economically 'mature'; nevertheless, Japan reached this level only recently as it really emerged in this sense only after the Second World War. The lessons of emergence are still relatively recent for Japanese corporations and institutions. Two countries, Korea and Taiwan, and the two smaller, more individualist-orientated states of Singapore and Hong Kong, are placed in the category of stage 3, having followed Japan in emergence. Stage 2 would include emerging Southeast Asian countries other than Malaysia, Thailand, Indonesia, the Philippines and one newcomer, India. Stage 1 includes China and Vietnam. Other Asian countries we position in the still-dormant heritage system.

A key implication of Asian emergence is that even if a country reaches stage 4, and so possesses a level of technology and economic well-being near to if not surpassing that in Western Europe or North America, the 'business system' may remain very different. Japan is an example: it has more than matched its Western European and North American

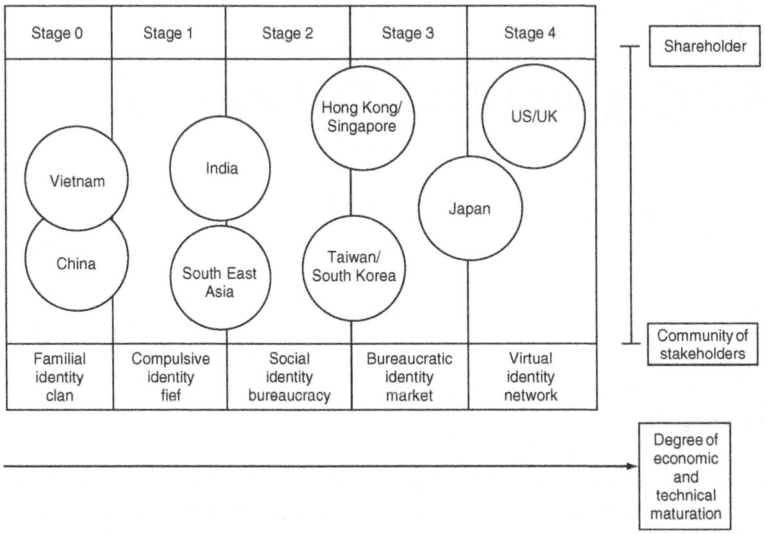


*Figure 9.1* Stages of growth model

competitors technically and industrially; a stage 3 country, Korea, leads the world in terms of broadband communications. Yet their business systems are still evolving.

This permits us to say that the business system prevailing at technical maturity is not a function of the stage of emergence the country is in: both the US and Japan are at stage 4, fully mature technically and have and sustain very different business systems. A factor may be the rapidity with which technical maturity was reached. Institutional growth and embeddedness are phenomena which take a number of human generations to become established. It may be that with very rapid and continuing development it is not possible for national political embeddedness to mature at a rate similar to that at which technology and wealth can. If this is the case then psychic distance may be sustained *ad infinitum*. Very rapidly growing and developing countries may remain psychically distinct from those whose maturation has been slower. The newly emergent global system seems to have become embedded in the virtual space created and spanned by global rather than national indices, and this raises new questions for how the emergence of the new global system is occurring.

This also raises the question of how applicable the traditional rules of international business are to success in today's knowledge industries.

# 10
# Bridging the Global Cultural Gap

## Introduction

If the conjectures in Chapter 9 are sustainable, then we must expect to see Asian development as unique. Psychic if not technological distance will be maintained but perhaps also transformed by the process required to sustain necessary global information exchange. This has clear implications for any collaborations that may be envisaged within the emerging global business system. Potential collaboration would seem to have to aim for the differences that undoubtedly exist between the individualist shareholder-driven system, the communal stakeholder-driven system and the emergent stakeholder-less business systems.[1]

## Psychic distance: I – shareholder, communal and emergent systems

The shareholder-based system of free-market exchange assumes that exchange occurs, indeed for reasons of probity must occur, at arm's length from any human relationships.[2] Exchange is perceived to occur impersonally. Little knowledge or identification of the partner in exchange is required apart from a bureaucratic registration of the individuals and enterprises involved. When dealing with the rapidly developing, technically similar, East Asian countries, account has to be taken of the social as well as the bureaucratic identity of exchange partners. We believe that to understand Asia's problems, there is a need to understand the evolutionary significance of this crucial difference.

These rapidly emergent countries are, and at the same time are not, at the same point in development as their individualist shareholder or their West European communal counterparts. Economically and technically they may even be ahead; but socio-politically they are not. Indeed they cannot be, because workable socio-political systems evolve less rapidly than the technology that explosively drives change during emergence. This is because socio-political maturation depends on the learning period of human beings. Generally, this covers the maturation period of a new generation of people that is unsullied by experience of legacy systems, and that is probably around fifty years: twenty-five years for a new concept to be matured and twenty-five years to pass it on as the way of doing things to the generation after that.

It is clear from observation that the shareholder and the stakeholder business systems can exist simultaneously in very different but equally technically developed economies. In any comparative analysis we must be careful not to consider the issue as one of developed versus emerging economies. However because of the slower maturation of socio-political embeddedness we would expect[3] the enterprises and institutions of the emergent market economies to show far greater overlap with the enterprises and institutions of communal systems.

We would also expect the above to be more true of institutions rather than enterprises. The latter can change more rapidly through quite fast birth (initial capitalization) and death (bankruptcy) or by suitably fast adaptation (investment in new know-how). Institutions, on the other hand, are in a way constructed to define boundaries and enforce them so they should by their nature be more immutable than enterprises. However, it is also true that there is a huge overlap in the way inter-organizational relationships exist in communal systems and the manner of operation of intra-enterprise relationships in shareholder systems.[4] This is not surprising. Transaction cost arguments drive one to see hierarchy as the preferred organizational structure in those areas of exchange where markets fail to operate, i.e. where the measurement of productive output is difficult and expensive to assess, as it is for example in the information industry.

It is important to understand the difference between enterprises and institutions, particularly as it exists between individualist and communal systems even when technically they are at the same level of maturation.[5] We notice very clearly that in some sense each has embedded in it elements of the other. These are perhaps situated differently but they are still there. As we have seen in shareholder anonymous exchange, nonetheless, human relationships are not insignificant. In communal systems due legal processes clearly also exist. Hence it is possible within one's own actions and context to see elements of the situation faced by others and develop empathy. If one has such awareness then both observer and observed can go some way to overcome psychic distance – within the system faced by each are the elements required to see the basis of the action taken by the other.

This has significant value as it enables each partner in exchange to develop an internally meaningful reference point, a focal point, from which to view the other's basis for operations in the other system and so see and understand how it works.[6] This is particularly important in attempting to understand an emerging business system such as exists in the rapidly developing economies in East Asia and the new global economic system now emerging.[7] Our key observation is that one can find elements of each system embedded somewhere in another, so that a basis for understanding by analogy is nearly always possible. If this is so then the psychic distance between potentially co-operating partners in different business systems can partly be overcome somewhat more easily than might be expected from casual observation.

Even within Asia's emerging economies some systems are more shareholder-based than others, the obvious example being Hong Kong. So it is necessary to couple the level of emergence with other factors to understand how to develop an effective approach to the exchange and co-operation required, if emergence and the new global economic system is to be effective.

## Psychic distance: II – emergence and unpredictability

The second major area of problem for psychic distance is embedded in the dynamic nature of emergence itself, and the impact this has on communication between enterprises in the emerging global network.[8] Does psychic distance increase or decrease in such circumstances?

The concept of trust is often called on to describe how the East Asian communal approach contrasts with the anonymous market-based exchange used in the individualist system.[9] The contrast is usually made between Japan and the US. In Japan, the organization is seen as owned by an entire community of stakeholders, which is in turn embedded in the community of the nation and is therefore, in some sense, socially trustworthy. In the shareholder, market-oriented individualist system, as it exists in the US, the self-interests of individuals rather than groups is its principal focus, and in some sense it is therefore socially untrustworthy. Analysis consequent on Enron, WorldCom, etc. suggests that this is in fact verifiably true, and it is changing the way such systems operate to be more communally transparent and so constrained.

Individuals and enterprises are theoretically able to pursue their 'self-interest' in this anonymous system where in a sense, apart from market transactions, social relationships do not exist economically. The social and political spheres are treated as distinct disconnected entities in which little interference of one by the other is allowed except in very clearly specified and constitutionally controlled circumstances.[10] Interestingly, this individualist self-reliant character seems also to prevail in the emerging global system as described in Chapter 9 – the difference being that in that case it is a self-reliance in the global communal interest.

In a communal system, it is thus argued, social obligation makes the predictability of an enterprise's behaviour less transparent to an external observer than in an individualist shareholder system. Here the transparency required of those operating under anonymous exchange makes not only their actions but also their outcomes as totally foreseeable as is possible in a more widely unpredictable world. Market risk cannot be eliminated for the latter reason but the facts are all there to allow the market to systematically eliminate any risk associated with a particular enterprise. However, recent events of the type described above suggest that such a reasoning is not sustainable and that a wider group of stakeholders has the right to some interest, or propriety, in the actions of enterprise in the individualist system.

## Co-operation and unpredictability

A major issue in international business environments is the unpredictability of the degree to which the parties to an agreement will truly fulfil their obligations and commitments as understood by the other party.[11] In an international business setting – and especially so in highly unpredictable emerging markets – not only does one carry the costs of identifying the other parties to an exchange but also those of measuring the content and value of the product or service being produced together over time, and of the share each has had in producing it.

Even where identity and agreed value to be delivered appear to have been ascertained to the satisfaction of all, in any continuing relationship discrepancies may creep in between what is perceived by each party to be occurring and what in reality is happening. This acts to amplify any communication problem. In escalation, things that are not true will be believed to be so and things that are true will be taken to be wrong. Such distortions are inevitable.[12] This form of psychic distance is one further complication in any effort to co-operate across the cultural divide that inevitably exists between the shareholder and the communal systems.[13]

In dealings with the emerging markets business system, transaction costs are, as said before, increased by the communication cost necessary to establish identity and to assess value. The transaction cost paradigm suggests that this will have consequences for organizational form. After the identity is clear to the parties to a deal they then need to determine how each values the deal and assess the gains due to each from the continuing transaction and how these should be distributed to each.[14]

Identity helps determine the boundaries of the enterprise's behavior and thus its attitudes to opportunism. Operating with a social identity undoubtedly lowers communication and co-ordination costs. With intangibles it goes without saying that a bureaucratic identity is of little value. No contract can be specified, so no savings are possible by this route. It may be appropriate to commodities, perhaps, but for information is unlikely to be so.

Where no identity exists one has to be constructed, as discussed in Chapter 9. By traditional routes, this generally takes time. As we have seen, this time can be foreshortened at some direct expense to the transactors by an exchange of hostages to fortune. This creates a bilateral identity from which social relationships based on trust, and thus a social identity, can grow.[15] However, as we have also seen, an identity can also be constructed using indices, determined either by external, specialist third-party intermediaries, or by other parties in one's social network or community.[16]

The key issue then is accurately to understand whether the transactors share values if they are both in the same type of business system or at least understand each other's if they are in different ones. Without either of these one needs a process to lock them together under some kind of self-imposed duress, mutual giving of hostages, or to buy time in which each can learn sufficient of the other to understand the other's values and so trustworthiness. Within the bounds of a closely-knit clan[17] identity is very closely shared, and the social exchange required is then arguably easier. In shareholder systems political embeddedness creates confidence in the use of bureaucratic state-created identities to regulate socio-economic activity: company registration records, certificates of competence, etc. These work only if what is to be transacted for is specifiable in a contract. With intangibles such as knowledge or knowledge-related products, this is less possible.

These barriers to co-operation in exchange brought about by psychic distance can be understood as a consequence of the parties' lack of a set of common beliefs which can lead to trusted identities and mutual understanding. If unpredictability remains high then only the mutual commitment of hostages to fortune can establish a compulsive bilateral identity as a basis to start a relationship that over time can lead to growing mutual respect and trust.[18]

Uncertainty as to whether measurement and enforcement costs will be high or low, as well as the uncertainty as to the identity of the transacting partner, adds to the difficulties of co-operating in exchange. However, our discussion helps to illustrate the realities of exchange in many emerging business systems, such as those in Eastern Europe and in parts of Asia and Latin America where there is high uncertainty about the value that can be placed on information in the business environment. Such unpredictability also characterizes exchange in the industries producing forms of information, where similar solutions to these dilemmas may perhaps be found. We believe they can be, and this will be the major focus of Chapter 11.

So psychic distances can be effectively bridged and in a manner that creates an incentive for the development of the identity required to participate effectively in what is an investment in knowledge as social capital. In emerging business systems the mores applied to outsiders may differ considerably from those applied to insiders. Paradoxically, the consequently high measurement and control costs drive a requirement for institutional change to lessen them and shift longer-term to trust-based exchange. It is the very magnitude of these costs relative to the value gain which can be made, and this is considerable during emergence, which drives the parties to construct a solution to the dilemma faced. Humanity seems to have a virtually unbounded capacity to create value in this way.[19] In fact, the information industries are the leaders in enabling this in the modern world, and not just for themselves. The effects are evident through all value chains in all industries and they are becoming increasingly evident, impacting hugely on costs everywhere.

Where value gain is high and the costs of measurement and enforcement are high, there will be a determination to initiate exchange to force the construction of means to establish long-term trust and so drive down these costs. The contractually based exchange of the individualist business system depends on political embeddedness to provide low measurement and enforcement costs. This is possible only for commodities and in reality one needs an exchange of intangibles to be socially not just politically embedded. The first is not conducive to the development of trust necessary between the contracting parties, because trust is simply not necessary. Fortunately this is not the case in emerging business systems, where by definition unpredictability is high.

In more general terms the paradox is that, by deliberately increasing the costs of measurement and exchange, one reduces the incentives for a partner in exchange to try to measure the value of the product or service being exchanged or transferred. The party providing the product or service has more information as to worth than the receiving party. By increasing rather than decreasing this asymmetry in information, any temptation the buyer might have to incur the costs of first identifying the seller better and then measuring the value both to be received and actually being delivered, is reduced. It would cost too much. If the would-be buyer wants the product, as he just might, then he either has to take a hostage to fortune and trust the seller in what could turn out to be, if the seller is trustworthy, a continuing and worthwhile relationship. This is precisely the context for a further expansion in the information industry where value can be added by a third-party acting as a specialist gatherer of information on identity and reliability and providing this information at a price to potential users of the service involved. This is the model developed earlier. It works again here.

## Overcoming psychic distance

A very simple way of overcoming psychic distance is to identify analogues of parts of another's system within one's own. However in international business enterprise seems to begin the internationalization process conservatively, by choosing partners in countries 'psychically' close to their own; and this is also true of the choice of business systems.[20] Working in countries that are psychically close reduces unpredictability. It may even make it possible for enterprise to operate abroad under conditions not dissimilar to those it enjoys in its home market. Unfortunately long-term this is not a good strategy. It may lock an enterprise into a pathway of easy future learning that prevents it discovering through diversity something which later becomes crucial to survival in the world at large. Companies from the politically embedded shareholder business system need to adapt quickly to the significance and implications for exchange of social communal-style relationships[21] and many are, through the adoption of value chain strategies that have been shown to work initially in the communitarian or communal system, such as partnership sourcing.

In the past enterprise has tended to reduce the impact of psychic distance through attempts at market penetration by multinationals from mature systems into others. Nowadays in the information industries the issue is not necessarily market penetration but the more effective exploitation of very tightly focused core competences wherever they may lie by a network of value adding global connectivity. This issue is fundamental to what we will be discussing in Chapter 11 – global value adding networks that form the basis of what is the emerging future business system.

## Summary

We have addressed the importance of overcoming psychic distance, in order to create an effective foundation for understanding the significance of communication costs. This would seem to be needed to effect the co-operative exchange required during emergence and on a continuing basis for enterprise to be able to create, exchange and exploit information. We have done so from two perspectives. First by looking at business systems and their supporting organizations comparatively, distinguishing between shareholder, communal and emerging value systems. We believe these differences are of an importance which goes beyond the implications for trading across the divide between these principal types of business system. Significant elements of all are embedded in the newly emergent global business system that we discuss in the Chapter 11. Secondly, by further examining the process of emergence we have emphasized the importance of communication as an additional cost of transacting in the information industries. We believe this has profound implications for co-operative exchange and its role in the developing global economy. The influence on transaction costs during emergence of unpredictability and interference patterns in communications across socio-cultural boundaries could be significant. An undue focus on the optimal results achievable in mature business systems neglects perspectives vital to understanding the development of industries and economies, especially during emergence. Knowing the ideal outcome gives little guidance on how to consciously assist the evolution of such maturity. Difference – or, more correctly, diversity – is as important a factor as sameness. Japan and Korea both have communal systems, Singapore and Hong Kong, while similar in many ways to the first two, are working more within a shareholder business system than either of them.[22]

There is no unique first-best path to development, there are just many that work. Economic and technical absorption makes possible a rate of technical catching-up which it does not seem possible to achieve in the socio-political realm. Their progress is dependent on the maturation and life cycle of human beings. This fundamental difference needs to be taken into account in analysing co-operative exchange which at base is dependent on some kind of social identity. This kind of transaction is fundamental to a new emerging global environment being driven by the information industries. In Chapter 11 we take these ideas to fruition by exploring their implications for the now-emerging global economy.

# Part III

# Synthesis

*This page intentionally left blank*

# 11
# Knowledge and the Emergent Global Business System

## Introduction

Increasingly value creation through enterprise is based on 'lean thinking'.[1] Each enterprise keeps 'lean' by situating itself in a value-generating network with others. Each enterprise concentrates on adding value for the ultimate customer. Each does this by focusing on its own area of core competencies and the role that it can play in delivering value to the network as a whole. Non-core activity is outsourced to others in the network. These all deliver JIT from the network's range of internationally situated global suppliers. The resulting value adding network of connectivity is organized much like the Japanese *Keiretsu*.[2] In this case, each is part of the web of cross-cultural connectivity spanning the globe. To survive, each sub-network within this whole has to operate co-operatively through market-like transactions to generate and pass on value for the system. In so doing, for incentive reasons, each should be receiving an amount of value proportionate to its perceived worth to the network seen as a whole. Each such sub-network competes with others for its share of the value they mutually generate for the global system. The more effective they are at attracting such value, the more net value they can generate. This is a self-reinforcing positive feedback system in which success breeds success.

The now available global infrastructure of connectivity makes this possible. It covers communication (e.g. email), distribution (e.g. UPS) and finance (e.g. Mastercard or AMEX). Infrastructures like this operating at the speed and reliability now possible emerged only in the last twenty-five years or so. Using them, globally dispersed enterprises can be co-ordinated to deliver high added value for all their stakeholders, including the ultimate customer.

Those interested in understanding the emerging global business system must focus on the dynamic forces driving the creation of such focused 'familial' networks. Unlike the traditional view of markets the ones that operate within such networks cannot operate on the basis of frictionless perfectly informed anonymous exchange. The knowledge needed to make them work is not free, but comes imperfectly, thus making communication costly. Additionally as its worth is intimately connected with knowledge on identity it carries the costs of establishing that this is from a trustworthy context within which it is socially and/or politically embedded.[3] Reality happens to be a complex of imperfections. Exchange within it has to be based on trust to be viable. If such a system is to exist in the global environment it will have to be constructed within the social network of connectivity described. There is no global polity nor a global socio-cultural infrastructure, apart from that provided too sparsely by the various Diaspora, such as the overseas Chinese in the Far East, the Jews in Europe and North America and the Palestinians in the Middle East and Africa. This is now supported by seamlessly connected banking, communication and distribution systems that now exist. Hence the need for indices and the dynamic identity with which they are associated.

In the newly emergent global system, the product being exchanged is knowledge, especially tacit[4] knowledge, and therefore it is absolutely essential to identify clearly the enterprise in which it is embedded. This enterprise will have co-evolved to support the knowledge's creation, exploitation and dissemination.[5] This is all intimately entwined with the *personae* of the transactors, both people and enterprises. Knowledge cannot be used without their assistance and then only in the particular social context in which it was created. In this sense, knowledge is an invisible asset[6] and one so thoroughly embedded in individuals who in turn are embedded in a specific socio-political context that it cannot be disentangled to be sold as a product that is distinct from the people within whom it is embedded. This creates problems for the specification, identification, measurement and replicability of such mostly tacit knowledge.

The exchange of knowledge to the extent it is thought about by managers is often in the particular context of a 'developed' country or, if internationally transferred, within the ambit of an internationally active enterprise.[7] In the emergent context we are discussing, our only existing point of reference is what we choose to describe as the emerging global business system and there the emphasis is on the socio-economic gains from transferring know-how from one of the mature business systems into this emerging global system. This involves mostly transferring necessary skills and understanding to people, seen as human capital – hence different from that just described.[8] This ignores the huge significance of the embedding context needed for it to be sustainable and accessible.

The role knowledge is playing in the process of globalization therefore creates very important issues, both in terms of generating self-reinforcing economic success and in handling the boundary crisis that always arises in emerging markets.[9] All this is highly relevant to the now emerging global business system:[10]

(1) Knowledge has to be seen as a distinct resource. It must not be seen as part of human capital. If it is, one gets a false focus on education and training policy when in our view it is as much the social and enterprise context in which it is embedded that is important to the value of knowledge as its intellectual content.[11]
(2) One has to see knowledge in the context of the new institutions and enterprises that seem to be co-evolving in the global system.[12] We need to give attention to the role knowledge plays in emergence and evolution generally, and not only how it is handled in specific enterprises, especially those in mature business systems.[13]
(3) Knowledge about generic technology has to be distinguished from the knowledge that supports the infrastructure in which it is embedded and this, as we have seen, is tightly bound up with the questions of identity and trust. We need to differentiate knowledge about technology from knowledge about the qualities of goods and services.[14]

All three of these have to be examined if knowledge is to be properly understood in an emergent context. To achieve such understanding one needs a synthesis of ideas spanning a number of fields and a means of surveying the field that allows us to see it from an individualistic, communal and emergent perspective. This is the reason why we constructed our three business systems in the way we did. It enables us to achieve the triangulation required.

## Knowledge/knowledge as a resource

In view of the distinction made between explicit or codifiable knowledge[15] (also called 'information') and implicit or tacit[16] knowledge, market mechanisms that work on the basis of precise knowledge may not be of assistance in trying to understand the processes required to exchange knowledge across networks of the kind described. Alternatives are required if we wish to transfer knowledge in the value adding and sharing way required to make such networks viable and effective.[17] We have already shown that while the traditional view of a market is quite effective for transacting in commodities it is imperfect when it comes to modulating exchange in most intangibles.

To effectively understand the system we are dealing with, knowledge has to be treated as a distinct category of resource and needs to be added to the three traditionally identified – labour, capital and land.[18] With these three categories alone the implicit and intangible nature of much knowledge inevitably drives one to treat it as part of human capital. If one then modifies the view one takes of labour market exchange one can see an effective mechanism supporting the creation, use and trading of knowledge as it is embedded in individuals – in effect, the labour market seen in social capital terms.[19] However, the nature of knowledge is such that it can never be known perfectly. Where there is reciprocal exchange as a means of dealing with this, each party has the advantage over the other in understanding the knowledge embedded in his own enterprise.[20]

## The power of the emergent knowledge industries: leveraging the power of knowledge

The strategies that are developing to assist this global emergent process are evolving from existing business systems. These are in the immediate sense both the individualist and the communal business systems. However, the changes envisaged are in dynamics. As such, they have far more commonality with the emerging market business system than either of the mature ones and would require an amalgam of features drawn from both of the first two, a lot from the third and clearly some new 'emergent' ones. This is the primary justification of our belief that it is now necessary to change the perspective from which we view business that transcends the boundaries defined by the nation state. The currently emerging system is distinct from existing systems as it is (a) as yet not fully mature, and (b) not, like the emerging markets system, regionally confined. It has thus to be treated as an ongoing process rather than being described as an existing entity. We agree entirely with Rugman's[21] position that globalization, the fact, is hard to substantiate, but take the view that globalization, the process, is well in train.

The main features of these emerging systems have in part been created by the need of enterprise in the individualist system to compete with that from the communal Far East. The new system started by absorbing key features of their systems of manufacture and distribution, particularly 'lean' thinking.[22] However, it is also a rational response to the observed failure of a market-based approach to business strategy and to the fact that the new economy is no longer nationally situated. It can move value about the globe in a manner unobservable to existing social or political institutions.

This overall approach has its genesis in the demise of the monolithic market-dominating corporate giants of the past. In the knowledge industries a key example would be IBM, Big Blue. IBM for a long time did dominate its market; it lost the battle by trying to continue using its sheer market size. In so doing, it created a very inflexible form of enterprise. The cumbersome beast that then matured was overwhelmed by new technology that in the end it could not control.[23] IBM carried within its hierarchy a mass of peripheral activities. This was not core to its main business yet added significantly to its costs. It tried to freeze out the technological advance represented by the PC until it had squeezed the last drop of monetary return from its existing asset base; in so doing, it lost control of the technology needed for the emerging market for distributed processing.

The effort to manage infrastructure ancillary to one's main business and focus on one's operations in existing markets, milking the returns from mature products, distracts management's attention from what post-modern enterprise sees as its point of main effort, the managing and exploiting of its 'core competences' as a learning organization that continuously creates and innovates new products and services.[24] Defined this way, core competence is continually evolving 'knowledge' of how-to, which we called earlier: 'knowing'. This is not replicable by a competitor. 'Knowing' is deeply rooted in the history and culture of an enterprise. Its physical aspects may be replicated. The intellectual content can be, but less so, but the spirit of the company – what it feels it is, or its meaning as an enterprise – can never be. The 'knowing' involved is embedded in its staff as individuals but also in their relationships one with another and in the spirit of commitment their leaderships past and present instil in them. 'Knowing' is deeply embedded in all of this.

Staff can be competitively recruited. The culture that empowers their capacity to deliver cannot. The classic stories here are of 3M, Canon and Apple. The solution to this dilemma is for each enterprise to focus on its area of core competence, outsource everything else and find a way of working communally with other enterprises to deliver value of mutual benefit to all stakeholders.

This clarity of purpose is possible only in the knowledge age. Prior to modern communication and distribution technology communication was facilitated by gathering people together, with the full gamut of skills required, within the hierarchy of one enterprise – and if this were not possible then in a local accretion of supporting industries in a city. The global network of communications, distribution and command and control now available makes impersonal dealing at a distance possible. The result is enterprise based in a large number of highly focused organizations working communally in a global network of connectivity. They operate independently with highly interconnected webs of supply totally interpenetrating, and effectively making irrelevant, existing geo-political and social boundaries.

A key consequence of this is not communal interactions nor arms-length anonymous market exchange, but something different. When done well it sustains co-operative not competitive exchange. For this to work well one needs to have very high levels of interconnectivity between the members of a network, as exists in the Japanese *Keiretsu*. This is coupled, as it is in the individualist systems, with low levels of mutual dependence. Two supporting global systems enable this new system to operate effectively:

(1) The extremely low-unit cost distribution systems that have emerged and are delivered by suppliers like UPS, TNT, Federal Express, DHL, etc.
(2) The international financial interchange and identity system now possible through the infrastructure set up by Mastercard, Visa and American Express, which in turn is supported by the global communication and command and control now made possible over the communally supported Internet.

Using this connectivity, the integration of all these systems makes possible good working relationships with all those with whom one deals.

You do not have to be politically or socially embedded in the traditional sense in a culture or a state. If a particular supplier in a system cannot help you there are other suppliers who can. No party relies totally on any other for survival. Risk is thus attenuated throughout the system and this again lowers costs. At the same time, by focusing on its own 'core competence' each enterprise increases performance and quality.

These combine together to produce the explosive growth in value the system is now demonstrably creating.

Something close to the emerging system that results from the above has been referred to as 'alliance-based capitalism'.[25] This is capable of initiating and sustaining very high rates of growth, and is still evolving very fast. It is for this reason that we feel a new perspective is required from which to view enterprise as it seems to be operating at the beginning of what is in our view a newly emergent business system. This has elements of both the communal and individualist systems as well as some of the emerging markets system, but operates globally above the level of any culture or state. This system bypasses the traditional competitive market served by hierarchical enterprises.

In doing so, it lays open a previously hugely under-exploited source of added value: the knowledge encapsulated in the 'knowing' within the minds of its constituent enterprises' employees. Every unit within this system is unique. Each can and is enabled to stay true to its own context, cultural or political, yet participate over the global network.

This is the essence of what we mean when we talk of 'core competence'. It cannot exist apart from the enterprise it emerged from and evolved within, or with support from the other enterprises it operates with within its particular web of connectivity. Robust diversity not soulless uniformity is the end result. Each enterprise in the network is independent of all others and focuses on its own narrow area of core competence. By networking with impersonal professionalism in open co-operation with others high-quality products can be conceived, created, produced and distributed with incredible economy. If it operates globally this system automatically works 24/7, 365 days a year. Many enterprises already do so, especially those supplying the distribution, communications and finance infrastructure that makes this possible.

This emergent global system is delivering such results in a manner that is slowly disconnecting from any reliance on the legacy-embedding institutions that made such activity national and so international. The system is in fact creating its own embedding infrastructure emerging from enterprises specializing in constructing the indices required for dynamic identity, not human social culture or politics. The outcome of this is in many ways similar to the emergence of the nation state and international trade out of the feudal systems at the dawn of the Renaissance. Here we have 'wormholes' in the socio-political fabric of the nation state that allow connectivity and exchange between any two points on the planet without the need to rely on the chance opportunities made available by a Diaspora, or the need for bargaining

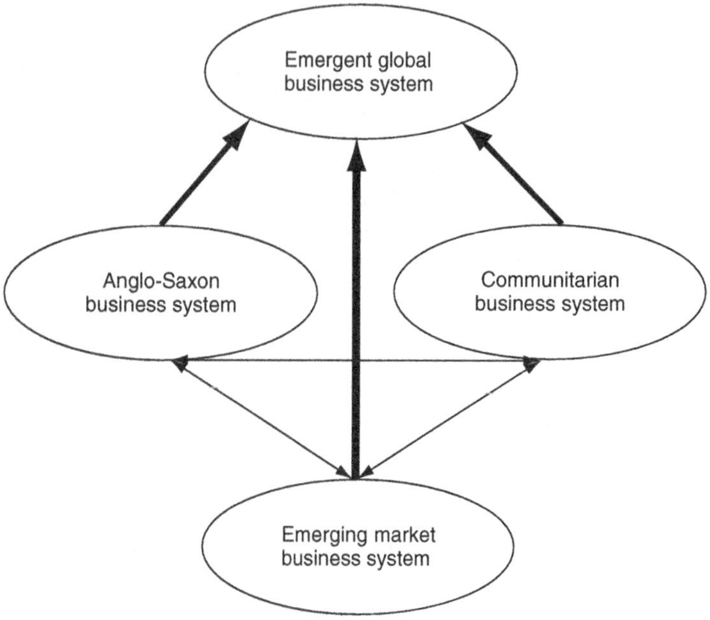


*Figure 11.1* The emergent global business system

between modulating national authorities. The system is simply growing so fast that it has to self-organize, as culture and traditional nationally based polities cannot adapt fast enough to be useful to its needs (Figure 11.1).

A model like Figure 11.1 makes clear what the processes are in the global business system that is emerging. It is essentially an emergent system. As such it has to 'use' a system which has an imperfect approach to handling knowledge. This must always be so when institutions are in transition. There is a lack of protection for the intellectual property that is being generated at an increasingly fast rate. The value of such knowledge in such an emerging context is huge, and increasing with time as its costs are plummeting – yet the net value it generates for successful enterprise continues to expand. Global enterprise thus enjoys a double success: it escapes from the limiting bounds of traditional social and political systems and reaps the rewards of policing the one that is evolving. For example, the value of knowledge may be contained in a technology licence belonging to a specific enterprise or in the institution developed for overseeing the certification of standards of quality.[26]

If we are to understand the nature of the global networks that are the fabric of the emerging global economy, we need to link together thinking on the processes delivering:

(1) The knowledge exchange fundamental to the value such networks add
(2) Propriety in the intellectual property (IP) they generate.

As regards (1): for networks to be sustained they need to exchange not only the products and services that knowledge in the sense of 'knowing' supports the production of, but also knowledge itself seen as a resource. One can only be first in class if one can co-ordinate one's own design, development and delivery while adding value for all one's stakeholders. For this to be effective one has to understand the needs of enterprises for one's efforts and vice versa. For that to be done well, one needs significant knowledge exchange especially of know-how across the network. Such intangibility of knowledge makes 'reciprocity' in exchange[27] inevitable.

As regards (2): if co-operation across such networks is to be effective in creating products and services in the common interest of the members of the network, then all parties concerned need to be clear about their individual and group interests in any jointly created intellectual property. It is however unclear how such propriety can be made effective when the object of interest (tacit knowledge) is mercurially intangible. As we saw when considering property rights a transactor's propriety is fundamental to his motivation, interests and capabilities.[28] If property rights are not protected there may be strong incentives for actors to break away with a subset of a strategic network's collective knowledge, and create their own, possibly competitive, sub-network.

Our approach is interdisciplinary[29] and our objectives twofold. First, we need to link our earlier discussions of knowledge measurement and proprietary enforcement[30] to the special circumstances of using knowledge effectively in an evolving network of connectivity. Secondly, reciprocity and social bonding are crucial for effective co-operative relationships.[31] This need appears to set practical limits to the potential size of any network, and may limit its effectiveness, if it is unable to span the full range of functionality to produce a product or service. This suggests a need for new thinking on the division of labour.

## Global exchange and networks

As a concept, exchange extends beyond the enterprise or even the enterprises sharing it as social capital in a network.[32] Best-practice economics and law usually treat exchange as involving the transfer of a consideration, generally money, to someone else in return for a product or service. The result is seen as producing a rational advantage to both parties.[33] To anthropologists, on the other hand, exchange is important not so much for its direct but for its symbolic function. They see it as creating and sustaining relationships of significance to a particular group of actors or enterprises.[34] In psychological and sociological research, exchange is seen as the joint outcome of a relationship.[35] Although a central definition of exchange is lacking, all this takes for granted that the actors transfer particular mutually understood things to each other. It may be that one of the parties demonstrably accepts the thing proffered as a mark of respect. In this case, what is transferred to the giver at the time of that acceptance is merely the fact of its acceptance. In the mature individualist system, this would be considered corruption. This has value in and of itself in traditional-style emerging markets where such tribute may be the accepted way of getting an export licence or even a licence to operate at all.

Knowledge-based networks raise two important issues that any theory on exchange has to address. First, how exchange in networks differs from exchange in markets. Secondly, the intangible qualities of know-how. Many see the first from a principal–agent perspective, but if the agents are of equal status who is the principal and who the agent? This is analogous to how such matters are dealt with inside the hierarchy of an enterprise. From this perspective, one is into management issues and costs, namely those of monitoring to control shirking within the hierarchy that effectively bounds an enterprise.[36] But how does this operate if the scrutiny function crosses enterprise, cultural and national borders? Each member of such a network ostensibly exchanges only goods and services with the others. But for the network to work there must also be an exchange of effective and valuable insights into each other's areas of core competence; this, however, occurs without any apparent mechanism to protect propriety in the know-how involved. There are therefore significant differences between the assumptions implicit in the analysis of atomistic commodity markets, and those implicit in the analysis of a network where the exchange has social as well as individual economic interest as its root.[37] The collective actions of the actors in such a network are inevitably linked by social bonds which affect the process of exchange itself, as well as its outcomes.[38]

We have already raised the issues of identity, communication and measurement costs[39] as clear features in such exchange. These factors are an even more significant potential cost in networks of the type we are now discussing – i.e. ones where the key products used and exchanged are undoubtedly knowledge. From a transaction cost perspective, this implies market failure. By such reasoning all required functionality should be carried out within a hierarchy[40] – i.e. a single enterprise. Clearly such an enterprise's resource management strategy would be to maximize the returns from the knowledge embedded within its processes, and to minimize its costs by leading, motivating, directing and organizing its staff in appropriate ways. If we are to make any sense of the existence of networks we have to explain why they are a better alternative to such hierarchies. The answer seems to be that the superglobal connectivity that is available, especially for knowledge as a product or service, makes networks practicable at exceedingly low cost. This enables management to have a very sharp focus on core competence so as to drive quality up and cost down. The enterprises in the network do trade goods and services with each other for money, but this is not a 'market' as commonly understood. Often network members only sell to each other, so there is no true competition in their transactions. The system is merely one for distributing what is perceived as an appropriate share of the joint value created. Some members of the network may deliberately have multiple sources of supply so as to keep each of their suppliers alert to the fact that there are always alternatives. There is generic competitive pressure, but only from other networks in the market for the final product existing in the global economy. Unlike traditional transactors, a network of enterprises is a virtual entity. It operates beyond the boundaries of geo-political or national social entities. Such truly global enterprises operate beyond existing states and are therefore politically or socially embedded in the traditional sense only to the extent they have a constructed dynamic identity.

We would hypothesize that global networks will have the following four characteristics:

(1) They involve significant knowledge exchange to ensure that value is driven as high as possible in the network as a whole.
(2) They involve relationships in a global setting whereby each node/enterprise in the network is well embedded in a distinct state and possibly culture. The psychic distance that has then to be overcome is dwarfed in its impact on value by the value brought to it from the robustness in the face of change brought about by diversity.
(3) They have to work to maintain a mutuality of commitment. Non-economic considerations – social, psychological and cultural – are fundamental to their cohesion. They are effective only if they provide

a pay-off to all stakeholders superior to that achievable by any other routes.

(4) To be viable and sustainable they need to be (learning) organizations continuously adapting to new circumstances to sustain their collective commitment to the values and propriety of each stakeholder.

## Property rights and knowledge

In Chapter 3 we explored the significance of propriety, that we posit is vital. It is perhaps the most vital issue for the viability of networks as the basis of the emergent global business system. There are two fundamental differences between the purely competitive nature of markets and the co-operative nature of networks. The first difference is that we need to understand the nature of the propriety that can be exercised if value is generated communally: how should the returns from it be distributed? The second difference is that to construct a co-operative network one needs a collective process to generate and sustain the values and institutions it requires.[41]

On the first, it is clear that exchange cannot be made effective without property rights. In the absence of a legal entity or even an enterprise to own them, the question arises as to who is the owner of these rights, if the collectivity creates them but has itself no existence in law? This is clearly a fundamental point and a fundamental problem. This is especially true in the knowledge age where knowledge is the principal fount from which enterprise draws the power needed to add value and remain viable. It is also important: it may be in an actor's interests to go outside the bounds of behaviour that the other actors consider just, but if such boundaries have not been defined then the morality or even the sense of any sanction protecting propriety is questionable.[42]

The second issue has always been fundamental in social anthropology[43] and in political science.[44] Exchange is a process where there is an inevitable divergence between incentives and interests. This is fundamental to any co-operative enterprise, from marriage upwards. The new and explicit role we feel has now to be given to knowledge, which as an intangible resource adds interesting complexity to our thinking. Knowledge is a strategic resource, a core asset, but it can also be a product or a service and so the subject of exchange. In Chapter 10 we dealt with the problem of exchanging knowledge as a resource, especially the tacit knowledge that comes with 'knowing'. One crucial new point in this chapter is that the value of knowledge is contextually, or situationally, specific to a particular organization or group of transactors.[45]

From this observation we can perhaps begin to get some inkling of why property rights issues may not be as large a problem as might at first sight be thought. One cannot steal something designed to fit its precise location like a dam across a river and get utility out of it elsewhere on a wider or narrower river, far less in the middle of a flat arid plane. The enforcement of property rights may not be an issue if the property simply cannot be moved, and arguably much tacit knowledge is precisely of such a type. The key point is that knowledge works only in its proper context. It needs that context to make it knowledge, because knowledge is always knowledge about something: one can be a genius, but one may not know how to repair a car as fast, accurately and effectively as a trained garage mechanic.

Past thinking in sociology and anthropology has looked into the role money plays in helping to determine and create markets, while at the same time it has shown that market-like exchange can take place in its absence.[46] Money provides a useful common measure of value for all tangible assets, goods and services that might be traded through a market. But intangible assets, such as some knowledge, tend to defy any objective attempt at market valuation, because the value of knowledge is specific to the people involved on both sides of any transaction and their situation and context. If I'm standing vacuuming the carpet, the phone rings and I go to answer, I can ask a casual visitor to carry on vacuuming. He could probably do okay. However, if I am in my office and the Head of Department comes in to say it is imperative that I come to an examiners' meeting and I ask the same casual visitor to deliver the lecture I was due to give in ten minutes, he probably could not do it – despite the fact that he is sitting in an office full of the right books on the topic of interest. The knowledge has to be absorbed, allowed time to be taken in, and then given time to mature into coherence. All of this would take a long time. Knowledge is not just knowledge instantly and effortlessly available to any passer-by – many would never be able to access some of it. It has to be systematically accumulated and assessed and understood and retained by a competent mind before it is usable. Who has bought it is therefore as important as who sold it – as both people have added value to the knowledge. Identity, the issue of who, would not be a necessary question for a typical traded commodity. It is here.

Some assets can have symbolic as well as tradeable value[47] in addition to any monetary value. In some societies where money as we know it does exist one can still find different yet parallel 'spheres' of exchange. In one such sphere certain items such as foodstuffs and raw materials are indeed exchanged for money, but other items such as a special cloth may by custom be given only as a gift with no monetary consideration permitted in return.[48]

The differences between such spheres of exchange could be seen as analogous to the difference between market exchange and social exchange where one has to pay one's communal share in a subscription or political exchange in which taxes have to be paid to cover social costs.[49] The spheres of exchange appropriate to trading an intangible like knowledge similarly have to be seen as distinct from those appropriate to many other commodities. Even in highly legalistic societies, such as the US, social punishment or reward can often replace legal contract and economic gain or loss. It must be remembered that property rights become significant only when a market value exists for the assets and this increases beyond some threshold value. However, even this assumes some type of singular and transparent market valuation. Networks need to provide the mechanism for co-ordination and exchange, and to take into account the transfer, capture and protection of property rights in the object of the exchange, knowledge.[50]

Property rights in knowledge are especially complex in the case of tacit knowledge.[51] Because knowing is often specific to a particular actor socially embedded in a specific enterprise[52] it has no direct market value – its value is manifest only in the product or service it ultimately helps produce. However, it shares that with all the other 'knowing' by other individuals who put time into the process. Of course, its loss would have an opportunity cost, that of giving someone else the right contextual experience and training to acquire it. So there is credible commitment of a hostage type built into such a network. I have 'knowing' that I could not have without the network, but the network will not function properly without me, and my 'knowing' is of value only when embedded in the network. This is the kind of situation where without continued co-operation both partres are guaranteed to lose heavily that typified our earlier discussion on hostage giving and taking.

The continual exchange that seems to characterize the success of a global network involves co-operation in knowledge exchange. Without leverage of the kind described this is unlikely to work; but for it to do so an assessment is needed of the contribution to the value ultimately created. The intangibility of the asset calls for measurement so we must have additional measurement costs, and even then the value of the asset, whether it is being transferred, exchanged or protected, may be unknown or imperfectly known to either its current or potential owner.[53]

In exchanging an asset such as knowledge, a transactor has reliable recourse only to those measures of value indicated by the virtual identity of the other actor in the exchange.

## Enforcing property rights

> How agreements are enforced is the single most important determinant of economic performance. (North 1991)

Having mechanisms to enforce property rights in global networks is crucial to their viability. Most work on this seems to assume enforcement is automatic.[54] A presumption of smooth property transfer and the full protection of rights before and after exchange must be suspect when knowledge is the resource. Such exchange might be relatively easy if all network members were from the same social or ethnic grouping, but in the case of global networks this is deliberately not the case. A common ethnic background can play a crucial role in the formation of successful networks.[55] Even scattered across countries and cultural milieus the Diaspora of an ethnic group can rely on its informal social codes of morality to form a bridge between the cultures in which the individual members of the network are politically and socially embedded. It is relatively easy for Jewish, Quaker, Chinese or Lebanese merchants to achieve co-operative trust-based relationships with their own peers, even those situated in diverse cultures.

The problem in today's global networks, especially in the knowledge industries, is the sheer diversity of the transactors in culture, location, legal obligations, etc. Global competition has created a need for networks to have 'wormholes' to facilitate cross-cultural entry to ease market access and put in place globally acceptable operating procedures. Such diversity complicates co-operative decision-making.[56] The continuing change and uncertainty inevitable in any emerging business environment intensifies this diversity. All this suggests that protecting property rights in intangible assets in global networks may not be easy.

Global networks pose a complex property right problem. There is great difficulty in translating or interpreting law across international boundaries, even prior to considering any enforcement problems.[57] Language is deeply rooted in culture, and if cultures are diverse then languages may be, too. The greater the psychic distance between the nations involved, the greater will be the difficulties in translating from one language to the other. A certain institution may exist in the US, but not in Italy.

References, or, more subtly, allusions to such an institution, may be very difficult to handle in translation. The knowledge of at least some Italians is precisely that of people in the US but there certain institutions exist that are not found in Italy, and vice versa. Knowledge in a culture is not just knowledge about that culture, but also about others. The development, transfer and protection of property rights is deeply embedded in large volumes of practical local cultural knowledge. This makes legalistic contractual-style exchange difficult, and socio-cultural exchange even more difficult.

Price and quantity are generally treated as the key variables in exchange. In consequence much thought on market exchange and resource allocation does not get connected with the social and cultural values of identifiable transactors.[58] Networks, like markets, allocate resources. Networks rely for their success as much on social relationships as they do on economic self-interest.[59] It is impossible to separate the nature of exchange in a network from the social milieu in which it sits.

Perfect transfer and protection of associated economic property rights[60] assumes underpinning the efficiency of pure market exchange. But much exchange, even in mature economies with strong legal systems, employs elements of 'reciprocal exchange'. This is as a result of uncertainty, of the existence of incomplete and asymmetric knowledge, and in order to create and sustain the social bonding and trust required for the truly effective exchange of such intangibles as knowledge.[61] Enterprises put resources, their own time, ideas, etc. into a communal pool for the benefit of all and are able to take out of the pool, as and when they require it, anything they like.[62] Reciprocal exchange has elements of other systems, and in some cases can resemble the 'gift' exchanges that occur in primitive and pre-modern societies as analysed by anthropologists.[63] However, gift or reciprocal exchange is also seen in modern societies.[64]

Gift, or reciprocal exchange has a number of advantages over anonymous market exchange, even in modern societies. It permits exchanges whose sole purpose is to build mutuality of trust, that is gifts with no directly evident return. Some such gifts would generally be considered corrupt in the individualist system. They can legitimately occur, provided they are publicly modulated – for example, social honours and/or general bonus payments made by an employer to all employees after a successful year. Trust can be vested in enterprises or states, independent of actions by individuals. The operation of trust in relationships depends on both the actors' knowledge and on perceived constraints on the actors' decision making and behaviour.[65]

In the case of knowledge-based assets within global networks it is hard to see how, in the absence of trust, the members of such a network can be assured of fair treatment in the transfer and protection of their economic property rights.[66] Taking a more social and institutional view of exchange, one can show that the exchange process has value in itself, independently of the intrinsic value of what is exchanged.[67] Thus, the nature of exchange and economic property rights has to be examined carefully, in order to find the most effective ways of exchanging knowledge within the bounds of a global network.

The issue of identification is complex, but it is crucial in knowledge-based global networks. We must now look at it again in the light of our examination of property rights and the difficulties of enforcing them – difficulties which arise not just because of the intangibility of the asset itself (knowledge), but also because of the diversity of social milieu in which such rights are to be established. In traditional Germanic law and economics, indeed in most of continental Europe's, an actor's economic property rights were linked to the community. Rights in this area were symbolic and an integral part of a wider process which generated closer relationships between individuals, objects, professional associations and communities.[68] In continental European countries operating on a communal principle, such important symbolic relations are often fundamental to understanding how ownership and property rights have been modulated in the past.[69] They are less important in the US and the UK (except as observed by gangsters, as illustrated in a movie like *The Godfather*[70]).

In thinking on management, unlike that in social anthropology or law and economics, the tendency has been to view identities as relatively unimportant outside the ambit of the enterprise. The two contrasting extremes are focused on the usual market place and transactions in socially embedded networks.[71] In most people's thinking there seems to be an implicit assumption that the asset or resource being exchanged is tangible.[72] But because tacit knowledge assets are intangible and more difficult to measure,[73] they require an analysis closer to the traditional German and continental European approaches to law and economics. There, there are close communal relationships between the transactors and the objects they exchange.[74]

Knowledge is by definition difficult to separate from the processes of community, not only because it is often contextual, but also because it is embedded virtually in relationships rather than concretely in individuals. In this it is similar to the concept of an 'inalienable gift'.[75] It should be clear from these arguments that some knowledge assets cannot be clearly defined, and therefore they cannot be freely exchanged and thus valued according to market criteria. The sorority approach to investment in social capital from which all in the network can freely draw is nearer to the reality of the manner in which the emergent global business system seems to be evolving.

# 12
# Cohesion versus Integrity in Global Knowledge-Creating Value Networks

## Introduction

At this stage we would like to distinguish between two major types of exchange that we find in knowledge-creating networks:

(1) Internal trade based on formal exchange for a monetary consideration
(2) Reciprocal exchange based on informality and mutual trust.

These echo the two business systems identified in earlier chapters, the individualist and the communal. It is unsurprising that in an evolutionary context elements of both carry over into the fabric of our thinking about knowledge-based networks. The emergent global business system is evolving from a context in which both the existing mature business systems are in vigorous commercial intercourse. In a very real sense one could view the emergent global business system as their offspring. The emergence we are now observing could be seen as the birth of a global system that Rugman[1] rightly observed was yet to be. As we saw in Chapter 11, elements of the two existing mature systems are embedded in what is now emerging. It is therefore not surprising that the nature of exchange as observed in this context exhibits a balance of the attributes of each of its parents.

A network with a relatively strong, explicit structure based on formal rules will have greatest transparency from the viewpoint of actors outside the network; such transparency will reveal the integrity of the network to outsiders. If this transparency is strong it will contribute to the trust partners in exchange can place in the services an enterprise renders. However, such strong emphasis on formal, explicit globally visible rules and laws creates dissonance within the network. The more comprehensive such rules are the less likely they are to be applicable to the specific circumstances of a single member or any small cohesive subset of members. Such subsets then have an incentive to develop their own local rules for their sub-network. These rules are likely to be more meaningful to them and liable to be more useful in support of their particular sub-set of functions.

The larger a network becomes, the greater the need for it to evolve a set of protocols and agreed standard operating procedures. Such legalism will tend to be rejected locally, as suggested above. There will always be tension between the need for global cohesion at the big network level and for integrity in the dealings required between closely interacting individuals locally. Such actors may discover through their interactivity that they can operate more effectively by becoming autonomous from some, if not all, of the larger network's rules. Such sub-networks will then spin off from the larger one, inevitably taking with them some of the collectivity's knowledge base. This creates a situation similar to the free-rider problem dealt with in economics.

The sub-network has used the vehicle of the larger network to develop a knowledge base that may be vital to the cohesion of the whole. It will take its sustenance with it and take the knowledge it has developed to date within the larger network. In a sense its departure has led to the collectivity losing an option in future intellectual property and having to accept a sharing of that already existing. It is not then clear who, if anyone, can properly claim to have propriety over the knowledge generated within the bounds of the now partially deconstructed collectivity or even the future knowledge within which it will become embedded. To decide about this there would have to be reference to the terms and conditions on which the network was founded. Even if this took the form of a formal legal agreement there would still be dispute. For example, witness the need for the American Civil War to occur to clarify the rules set up under the American Republic's Constitution to respect the rights of individuals and its constituent states at the time they broke with the British Empire.

A larger network clearly has some claim to a share in what has been, at the very least, collectively facilitated[2] when a sub-network becomes detached from its parent. This may or may not be a bad thing. Whether it is or not depends on how it is handled. If the spin-off group remains a sub-network attached to its parent in some manner then the previous reciprocity and mutuality of benefits need not be lost at all. After the Revolutionary War the US and Britain became even stronger trading partners in the short term and have had a mutually supportive symbiotic relationship ever since.

If a network is socially and informally policed, a result similar to the above may occur. It will do so for different reason. Socially and informally policed networks are likely to have strong collective ideologies and cultures. They will tend therefore to place greater emphasis on informal rules and norms than on formal or explicit rules.[3] Here, reciprocity is very important. However the more parties there are to the reciprocity the more difficult it is to sustain. The number of people with whom one can sustain productive propriety reinforcing reciprocity is quite small. Thus some actors in a large network may find themselves having more and more contact with a like-minded sub-group. As their interactivity with this group increases their joint productivity may increase to the point that they become more and more detached from the parent network. Thinking on collective ownership and interests confirms this. For these reasons, groups or communities driven by social bonds and reciprocity in exchange tend to have an upper limit to their feasible size.[4]

We therefore find that under both systems of governance there is an upper limit to network size. As output grows and production rates increase, sub-networks will inevitably spin off.[5] In such circumstances the larger network needs to find a manner of operating which combines formal and informal rules. These perhaps need to regulate only the interface between sub-network members and their modes of communication. This allows smaller more integrated groups within the larger network to have their own sub-network, which will be limited to a size able to sustain the level of reciprocity necessary to maintain the social bonds required for a well-integrated approach. Generally speaking, actors in such strategically focused networks can stay linked, provided they follow a common set of protocols and have a collective value system generating sufficient mutual benefit to sustain the cohesion of the larger entity defined by a boundary effectively excluding others.[6] The added value across the network can then be contained within its bounds, and the individual propriety of its members recognized for the collective good they help generate.

## Communitarian collective ownership and strategic networks

If it is to remain successful over time, any strategic network has to decide how to establish and enforce the propriety associated with the cohesive community it sustains by creating trusted useable valuable knowledge. The traditional view is that as individuals each pursue their own interests an 'invisible hand' helps the pursuit of the collective interest. The law gainsays this. Social anthropologists and political scientists are clear that such benign collective outcomes are by no means assured. This is especially so when the size of any group, network or community is large.[7] In such a case it has traditionally been possible to create a geographically defined entity, the nation state, to define, decide and enforce the collective interest. Collective ownership in the network requires co-operation between actors in either formal or informal settings, where the actions of the actors are interdependent.[8] The traditional answer to this has been to create a polity with the *force majeure* required to enforce the recognition of the existence of individual legal entities and to regulate and control their activity, especially in exchanges with others.

However the network collectivities common in the emergent global business system inter-penetrate the boundaries of existing nation states. The power of any individual state is then of little use in providing a framework for political embeddedness (a judicial system, commercial law, company registration, etc.), unless the state enters its own collective agreement with other states to respect each other's institutions, as, for instance, the EU. However such agreements are problematic where the states are of the kind existing in emerging markets. And enterprises connected together by the now extended global infrastructure have means of connectivity that are invisible to the states in which each of their members is already embedded. These connections across the internet, telephone or finance networks continuously inter-penetrate the legal and socio-political boundaries that have been drawn up by agreement between traditional nation states.

At the enterprise level new global collectivities need to rely on social identity, based on some cross-national characteristic: the overseas Chinese community, for example; or *in extremis* the compulsive identity created by hostaging.[9] However, the larger the network, the more difficult it is to sustain social bonding through reciprocity, augmented further when there are significant psychic distances between the members of the network. In today's global business environment successful strategic networking is often achieved by deliberately seeking out members from different countries, regions and professional backgrounds, to ensure a robust structure with the maximum potential to generate new ideas and adaptive solutions to existing ones. To incorporate the value such diversity brings is a key objective of the virtual entity such a network represents.

In such circumstances, the network as a virtual entity has some expectation of the loyalty of its members despite the heterogeneity described and the inability of the network to enforce by law its interests over those members. The cohesion of the system comes from the co-operative game it is possible to play in an expanding market. This provides huge pay-offs to those sustaining the integrity of any neighbourhood within its ambit. In other circumstances, things can become more problematic.

In this case, the only remaining alternative is hostaging, the tool of the emerging market business system. In the absence of a geographical boundary in which collective authority can be homogeneously maintained, a successful network may have to accept that it can be only a holding enterprise for the hostages to fortune made available to it by each of its supporting family of sub-networks. Each of these sub-networks can then be made as small as necessary to support the integrity required to sustain the high levels of reciprocity needed to support the social bonding and trust required in knowledge-based industries.

So far, we have developed a typology for exchange relationships. First, the traditional market exchange as followed in atomistic competition. Secondly, the social network of exchange covered by the non-economic social science literature. We have suggested that no matter which of these prevails there exists a critical size beyond which the network will not be sustainable. Notwithstanding this, there is a strong potential for most networks to break up into sub-networks.[10] We have provided a framework which accepts that social bonding and trust-based exchange can be truly effective only on a small scale.[11] This all suggests that one has to embrace the inevitable and assist sub-networks to flourish and not try to contain or constrain them. To do so is to limit their creativity, and the value that can be released by the knowledge they liberate. One needs to sustain diversity by allowing them to follow their own norms and social bonds but to do so within a very general framework that sees value as created by the cohesive generation of the social capital that is knowledge.

The incentive of ownership as envisaged in past economic analysis was about effective markets exchanging 'private' rather than public assets or resources. The private resources dealt with could be private precisely because they were tangible and marketable. The resource and product/service which is the focus of interest in the post-modern age is knowledge. This is intangible and so has to be marketed differently. Traditional economics can deal well only with resources which have clearly defined property rights attached to them. For their ideas to work, ownership must be capable of being exclusive to a particular actor and there needs to be competitive rivalry for the equally definable resources used to create the knowledge required to operate.

Some required public resources or assets, such as scientific discoveries, weather forecasts and the position of oil reserves may not be subject so easily to competitive rivalry or to exclusive ownership[12] but their delivery may still be constrainable within the bounds set by a nation state. These goods are therefore capable of being paid for out of general geo-politically raised taxation. The inalienable collective nature of more general knowledge seen as an asset means that it resembles such publicly owned and financed resources or assets – which has the added complexity of being difficult to confine within the geo-political boundaries set by the ambit of a nation state. This leaves its control, financing and exploitation in the hands of those throughout the world who choose to communicate with each other. In such circumstances, they can be encouraged to pursue collective interests only if social reciprocity can be sustained at a reasonable rate. This restricts the sustainable size of any network, and probably the amount of finance it can obtain to develop its knowledge base.

To be successful, such networks require collective interests to be respected and for incentives to exist encouraging sharing among the network's members. To promote themselves they also require mechanisms to exclude outsiders from the benefits the knowledge they generate provides.[13] Knowledge and its creation is embedded in the relationships between those in an effective network, and is inalienable. It can exist only in its special context. One does not need laws or social mores to protect the network's IPR. It is simply impossible to alienate it from those who generated it. The knowledge a network generates can, however, be used to provide value to others indirectly through the products or services in which it can be incorporated. The result alluded to is similar in concept to the 'club goods' considered in law and economics. Members of a strategic knowledge-based network pay an analogue of a club fee for membership and share the inalienable benefits of membership collectively. Non-members cannot free-ride,[14] for even if they can apparently access what the network 'knows' it is meaningless outside its context and useless without the assistance of the network itself. In such circumstances the threat of exclusion from the network is sufficient for policing its collective resource.

This type of knowledge creation and sustenance is similar to the hostaging typically used in emergence. Knowledge creation is assisted by deliberately choosing network members from heterogeneous socio-political backgrounds and value systems.[15] Each gives his or her knowledge to the network and the network operates to integrate it with that of others to generate collective understanding that can be accessed only by those choosing to stay connected to the larger system. To sustain such a system one has to underpin the growth of sub-networks, but to do so within a framework of mutual commitment, hostaging, which makes it worth their while to stay attached to the larger network. This is precisely what franchisers do successfully in the global market place: MacDonald's, Benetton, etc. They sell 'know-how', not products or services.

## Conceptual frameworks of analysis

Here we have re-emphasized and analysed the importance of understanding the nature of the process of exchange. This is necessary if we wish to develop our understanding of how the strategic knowledge-based networks characterising the emergent global business system operate. We wish to see how it deals with its principal intangible asset, knowledge; and how in doing so it can support the propriety of all stakeholders including the virtual one, the collectivity they support. We have made a tentative effort to develop a framework by which to understand the exchange mechanisms that may emerge to deal with that particular intangible and inalienable asset, knowledge, that is so vital to the whole process we are describing in this book.

We have provided alternative perspectives by developing the idea of reciprocity traditional in pre-modern societies.[16] However, these societies have developed exchange mechanisms for differentiating between commodity-type assets, which are exchanged through the market, and tacit, implicit assets such as knowledge, which are exchanged through reciprocal arrangements. We also argued that strategic knowledge networks need to address the problems of collective ownership[17] but within this sphere of ownership one needs to be clear that this will lead to fragmentation and the spinning off of sub-networks integrated by tight social bonds. There is a need to consider what processes need to emerge to maintain the loyalty of sub-networks to the collectivity which spawns them. The answer seems to be by an emergent process of hostaging. We will call it the power of 'contextual knowledge'. This is essence of the emergent global business system which is an amalgam of key elements of our new analytical triad of business systems. As we will argue, an element drawn from each operates to enforce propriety in knowledge at different levels of its emerging institutional context.

The market is used to discipline networks at the highest level. Each larger network has to sustain competitive advantage in the global market place in competition with other such networks. They use multi-purpose money for some exchange and trade between their constituent sub-networks. However inter-network trading is envisaged as being regulated by an informal set of agreed values, and by official and unofficial rules policed by the use of hostages to fortune, given both by the collectivity to the sub-networks and by them to the collectivity. Finally at the lowest level one finds reciprocity and social bonding alone used to regulate behaviour and performance at the level of each sub-network.

# 13
# Socio-Economic Emergence of Man and Society

## Introduction

Only time will tell whether our analysis provides the right means to interpret events in the globalising business environment. But it is clear that dramatic change is already happening in the global networks now made possible by the emergent knowledge industries. New technologies, new industries and new markets will succeed existing ones. They themselves will either thrive or perish in the socio-economic turbulence inevitable with emergence.

This book has revolved around three distinct ways of looking at the socio-economic world. All are helpful in developing perspectives on development:

(1) *Rational economic man*: encourages the shareholder-focused, personal gain-driven, individualist business system view. It seems to promote an inventive, reactive and resilient style of behaviour that can ignite emergence. It does so, however, from a questionable, static basis.
(2) *Social man*: encourages the key stakeholder-focused value, driven by the stabilizing negative feedback typical of a communal business system view. It seems to promote an innovative, responsive and compliant style of behaviour. It does so from a basis firmly rooted in the status quo.
(3) *Evolutionary man*: encourages a thrusting creative enterprise perspective driven by the positive feedback typical of the emergent business system view. It seems to promote a creative, proactive, explosive behaviour that naturally destroys the status quo. In its essence, it is dynamic and revolutionary.

We co-join all three to provide the triangulation necessary to gain a perspective on the kaleidoscope of possibilities evident in real-world business systems and to help us gain some insight into what we have called the emergent global business system.

## Rational man and rationality

Examples of rationally conceived approaches to emergence include the merchant guilds of the Middle Ages and the Technology Foresight Committees in the modern UK. Each of these is an attempt to lessen the uncertainties of emergence. By its nature, emergence is full of contradictions. Without them, the new and radical will not be born nor mature. With them, the chaos of creation arrives, and the unpredictability of adolescence. These can threaten the survival of both old and new. During emergence the failure rates for enterprise can be very high and entirely arbitrary. Some of the new institutions and enterprises that do not survive the initial turbulence to maturity may have better potential than those that do. In emergence success reinforces success, even if sub-optimal. In this, the adequate can be as successful as the good and although the good may drive out the bad there are no guarantees that they drive out the adequate. Humanity's capacity to adapt in response to events holds out some hope that rational collective thought can shift the balance in the direction of the good, but there are no guarantees. Tsarist Russia was succeeded by rationally conceived Stalinist Russia. Some Russian people have recently attempted to thrust American free-market libertarian economics institutions into the simultaneously warm and cold communal soil that is the essence of Russia. This is unlikely to take root, as to the extent anything has rooted so far it has adopted a distinctive Russian flavour: a minute number of Russians becoming exceedingly new-wealthy, and the vast mass of ordinary Russians left serf-like with no option but to accept the unhappy uncertainties that fate and 'they', whoever 'they' may be, hand out to them.

## Social man and sociability

The social analysis of emergence suggests that if repeated transactions occur between actors reputations will emerge that will aid the development of trust between them. Using this trust, they then form into a communal association endowed with appropriate social capital and they can build stability and sustain it to maturity. There are two principal means for this to be achieved, one constructional that we have already examined and one over which little control can be exercised. The first is by deliberate direct inducement, the taking and giving of hostages. Through this, as we have seen, it is possible to make commercial progress even in emergence. The second means is indirect and dreadful for individual humanity. It is the process by which social, ethnic or religious groups are scattered about the globe as 'refugees': the Jewish Diaspora, the overseas Chinese, etc. Such scattered groups are created either by the directed brutality of men or the unyielding arbitrary process of universal evolution. 'Ethnic cleansing' produces an outfall of refugees. In addition, the unbending forces of natural evolution produce similar results through famine, disease, earthquake, etc. Both human action and nature can thus deprive whole communities, in their existing context, of access to subsistence sufficient for survival. In this process dispersion and flight offer the only route to survival. This, too, is evolution.

## Evolutionary man and evolution

The evolutionary view of an emergent context sees in its essence a big role for chance. Small random variations in initial conditions can be magnified by the subsequent explosive growth brought about by self-reinforcing positive feedback. We considered institutions to support change (guilds, trade-fairs, alliances, counter-trade, etc.). These could have been 'selected' randomly and left to be replicated if seen as useful. Emergent institutions are not necessarily the outcome of conscious rational choice.[1] Often institutions that are the outcomes of conscious choice can be locally sub-optimal or even detrimental – for example the Tsar's *pogroms* against the Ukrainian Jews, the Spanish Inquisition or the Nazi concentration camps. While absolutely detrimental locally, globally they are seen as playing a vital evolutionary role. They created the Diaspora that have driven past waves of emergence (e.g. that producing the huge melting-pot of individualist humanity that is the US). Uniquely, the US is populated by the descendants of those who originally fled persecution, poor prospects or natural disaster in their homeland. They therefore put little faith in government and a lot in themselves and in God.

## Discussion: three perspectives using our analytical triad of business systems

However, the adequate always suffices and while the most effective may be replicated at a high rate if its virtues or qualities are noticed, it is as likely that success stays concentrated by low rates of replication. In the absence of anything else the unsuccessful may replicate at a high rate. The random distribution of attributes in the mass that results may generate a few rags-to-riches success stories. In the right context this process reinforces the explosive growth symptomatic of emergence that we have considered as occurring in emergent states, in networked capitalism and in the knowledge industries.

Traditional rational choice provides only a plausible picture of the system in being. It is about maintaining beneficial institutions and enterprises once established in a static non-evolutionary equilibrium. In emergence, such stasis is the enemy of progress. The collective rationality of the old enterprises and institutions treat emergent activity as detrimental to their vested interest in the stable status quo. It was to escape from the tyranny of just such a status quo that the Founding Fathers and their successors over the generations in North America were led to create and sustain the US Constitution. This contains an aversion to government diktat and an unbending faith in the enterprise of the individual to survive if given the right to protect himself and a right of access to his own God and his own devices. It is unrealistic therefore to believe that the system that then evolved among this uniquely diverse body of multiple Diaspora in the fertile anti-social soil of North America can be transplanted back into the places from which previously its creators had been rejected. The history, culture and extended family in other societies that visiting or cultured Americans admire are in reality hugely constraining influences on what it is practical to achieve within them. One can also argue that the set of institutions and the style of individuality in enterprise that has evolved out of the US constitutional context may be uncomfortable in coming to terms with the idea that in the new world wealth is created by the social infrastructural capital of a growing knowledge base. This does not necessarily find fertile soil in which to grow in the libertarian parts of North America.

In order to support new enterprise there is always an increasing need to create new communal institutions with roots in the new rationality. The growth of such a new social matrix is necessary to provide the communal socio-political embeddedness supportive of the new institutions and enterprises of the new emergent age.

We argue that effective collective social action, which is a prerequisite for turning opportunities into self-reinforcing institutional change, can evolve out of turbulence. But when it does there is no guarantee that what emerges will be optimal, only that it is what has evolved. A rational designing collective helping hand may be more helpful than a disparate invisible one but it can as easily tilt the evolutionary game in the wrong as in the right direction. How effective is the US Constitution as an institution for the new age? It was a rational approach to limit the problem of intolerance and oppression that the Founding Fathers and their successors had experienced and wished to protect themselves from. However by almost sanctifying the individual in union with his own version of spirituality at the expense of the wider community and the state, can one expect this soil to produce good results in an age where ownership of the key resource is inevitably communal rather than private?

Logically, communal cultures can absorb pre-existing routes to success more easily. Absorption does not require the massive creativity released when you empower individuals. Their creative success can be socially replicated to the advantage of all by well-directed community action, as has been achieved by the Japanese or Korean communal system of governance. However, there are no guarantees. The Soviet case illustrates a recent failure of a state that was rationally constructed. The Soviet state itself came into being because of Tsarist Russia's failure to emerge, despite strenuous efforts by many of its leaders from Peter the Great onwards. Arguably in the Russian social context the Soviets merely re-evolved the same flawed thinking of the Tsars.

Thus a social values-driven approach to analysis has a tendency to be biased towards the status quo *ex ante*. But on reaching a critical mass of changed approaches to enterprise it can switch to re-enforcing the status quo *ex post*. It then acts to accelerate change, but now on a path that in the end produces decreasing returns to its continuance and so a new status quo. So while it is putting in place new values and new institutions to sustain and stabilize new enterprise it is in effect specifying a desired end state for the consequences of change. It is true that an approach driven by pre-existing social values supports their continued existence and this may induce individual players to forsake some of the opportunities that enterprise might find if left to its own devices. But it is just such social satisfying of the sorority type that is essential to the process by which people establish bonds of trust. This is done by demonstrating a willingness to sacrifice one's own immediate interest for that of the community one is embedded in. Such behaviour is the route to identifying and eventually putting in place new socially useful stabilizing institutions. The stabilizing negative feedback of social constraints that eventually emerges from the process of emergence can sustain similar sets of values and normative pressures in different places, and thus produce similar behaviour by diverse means. The institutions and enterprises that co-evolve to create stability out of the chaos of emergence can be very different indeed. As an analogy – the grass-eaters of Australia, the marsupial kangaroos, have no direct genetic relationship with, and do not at all resemble, the deer and horses that inhabit the African plains; but they do share behaviours adapted to the similarity of their context.[2]

Diversity in social institutions and enterprises is an inevitable consequence of the chance events that initiate evolutionary processes at the local level, and of the high rate of positive self-reinforcing feedback typical of emergence. A very small variance in context can lead to small changes in individual behaviour which through positive feedback result in large-scale transformations. In the process of innovation development is initially chaotic, but then grows very swiftly with one or two ideas dominating and driving out the rest before the process stabilizes.[3]

## An integrative icon

We now wish to bring these thoughts together with those of the earlier chapters to show how the triangulation we have used provides the perspective from which to see a possible way ahead for international, or more correctly in our view, global business. In the adventure of the emerging global economy this is driven by the networked capitalism made possible by the social capital created by the knowledge industries.

Emergence is like an ascending spiral. To understand it, we distinguish three features and posit that an integrated theory of emergence has to be able to model:

(1) An initiating spark which leads to new enterprise and institutional crisis
(2) The explosive positive feedback creating the industrial and social diversity and chaos that is emergence
(3) The evolution of a system of governance producing the stabilizing negative feedback necessarily for socially useful enterprise to accrete out of the chaos as new industries and communities.

The spiral icon fits this well. From one oblique perspective it is an ellipse symbolizing stability. No matter how far you try to move you find yourself constrained back to your point of departure: social man. From another cross-sectional perspective it can be seen as making evident progress, but by moving directly from one extreme of possibility to another: economic man. In another necessarily oblique view it displays a progressive cycle: evolutionary man. So we have order and stability, disorder and growth, and evolution and development encapsulated in one icon.

The natural way to assess the scope of such a model is by looking in more detail at the three approaches outlined. Our task has been to examine how dynamic evolutionary competition leads to co-operative exchange in a dynamic way to produce the highly successful knowledge-driven industries now providing the explosive forces propelling the emergent global socio-economic system forward. By doing this we have presented the beginning of a new view on an emergent social order which will contribute to all of our capacities to consciously assist the evolution of the new global system of communal wellbeing now being born. The general theory of this has to explain the evolution of co-operative institutions beyond the reach of individual states. These will have to have the power, despite initial chaos, to generate the enforceable norms required to provide the stability required for new enterprise to flourish into a maturity that will not include the total suppression of dissident pressure. These new institutions have to have safety valves built into them that allow social pressure sufficient to keep them stable in normal times but release pressure in emergent times. Thus theories of social order typically imply a theory of emergence, often contained in thought experiments about a condition of disorder. Such efforts have been undertaken by many disciplines: economists, economic historians, sociologists, applied mathematicians, political scientists, philosophers and anthropologists have all tried to solve the puzzle. All fail on their own, because by its nature evolution is integrative not reductionist like the 'traditional' academic disciplines that emerged at the beginning of the Newtonian 'Clockwork Universe'.[4] The explanations reductionist thinking brings about can be grouped into the three broad categories, which interestingly do not divide neatly along traditional disciplinary lines. Reality is such that institutional change can only partially be explained by any one of the three perspectives suggested – rational, social and evolutionary. We now review these three perspectives before using the building blocks from earlier chapters to construct the integrative model we present in the final chapter.

## The dynamics of social order: the paradox reviewed

### The maximization of dampened rational personal gain

From this perspective, men are supposed to be rational maximizers of their interests constrained within bounds set by the limited resources available to them from nature, their intellectual capacity to conceive of what can be done and their spirit's willingness to take on the challenges they face. Their preferences are seen to form a rational ordering. People always do what they prefer. People are then seen to adopt the best means to satisfy their aspirations and people's actions reveal their preferences. If you reach for a glass of water and not a piece of bread you are taken to be thirsty. No gap remains between preference and choice. We cannot ask the normative question: why should your preference be satisfied this way in preference to another? A gap between selfish preference and choice may appear only through irrationality – i.e. if no maximizing interpretation can be given to your actions. For example, you may insist that you preferred the bread but nevertheless you chose the water.

To admit such irrationality is to accept the impossibility of giving meaning to man's existence through rationality. However, the stark fact is that to achieve such a rational approach you have to assume away most of the human condition – love, hate, envy, greed, self-sacrifice, etc. Is this not then becoming rather empty? It is precisely these things that lead to the reputation and trust we have described as so essential for the sensible accumulation of knowledge that is the 'knowing' part of social capital. A view on the mores and values that have to go into sustaining and exploiting such social capital is needed, and this requires a judgement of the wider social interest. One can use a rationalist approach to argue for social institutions, and we have used elements of this approach in discussing the costs of transacting and how those costs drive institutional co-evolutionary change.

As we have seen, to understand part of the evolutionary process the cost of transacting provides a very important means for using rational analysis, particularly that providing a rationale for the growth of the non-market socio-economic behaviour that is created within the bounds of the hierarchies that enterprises are.[5] But as we have seen, too, the hierarchy of enterprise may not be as economically efficient as networking. If such is the case, and the modern world suggests it may be, then the costs of transacting – typically, knowledge, contracting, governance and associated communication costs[6] – must be driving us – as we suggest – to a new networked kind of global capitalism.

Hence, we can provide a rational argument for the emergence of new socio-economic forms of enterprise and institutions and we can take rational analysis a stage further by arguing that its use is justifying social reciprocity as a means of exchange.[7] It is then undoubtedly clear from our previous analysis that in a dynamic context one can make an argument for developing oneself as trustworthy:

> The disposition to keep one's agreement, given sufficient security, without appealing directly to utility-maximising considerations, makes one an eligible partner in beneficial co-operation, and so is in itself beneficial. (Gauthier 1986)

Here, one has to take two distinct actions, one to choose to set out to be trustworthy and secondly to use that trust to make a deliberate strategic choice. Unfortunately the first may be rational but the second may not. It may be good to be seen as trustworthy but if one subsequently faces a situation where to be trustworthy will result in damage to oneself, is it still rational to be so? For example, if one has always been willing to help a certain group of people and they you, and you can both be relied on to do so, and then one day 'they' give you a large heavy package that ticks to take on a plane journey to deliver to a friend of theirs, should you do it?[8] The difference between disposing oneself to be trustworthy and actually performing specific acts is thus clear. However, it is important to see that this approach admits of a dynamism and of a process for becoming trustworthy, and not just the existence of trustworthiness as a constraining envelope on a static choice. Understanding of such dynamics has recently been taken a step further in the mathematical modelling of games that has demonstrated that rational co-operation can (*though note*: not 'must') emerge in repeated plays of a game.[9] But in fact this is not a new way of seeing things in rational terms but an example of integrating thought arising out of rational man with that more apposite to evolutionary man.

## Social value-driven dampening feedback

We have suggested above that it is possible to provide a rational argument as to why social norms arise institutionally as rational responses to incentive structures. This integrates the rational approach with the evolutionary one, as we have done in the body of this work. Our second approach in observing things driven by values sees social institutions as autonomous.[10] Early thinkers in this field see social order rooted in a natural tendency to solidarity that arises out of a human need to be concerned for others. This leads men into a natural sense of obligation to each other that is sustained by naturally occurring moral pressure.[11] However, more realistically we could argue that an evolutionary dynamic of the type we have introduced in this work generates a requirement for the stability that a socially structured context for decision making can bring.[12] Within such a framework the cost of transacting can be lowered as one has little choice as to what one is able to do.[13]

From this, one is naturally led to the concept of social and political 'embeddedness', we developed in Chapters 2 and 3, to provide the situational constraints one needs to stabilize explosive emergent growth. We would understand 'embeddedness' as arising out of the stabilizing feedback derived from repeated transactions. This is attractive to our task of reconciling the three perspectives we are developing, by permitting compatibility between two distinct processes essential to the evolutionary models of the development of business systems, namely that of becoming embedded and the process of creating embeddedness.

## Evolution and the self-reinforcing feedback of emergence

This is the ultimate account of the paradox we have to wrestle with, how to reconcile social co-operation with huge change. As we have seen, the specific spark which ignites explosive growth may remain elusive but the process that leads to its initiation is not. It simply happens. The process involves transactors, and groups of transactors, with the same preferences and the same starting point, but with randomly generated differences in their initiating event. History then unfolds and the experiences of that can lead to perceptually very different solutions to the same problem. It is also true that similar outcomes may materialize naturally from very different starting points.

At first sight, this may seem surprising, but if the same problem has to be solved similar outcomes do make sense. Only the players, the processes and the starting context differ: the kangaroo and the deer can both successfully exploit savannah. Political scientist Thomas Schelling's theory of focal points (1960) is the *locus classicus* of iterative processes of social interaction. In the game of life co-ordination can come simply from the players, us, picking out what they might see others doing faced with the situation they face, and so on. Schelling asked a sample of test subjects to name a place in New York City to which they would go in the hope of finding a partner with whom they had lost contact but whom they knew would wish it to be re-established (e.g. a husband who had missed his wife or a planned shopping expedition). More than 50 per cent chose the same place: Grand Central Station. This was in the late 1950s. The result might be different today. What one generation see as a social icon all understand may, or more probably will, change.[14] A repetitive history of experience set off by chance will tend to unfold in a predictable way once socialization of the type discussed above generates the required social and political embeddedness to direct our choices; then co-ordination can turn into convention.[15]

The Santa Fe Institute's work on complexity using advanced mathematical techniques for modelling dynamic feedback phenomena, in both the natural sciences[16] and in economics, has provided a confirmatory perspective on this. As with the co-ordination game of control, economic change may come about when random variations reach a critical level, at which processes become self reinforcing and then display the explosive exponential increasing returns we have come to expect of emergence. This is destabilizing and is in violation of the stasis on which most discipline-based subjects advance their thinking.[17] In emergent contexts, profits rise very steeply and the more the process goes on, the faster the profits rise. Very many very different flowers can then bloom. And they do. The consequence is the diversity of structure and performance we observe rather than the unique best outcome the old thinking brought us to expect.

High-technology markets provide good examples of how network economies can lead to huge and ever-increasing returns – often to a sub-optimal solution. The success of Matsushita's VHS in beating Philips' Video2000 and Sony's Betamax to become the video standard in the early 1980s, or Microsoft's current dominance of the software market, despite its operating system being initially adjudged as technologically inferior to that of its competitors, are examples. Success breeds success, even if it is the success of the lesser kind.

Two main reasons exist for the occurrence of increasing returns available to emergent knowledge industries:

(1) *High up-front costs*: 'The first disk of Windows to go out the door cost Microsoft $50 million; the second and subsequent disks cost $3. Units costs fall as sales increase.' (Arthur 1996, p. 103)
(2) *Customer groove-in*: 'The costs of buying into a new product include the costs of learning how to use it and own it, and these can be considerable for the high-tech products of the knowledge industry age we are now in.' (Arthur 1996, p. 103)

Feedback-driven accounts differ from rationality or value-driven views of decisions in their insistence on a multiplicity of possible results, all totally consistent with viability. In this view of the world present order is always a consequence of random historical developments. As in the end this leads to social embeddedness, one could argue that the positive feedback models of evolutionary man can be at ease with the value-based ones of social man. Despite the mathematically trained modellers such as those working at the Santa Fe Institute, we still are congenitally incapable of building models that do other than confirm the intellectual status quo. This, then, is in line with Keynes' observation: social order may be beyond mathematical reach or any formal representation, as it would appear to introduce too many variables.

# 14
# The Paradoxes of Global Emergence

## The challenge

In emergent contexts, opportunity and crisis, co-operation and competition, and order and disorder, are three different perspectives on the same thing. In response to opportunities, enterprises operating in emerging industries or markets quickly abandon the previous institutional legitimacy for any new ones that might support their activities. This throws the old institutions into crisis before any agreement exists on successor institutions. There is then a vacuum. In such conditions, which typify emergence, exchange is parlous. This seems to limit the ability of transactors to co-operate outwith a hierarchically controlled enterprise. Outside such isolated fiefdoms there is no collective framework in which to embed enterprise and mobilise the resources for accruing social capital. Both producing for emerging markets and trading in them is fraught with uncertainty and subject to extortion and to political hostility, all of which would seem to make them less attractive than the safer returns offered by existing systems. Yet both emergence and the associated institutional change comes about in the world in which enterprise is situated. How? The answer appears to be that short-term the vacuum described is bridged. This is done by any practicable scaffolding that can be found to support the constructive evolution of future co-ordinating institutions. The value that can be created during emergence is so high that in the short term the pay-offs dwarf the costs and the risks.

## Trust again

To understand emergence one has to understand stage (1), the initial spark, then stage (2), the process of reinforcing positive feedback, and finally (3) how stabilizing dampening institutional factors emerge from the chaos of stages (1) and (2) (see Chapter 13). Consider an analysis put forward by the philosopher David Lewis (1969) to explain how institutions or conventions can become established. Lewis reports that in some areas of America in the 1950s (including Oberlin, Ohio) the telephone company decided to control capacity by arbitrarily cutting off without warning after 3 minutes all local phone calls. Soon after this practice had begun, a convention established itself that when a call was cut off the original caller would call back while the called party waited.

The introduction of the obligatory cut-off was like an igniting spark that triggered an institutional crisis. There was then a second phase in the evolution of this context, in which caller and called party tried to work out how to match their expectations of each other. Once they encountered success with the call-back process, which might take several attempts and a little time, the call-back convention spread rapidly. This is a phase of rising social capital. In a third phase, patience after being called and cut off would become a way of life in Oberlin, Ohio. People would trust the other party to call-back. People moving into the area would be initiated into, and adopt, this convention. This behaviour, trust in the call-back, has then become an institution.

Hence, after the initial shock, this whole process is driven by nothing but expectations feeding back on themselves: I do what I expect you to expect me to do.[1] Even the sudden institutional breakdown of phase (1) can be incorporated into this model. If the seeds of disruption were planted – e.g. if a called party persisted in calling back – Oberlin's conventions of calling would quickly falter.

Such institutions are of course pervasive in socio-economic life. Following this analysis they can be understood as evolved solution to a co-ordination problem. All parties to the acceptance of an institution have preferences they can satisfy only by working together. This is evolution seen as a co-operative, not competitive game. In emergence, industries and economies follow this pattern exactly. They overcome the difficulties they face because as they operate within a short-term virtuous cycle of positive feedback all can win, as competition for living space for each enterprise does not exist. Opportunities abound in truly emergent environments. By their very nature they constitute an interconnected set of bull markets. In such a context win–win, or co-operative, games are easy to set up and to find. I sell you something, someone else will buy it from you. If it does not quite fit their need they will easily sell it on at a profit. At the time it seems this process of value adding 'pass the parcel' can go on indefinitely. If one sees knowledge as the currency of this process rather than money the same idea follows through. If I give you my latest idea for free you may use it to compete with me. First, this does not really matter to me, since it was my idea in the first place, and being inalienable my version of the idea will always be different from that you feel you have acquired; and furthermore there is enough business for everyone. Second, to make that knowledge useful requires knowing how, and by the time you have developed that to absorb what I have passed on, I will be working with an entirely new idea based on the 'knowing' I already had, and which I have now transformed anyway. I gain in every way from helping you. I win your goodwill and trust while diverting you from developing new things for yourself which might threaten my position.

So you switch to absorbing my old idea and I create a new one. This idea will outcompete the ersatz version of the old which you are then putting on the market. But you can still gain. You had lower development costs than I had on my old idea. You can therefore sell it at such a large discount in comparison to my new version that it may be attractive enough to create a previously unexploitable market segment. For example, in the history of computing we moved from a tiny number of very large inefficient machines affordable only to the state, to large mainframe machines used by big businesses only, to PCs, manufactured from chips invented for the large business machines, used in business generally. Thereafter came PCs sold in huge numbers to individuals who are now massively increasing the connectivity of the planet by communicating with each other using broader and broader band widths. Where will this end? All the feedback in this system is positive.

The above story describes precisely the corporate strategy of INTEL over the years since 1985 in the very narrow market for microprocessors. They continually innovate their chips, so that by the time their competitors are in a position to enter the market with a replication of the capability of the last INTEL chip INTEL themselves are already selling the next generation. They make sufficient return out of this process to pay for their sunk development costs and keep ahead of the competition. Those who replicate them make a handsome profit by selling the previous generation of capability very cheaply into previously unexploitable markets simply because they have minimal development costs. This is a win–win situation yet again. It has all the classic characteristics of positive feedback of the type characterizing emergence. It runs counter to the intuition of those brought up in the mean intellectual environment created by social and economic stasis. This is regulated by constraining negative feedback to such an extent that all situations are win–lose and so inevitably aggressively competitive.

Thus positive feedback is available even in highly competitive markets, as long as we do not see markets in static terms. In the example just given, the very long run – i.e. the period over which technology changes – is much shorter than the long run in which the balance of all input resources can be changed. INTEL may not necessarily have written off their production plant before they have replaced what it produced with new technology.

How does this work in the case of trust? As we have seen, trust is essential to the achievement of social order.[2] As a late medieval merchant venturing beyond the legitimacy of feudal borders, how am I to mediate the hazards of my opportunism? Often I can't check the identity of a transaction partner reliably, or only at excessive cost. Rationally it might seem I am compelled to take and be taken advantage of, appearing trustworthy but never trusting. But such behaviour is likely to lead to permanent institutional crisis, as implied in Plato's recommendation never to trust a seafaring trader, because he might not come back (Plato, *Laws* 4).

One response is to deny or ignore the futility of increasing one's vulnerability:

> since the output and objective of collective action are a public good available to all, the only way an individual can raise the benefit accruing to him from the collective action is by stepping up his own input, his effort on the behalf of the public policy he espouses. (Hirschman 1982)

But this is a reasonable option only if I can expect those efforts to influence the expectations of others.[3] If this can be brought about, one can model trust as a convention. If two (slightly) trusting and trustworthy individuals are paired by chance, mutual expectations will rise. Personal trust can thus spread to institutional trust, at least in a confined context.[4] This will start a further positive feedback loop. Trust seen as a resource can generate value from the process of transacting it enables. It is a very special resource indeed. It is has the rare value that it is one of those rare resources, 'whose supply may well increase rather than decrease through use' (Hirschman 1984; p. 93). It is infectious, for if trust can be seen as a strategy that generates wealth it is likely to be replicated as a strategy by others. This is extremely likely to be the general case in a bull market where virtually all transactions are win–win and in their essence co-operative not competitive.

An integrative theory of emergence thus has to deal not just with positive feedback derived from the economic and technological improvements normally characterizing development, but also with the processes generating trust within and between enterprises. These are absolutely necessary for the growth and stability brought about by the co-emergence of the institutions of which that trust aids the evolution. These in the end provide the stable base of operations which will sustain a level of development once achieved. Win–win games and the hostage games discussed earlier generate this prospect. It is part of the self-re-enforcing cycle of development that produces the ever-upward spiral of opportunity that is emergence. It leads to diversity and to the paradox that competition is almost synonomous with co-operation in the complexity that results.

## The knowledge industries and complexity

The cost of transacting makes the monolithic hierarchy of a single enterprise[5] an apparently attractive way of proceeding. The costs of a management hierarchy are substituted for those of transacting. This works well if management is focused, clear, comprehending and accountable. However as we have seen, conglomerate organizations, especially those producing an intangible like knowledge, often find it hard to achieve focus. They are also faced with major measurement and performance evaluation problems that make any system of governance problematic. However, there does exist a third way. This is based on the idea that managerial focus on 'core competence' can achieve excellent results. This can in addition be brought to social account by appeal to indices generated by market-financed institutions which themselves are enterprises in the knowledge industries. Through this focus managers earn a learned capacity to exercise judgement on the effectiveness or not of the processes within an enterprise The transacting that occurs in the market is not that normal to a traditional view of trade. Generally it involves 'lean manufacturing ideas' but more importantly yet another value generating a positive feedback loop, that of mutual self-endorsement of the successful by the successful in the emerging business system we now belong to:[6]

> The pursuit of economic goals is typically accompanied by that of such non-economic ones as sociability, approval, status, and power. (Granovetter and Swedberg 1992, p. 25)

The knowledge industries are thus the powerhouse of the emergent global system and are themselves emergent towards higher and higher levels of capability that are connecting up the globe.[7] In the process, they are destroying the relevance of old-style enterprise as well as industrial and national boundaries. The ever-accelerating pace of creativity, innovation and wider resource exploitation this is enabling is phenomenally increasing the competitive forces which drive the further invention that produces the positive feedback of increasing returns observed in the INTEL case.[8]

This new market environment is not one of impersonal commodity trade between anonymous parties, but is a series of interconnected networks of agents. Each is made up of all stakeholders and the knowledge and resources over which they have propriety.[9] These networks become ever-more complex. Successful enterprises in network terms will be given a disproportionate advantage and will be continually forging or re-forging more and more links in and to them. The volume of communication that goes on in any of these links determines the volume of resources each node connected to it will receive as its share of the value the system is creating. The pattern of such links defines the collective knowledge of the global network.

Through the self-reinforcement processes that produce dynamic virtual identity highly interconnected groups can be seen as distinct objects within the global network and will as a result of the processes described have a distinct value to it. Too many connections for any such entity entail an unsustainable communication overload. As we saw in Chapter 9, the tendency will be to constrain local network size to that able to sustain reciprocity. To contain the number of connections a node is able to manage, the system will create cross-connected hierarchies. The degree of connectivity at each enterprise node will roughly determine the resources the system will automatically allocate to it. The ties between nodes on the network can be based on the exchange of resources, of knowledge, of authority, of kinship, or of anything that can be regarded as advancing relationships.[10] Networks are thus not strictly hierarchies, nor are they markets. They are a new species of emergent organization serving the evolving socio-economic needs of a new global system of being.

In adopting the network conceptualization of economic activity, it is important to focus on the connections between the networks' constituents rather than on the constituents themselves. It is in the connections between seemingly disparate parts of the global network that one will find the power engine driving dynamic positive feedback loops. The explosive growth that results and the complexity of the interconnectivity self-organization brings is so blurring the observable relationships between cause and effect that reductionist analysis of such networks becomes virtually impossible.[11] The explosively growing connectivity of the individual people and enterprises on the planet that is now emerging is impressive. It creates a communal pooling of knowledge, information and know-how that is so massively transforming that it is difficult to see where it will end.

Hence, one can talk only of a multiplicity of causes and co-evolving outcomes.[12] Attention must be shifted to understanding the co-evolutionary process of the search for a fit between enterprises and their institutional environment, and vice versa. As we saw in Chapters 2 and 3, enterprises cannot separate themselves from their institutional environment, because that environment and the reality of the enterprise are participating in the co-evolution of each other.[13] They are realized to generate or sustain the potential that comes from their interconnectedness.[14]

Enterprises and individuals develop mental models of the identities of those with whom they would like to exchange. These mental models determine their ability to transform knowledge into understanding capable of resolving any uncertainty they feel about an exchange that may lead to an improvement in their capacity for creating and then sharing knowledge, and for articulating its significance for the enterprise's actions, including those of further discovery.[15] It can be argued that the knowledge so generated is knowledge about the structure and the patterns of interaction in the network. These interactions reveal sufficient about the interrelationships within and between enterprises to enable them to co-ordinate all their value adding activities with each other.[16] Such knowledge is held in the 'knowing' of the enterprise's individual stakeholders[17] and exists often as a

> set of heuristics used by the stakeholders to solve the problems they face in co-ordinating their activities and when the right levels of trust develop and those working together understand the outcomes of each others heuristics a collective competence in knowing emerges that economises on further cognitive effort. (Orbell and Dawes 1991)

This arises out of the evolving iterations of experience that lead to the enterprise's history and allow one to link the present to the past in a way suggestive of what the future might bring.[18]

An enterprise which keeps itself open to external contact, and which constantly fosters external relationships then arrived at receives a continuous stream of knowledge from them that during emergence drives the whole system forward to a different state of being. The positive feedback that results leads on to the emergence of a newly configured enterprise. This is the process currently driving the creation of the emergent global business system, which as a form is neither a market nor a hierarchy. It seems to defy classification and seems designed to avoid embeddedness in existing social systems of value or political control.

Transactors formulate their behaviour according to their cognition. This is formed in conjunction with their network of acquaintances and according to some developing collective purpose.[19] From such an evolutionary perspective people develop mental models of the world,[20] basing them on their own pattern of experience. This history creates very different expectations for each individual[21] because even if two or more individuals start from the same place, or are situated in the same containing context, their experiences, and therefore their perceptions, can be very different indeed. The same knowledge can then be interpreted very differently but for tight-knit groups in the network a new overarching order can emerge in which the individuals become embedded.[22] The organic process that is then set up of dynamically building and re-routing interconnections is a very powerful one for creating thinking at a global level. This process also propagates redundancy when apparently irrelevant contact is made.[23] As we have already seen the latter brings together agents with diverse cultures, attitudes, ideas, expectations and behaviours. This may create the spark for further new relationships and responses to emerge spontaneously.

Complexity puts emphasis on the process, as controlling the development of cognition and providing a dynamic identity for the knowledge bearer. In the same vein, we have developed a means for constructing the essence of a business system by defining its containing institutions for enterprise.

Identities are an essential part of the process described – nowhere more so than in the emergence of the knowledge-based industries. Dynamic identity is a key to this process. It provides the means by which positive explosive feedback can be set up in the industry. This drives not only the emergence of the industry but also that of the business system of which it forms a leading sector, global networked capitalism and, through it, the emergent business system.

## Dynamic identity and disproportionate competition

Our next subject is the four truthful signals of dynamic identity introduced in Chapter 4. These show how enterprises can be ranked, by themselves and by others, in terms of their utility as potential partners in exchange. Enterprises which are ranked high on all the dimensions of a dynamic virtual identity become embedded in a dense network of inter-firm relationships which serve 'an important function in the development of social constraint directing knowledge flows in the building and maintaining of social capital' (Walker, Kogut and Shaw 1996).

Moreover, they have the incentive to support other ranked enterprises in the market, because a ranked enterprise's success benefits all other ranked enterprises associated with it in the network. This is reflected by the 'truthful' signals they each send out to their associates. This broadens the bandwidth over which any signals can be received, creates redundancy in transmissions and thereby increases the probability of any particular party receiving it. This is clearly a very powerful positive feedback loop. When it gets into top gear enterprises move together in an upward exponential spiral of success. This is not enjoyed by enterprises which fail to get so ranked. Thus ranked enterprises appropriate the social capital associated with the network of stakeholder alliances, within which they have become embedded.[24] By this process of indirect co-operation the mutually certified goods achieve disproportionate competitive advantage. Unranked enterprises find it more and more difficult to establish networked relationships of their own, and lag further and further behind in the world defined by the mental images of potential transactors. Success breeds success in the knowledge industry's game and perhaps more so than would be the case elsewhere.

Unranked firms in knowledge-based industries face two important challenges. First, they have to compete with ranked firms in head-to-head market competition in the conventional sense. Second, to succeed they need to develop relationships with these very competitors, in order to achieve some kind of virtual identity to aid them in getting business. Through the indices of dynamic identity, the ranked firms are then definers and measurers of success. They thus assume powerful positions in their market. They can exercise control over the process of constructing and communicating dynamic identity and as this creates a virtual landscape in the mind of potential transactors they effectively orchestrate the whole sub-network within which they operate.[25]

So some enterprises succeed disproportionately, to the detriment of others. However as the indices system used is dynamic and not static it is not an exclusive one. The ranking mechanism does not lead to permanent exclusion, as does identity in terms of ethnic background or height. This is a principal advantage of hostaging over Diaspora in support of business and trade. Even if you have a means to use a Diaspora to spread connectivity it cannot be expanded beyond its distribution and size. But dynamic identity, by definition, acquires meaning within the context of an enterprise's network of interconnections with its stakeholders: customers, clients, partners, competitors, banks, shareholders, the state and external intermediaries. If one is determined enough, it is nearly always possible to become a member of an exclusive club by mutual consent. This is why dynamic identification needs to exist in the emergent global economy.

The market provides a co-evolving institutional environment, and as enterprises fill existing niches in it new niches tend to emerge.[26] This enables the diversity we see as typifying the emerging global system. Therefore, laggards determined to survive can achieve success by filling the gaps in the market. These exist in large numbers at a time of explosive growth and such gaps present immediate opportunities. This in turn creates the potential for further new niches to open up in activity supportive of the new sector. These niches are often the spark that leads to the positive feedback that creates yet an other emergent industrial sector. Dynamic identity tracks this process. New sub-networks with their own mutually reinforcing indexing can start up alongside the existing networks. These new networks can as easily destroy the old ones as be overcome by them. Enterprises can appropriate the benefits of the virtual social embeddedness which a dynamic virtual identity bestows.[27] They can also use the same notion to identify suitable new exchange partners using the 'structural holes' created in their embedding institutional infrastructure.[28] This then provides identification based on new inter-enterprise exchanges operating as gateway events[29] or sparks from which emergent grouping appear: 'small changes escalate into major qualitative changes in outcomes' (Stacey 1995).

Such new enterprises enter into their own upward spiral of success. This generally brings rapid connection with existing self-defining high performers, and a new well-embedded niche emerges.

## Conclusion

We have provided an analysis to assist the understanding of the process of global emergence now going on in the business environment. This process is vital to delivering a modern perspective on trans-national business. There are two levels of emergence, and it is very necessary to understand both. Emergence is occurring in the emerging markets, and the global system is emergent because of the emergent knowledge industries. Knowledge and knowing encapsulate the fundamentals of core competence in all industries. As we posit that all industry is knowledge-based, our conclusions apply to all enterprise.

In Chapter 2 we defined three ways of looking at the business systems in which enterprise is embedded. We deliberately constructed these artefacts to provide the three-dimensionality required for triangulation to understand the dynamics of the new global as opposed to international business system. The result was our new analytical triad of business systems – that of the individual shareholder-focused, the communal key stakeholder-focused and the stakeholder-less emergent models which to only a limited extent can be related to the mature inputs of the Anglo-Saxon, communitarian and familial systems of the descriptively based more traditional triad of business systems.

To make these coherent from an institutional perspective, we had to show how our three business systems affected propriety for their respective principal stakeholders. We then argued that for success to be possible in this an identity for each enterprise was vital. Identity was explicated in Chapter 8. With identity defined, we next dealt with interpersonal and inter-enterprise communication. This is an issue to be managed because in global networks distinct identities within it operate in different business systems with very different cultures, which puts psychic as opposed to geographic distance between them. Communication has to carry across this kind of distance.

The solution emerging in practice is what we have chosen to call the emergent global business system. This emergent form of system transcends any need for traditional political or social embeddedness within the bounds of existing states or social groups. This produces pressure on existing states and enterprises to find new ways of interrelating with each other – for example the EU – but such accretions are as yet regional not global. (One limited exception might just be the old British Commonwealth of Nations.) Such groupings of nations try to assist the legacy systems to stay in touch with the emergent global system and assist it find reliable means first to produce and then sustain stability. However the nature of the emergent global business system is that it is in fact emerging in a manner that suggests that it is blurring the distinction that existed in the past between enterprise and other organizations. A characteristic of this new system seems to be its use of a system of self-reinforcing indices of an enterprise's performance and identity.

Here enterprise seems to be self-organizing its own embeddedness in the absence of an embedding society or polity.

Finally, in this chapter, we have taken these ideas and shown how they can be coalesced into a useful model of the process of business system evolution. Those interested in emergence use the ideas coming out of thought on the nature of complexity. A key feature of evolving as opposed to rationally constructed systems is that they display explosive growth along knife-edged trajectories of experience. This means the end state achieved from a unique initiating spark of change can be a conglomerate of hugely diverse industries, sectors, states and business systems. A large number of possible results is what one must learn to expect from emergence, not a unique optimal solution to the challenges posed. It is not surprising that one does not find sameness across the modern industrial landscape now spanning the globe. The huge variety of shapes and forms of enterprise and business systems is just what our approach to analysis would lead us to expect. This is of the essence in an evolutionary process. Rain forests are marked by their diversity, not their uniformity. The same is true of enterprises and their containing business systems. We believe that this will remain so despite – or possibly thanks to – globalization.

The categorizing system we have used is a useful analytical tool rather than a description of reality. In the real world, uniqueness is everywhere, but so are useful similarities which can be used to understand and bridge psychic distance. Diversity leads to robustness, sameness to vulnerability from the unforeseen. Uniformity is easy to manage – the complexity of evolution is not. Evolution countenances the sub-optimally adequate or satisficing strategy. This is inevitably less efficient than what is theoretically possible using a rational approach. Emerging markets are of their nature disruptive of any concept of sameness or best; what exists is simply what has survived and this always entails creative diversity. International business systems and their constituent institutions and enterprises seem to span a kaleidoscope of possibilities, and nowhere more so than in the emergent global business system.

Let it be.

# Notes and References

## 1 Introduction

1. Rugman (2002).
2. Beamish and Banks (1987).
3. Haber, North and Weingast (2002).
4. Smith (1776).
5. Marx (1887).
6. Rostow (1991).
7. Olson (1991, 1992).
8. Ohmay (1996).
9. Bobbitt (2002).
10. Dunning (1996); Prahalad and Hamel (1994).
11. Choi (1992, 1994); North (1990).
12. Hofstede (1980).
13. Bobbitt (2002).

## 2 The seeds of business system diversity in knowledge and governance

1. Haber, North and Weingast (2002).
2. Ohmae (1995).
3. Dunning (1996) has suggested that the socio-institutional structure of market capitalism is undergoing extensive change brought about by new approaches to:

   - *Knowledge creation*, or invention
   - *Knowledge mining*, or innovation-led growth
   - *Knowledge 'voiced'* to identify it to enable propriety to be exercised over it
   - *Knowledge communication*, used to increase co-operation and enhance competitiveness.

4. Ohmay (1995): Bobbitt (2002).
5. Bard and Soerquist (2002).
6. Albert (1991); Boddewyn and Brewer (1994); Kogut (1993); Roe (1994, 1997); Toyne (1998).
7. Zubkin and DiMaggio (1990).
8. Boddewyn and Brewer (1994); Hillman and Keim (1995).
9. Boisot and Child (1998); Choi (1994); Choi, Lee and Kim (1999); North (1990); Olson (1991, 1992).
10. Nelson (1992).
11. Brewer (1993); Buckley (1996); Choi (1994); Choi and Lee (1997); Hill (1995); Kogut (1991); Lenway and Murtha (1991); Shan and Hamilton (1991).

12. Boddewyn and Brewer (1994); Dunning (1996).
13. Franks and Mayer (1997); Gerlach and Lincoln (1992); Roe (1994), (1997).
14. Roe (1994), (1997).
15. E.g. Holland, Belgium and Scandinavia, see Albert (1991); Lenway and Murtha (1991); Noorderhaven (1995); Nooteboom (1996); Sorge (1991).
16. Hillman and Keim (1995); Sorge (1991).
17. Albert (1991); Franks and Mayer (1997).
18. Roe (1994, 1997).
19. Zubkin and DiMaggio (1990).
20. North (1990).
21. Albert (1991); Brewer (1992); Roe (1994, 1997); Whitley (1990).
22. Buckley (1990); Choi (1994); Choi, Lee and Kim (1999); Elster (1989); Lecraw (1989); Madhok (1995); Olson (1991, 1992).

## 3 Enterprise and the state: individualist versus communal interest

1. Smith (1776); Porter (1990).
2. Reich (1991).
3. Boddewyn (1998).
4. Dunning (1996).
5. Wade (1985).
6. Hartford (1990).
7. Wade (1996); World Bank (1993).
8. Hannan (1997, p. 198) distinguishes prescriptive and constitutive senses of legitimation: 'An organizational form is legitimated in the *prescriptive* sense when its ostensible purposes, structures, and observable routines conform to a social system's formal rules. A form is legitimated or institutionalized in a constitutive sense when it has the status of a taken-for-granted social fact.' The latter sense is adopted by the new institutionalists (Meyer and Rowan 1977; Meyer and Scott 1983; Zucker 1989). Taken-for-granted social facts are conceptually prior to the prescriptive sense. We are interested precisely in the processes by which social facts take on a prescriptive character.
9. Hannan (1997, p. 198)
10. Hart (1997).
11. Greif (1993); Epstein (1994). Note that these changes did not take place everywhere and at the same time. Foreign trade first took off in the Mediterranean basin and some parts of Germany. After a period of Spanish expansion, the Low Countries and England became the most advanced centres of commerce. Our focus, naturally, is not on the details of economic history but on the institutional features of early trade. Historical details are mainly taken from Berman (1983), Epstein, (1994, 1995), North (1981).
12. Berman (1993, p. 541).
13. Epstein (1994, 1995); Greif (1993); Milgrom and Roberts (1990).
14. Hart (1997).
15. Boddewyn (1998); Choi (1994); Choi, Lee and Kim (1996); Kogut (1993); Yarborough and Yarborough (1992).
16. Boddewyn and Brewer (1994); Hillman and Keim (1995); Kogut (1991).

17. Freeman (1984).
18. Easterbrook (1997) and Roe (1994, 1997) make this point.
19. For example, Roe (1994, 1997).
20. Buckley (1997) shows this.
21. Roe (1994, 1997).
22. Roe (1994, 1997).
23. Roe (1994, 1997).
24. Bard and Soderquist (2002).
25. Carroll (2002); Evan and Freeman (1998); Graves and Waddock (1994); Harrison (1999); Hill and Jones (1992); Jones (1995); This interest includes publications by Sirgy (2002). These all either elaborate different aspects of stakeholder theory or combine it with corporate governance, ethics or agency theory.
26. Gray (1989); Mallott (1990); Polonsky (1995); Post *et al.* (1983); Preston and Sapienza (1990).
27. Cochran and Wood (1984); McGuire, Sundgren and Schneeweis (1988); Spencer and Taylor (1987); Upperle, Carroll and Hatfield (1985).
28. North (1990).
29. Hosmer (1995); Spender (1997).
30. Grant and Spender (1997) provide a comprehensive review of recent developments in knowledge-based industries.
31. Albert (1991); Fruin (1992); Gomes-Casseres (1990); Kogut (1991); Uzzi (1997).

## 4 Institutions, organizations and enterprise: their co-evolution

1. North (1990).
2. Choi (1994); Choi, Lee and Kim (1996); Fruin (1992); Orru, Biggart and Hamilton (1997).
3. North (1990, 1994).
4. Hart (1994). Secondary law is the law that legitimizes sovereignty and its delegation to others of its power to create and modify the primary laws which day-to-day behaviour.
5. Hart (1994).
6. Albert (1991); Choi (1994); Choi, Lee and Kim (1996); This has been raised by authors such as Hill (1995); Kogut (1993).
7. Sachs (1999).
8. Hart (1997).
9. Kogut's (1991) analysis revealed this.
10. Boddewyn (1988); Hillman and Keim (1995); Kogut (1993); Row (1994, 1997).
11. As Roe (1994, 1997) pointed out in his in-depth review of governance systems.
12. Choi (1994); Choi, Lee and Kim (1996); Lenway and Murtha (1991).
13. Easterbrook (1997).
14. Fruin (1992).
15. Fruin (1992).
16. Womack, Jones and Roos (1991).

17. An excellent modern interpretation with extensive data can be found in Foster and Kaplan (2002).
18. Gershenkron (1962).

## 5 Socio-economic emergence and complexity: containment, ignition, explosive release and maturation by restraint

1. Jacobs (1994).
2. Mitchell *et al.* (1998).
3. Chandler (1990).
4. Hart (1994).
5. Hart (1994).
6. Arnott and Stiglitz (1990); Besley (1995).
7. von Hayek (1945).
8. von Hayek (1945).
9. Olson (1991).
10. Prahalad (2002).
11. Bourdieu (1980); Coleman (1987).
12. In the transaction cost economics (TCE) tradition, this is the term used.
13. In the sense of Burt (1992, 1997); Nahapiet and Ghoshal (1998); Walker, Kogut and Shan (1987).
14. Landa's (1981) research on ethnically homogeneous middlemen and Landa and Grofman's (1983) research on networked trading structures in primitive societies proposes TCE models for the second phase of emergence we describe.
15. Exploitation can be formulated in a number of ways (Porter 1990; Saxenian 2002; Pouder and St John 1996).
16. Here, social capital would take on a cognitive function for each networked individual (Albert 1991. Aldrich and Fiol 1994, p. 649; Ellickson 1991; Roe 1994, 1997;) Empirical research substantiates the importance of knowledge infrastructure for processes of innovation (see Van de Ven 1993).
17. Aldrich and Fiol (1994); Hannan (1997); Meyer and Scott (1983); Walker, Kogut and Shan (1996) argue that '[t]he formation of a network is determined by the opposition of two forces. The first is the reproduction of network structure as a general social resource for network members. The second is the alteration of network structure by entrepreneurs for their own benefit'. This can be read as a variation of the paradox of emergence. Population ecologists, again, try to model the two competing forces as functions of 'density': 'According to the theory, increased density initially enhances a population's legitimation, thereby raising its founding rate and lowering its mortality rate. These effects initially induce further growth in density. However, persistent increases in density eventually generate intense competition, which depresses founding rates and elevates mortality rates' (Hannan, 1997, pp. 194–195).
18. Organizational fields have been defined as networks of transactions, knowledge flows and personal linkages, or culturally from normative and cognitive belief systems (DiMaggio and Powell 1983; Meyer and Scott 1983).
19. Stinchcombe (1965).
20. Following DiMaggio and Powell's (1983) seminal article, 'isomorphism' has become the concept of choice, capturing processes of involuntary

homogenization in the face of efforts to change. This has received its fair amount of attention for empirical support (see, for example, Porac, Thomas, and Baden-Fuller 1989).

21. Note that much of this literature starts from a conditional clause ['once a set of enterprise emerges as a field', DiMaggio and Powell 1983, p. 147] which has received too little scrutiny. Following relentless isomorphic pressures it appears almost miraculous that the sprial of emergence keeps turning – and never more quickly than at the end of the twentieth century.
22. In Abrahamson and Fombrun's (1994) work on macro-cultures, homogenity is seen as a source of social capital; they prefer to use the term 'value-added network ties', facilitating negotiations, increasing trust and generally reducing transaction costs (e.g. 1994, p. 750). At the same time, they hold macro-cultural homogenity responsible for dangerous limits to collective adaptability and 'outdated strategic postures' Abrahamson and Fombrun 1994, p. 728).
23. Works highlighting such differences include Arnott and Stiglitz (1999); Choi (1994); Choi, Lee and Kim (1999); Yarborough and Yarborough (1992).
24. Haber, North and Weingast (2002).
25. Note the same topic in Smith (1776) over 200 years ago in Scotland.
26. See the analysis by North (1990, 1994).
27. Boddewyn and Brewer (1994); Choi (1994); Olson (1991, 1992); Zubkin and DiMaggio (1990).

## 6 Markets, individual interest and social governance

1. The nations one might describe as 'emergent' are most Asian countries apart from the three 'tigers' (Korea, Japan and Taiwan) and two cities (Singapore and Hong Kong), some Eastern European countries (such as Poland, Hungary and the Czech Republic), and some Latin American countries (such as Mexico, Chile and Brazil).
2. Choi, Lee and Kim (1996); Olson (1991, 1992).
3. To do so, we use a modification of work by Hennart (1990), which uses a transaction cost analysis of counter-trade.
4. Hennart (1989, 1990) addressed the importance of unconventional trade practices in today's global business environment. He did so through a detailed analysis of various types of counter-trade, and distinguished two types in particular: barter based on clearing arrangements, and switch trading. The latter is used to avoid money-based exchange. The former includes buybacks, offsets and counter-purchase, which are used to impose reciprocal commitments (Hennart 1990, p. 244). Schelling (1960) articulated the concept of 'reciprocal commitments' as early as 1960, and it has been raised again in attempts to understand the raison d'être of counter-trade and other unconventional trade practices (Casson and Chukujama 1998; Choi, Lee and Kim 1996; Choi and Maldoom 1992; Hennart and Anderson 1993; Lecraw 1989; Kogut 1986; Mirus and Yeung 1986; Williamson 1985; Yoffie 1984).
5. Beamish and Banks (1987); Buckley (1990); Madhok (1995); Parkhe (1991); Ring and Van de Ven (1992, 1994), among others, have emphasized the role of trust and other relational attributes in international business.
6. Fruin (1992); Gerlach and Lincoln (1992).

7. This has been called 'alliance capitalism' (Dunning 1996).
8. Williamson (1996).
9. By elaborating on Hennart's (1989) transaction cost rationale for counter-trade.
10. This idea is from Schelling's (1960) framework for negotiations under uncertainty which is applicable to the international business transactions sought by emerging economies.
11. Williamson (1983) recognized this; he suggested that a study should be made of the feasibility of crafting superior *ex ante* incentive structures.
12. Caves and Marin (1992); Choi (1994); Fletcher (1996); Marin and Schnitzer (1995).
13. Williamson (1985).
14. Williamson (1985, 1996) extended the underlying logic of Coase's (1937) seminal work on transaction costs economics, and looked at what observable attributes of transactions make a particular set of institutional and organizational arrangements optimal in one instance but not in others. Williamson's use of transaction cost analysis to operationalize the merits of alternative institutional and organizational arrangements has led to a considerable body of research along these lines.
15. North (1990) has pointed out that transaction costs do not incorporate the costs of enforcement ( Choi 1994; Choi and Maldoom 1992) and measurement (Bazel 1982; Bernstein 1992; Hirsch and Lounsbury 1996).
16. As Bazel (1982) suggests.
17. Schelling (1960).
18. As Bazel (1982) suggests.
19. See Beale and Dougdale (1975); Macaulay (1963); MacNeil (1974).
20. Dore (1983) pointed this out in his analysis of obligated relational contracting in Japan.
21. Williamson (1985); North (1990, 1991); Olson (1992).
22. Choi (1994); Choi, Lee and Kim (1996); Murrell (1982).
23. Hennart (1989, 1990) suggested this.
24. Williamson (1985) stresses this.
25. Williamson (1985, p. 22) defined it this way.
26. Ellickson (1991) showed this.
27. Dunning (1996); Gerlach and Lincoln (1992).
28. Peng and Heath (1996) suggested this.
29. According to Williamson (1994).
30. Olson (1992).
31. Williamson (1983).
32. Olson (1992).
33. Caves and Marin (1992) and Marin and Schnitzer (1995) pointed that out.
34. Fletcher (1996).
35. Hammond (1990).
36. Marin and Schnitzer's (1995) detailed empirical investigation argued that counter-purchase is motivated by hostage-style exchange, rather than by financial or foreign exchange constraints.
37. As presaged by Hennart's (1989, 1990) empirical analysis.
38. Choi (1994); Choi and Maldoom (1992).
39. We argued against the traditional explanation based on foreign exchange shortage, but in line with the empirical work of Caves and Marin (1992) and Marin and Schnitzer (1995).

40. North (1990, 1991).
41. Choi and Lee (1997).
42. Choi (1994); Inkpen and Beamish (1997); Simon (1991).

## 7 Knowledge exchange: the role of identity and trust

1. Recent exceptions to this tendency include Choi and Lee (1996); Oliver (1990); Ring and Van de Ven (1992, 1994); Spender and Grant (1996).
2. Burt's (1992a) pioneering work helped to show this.
3. Burt (1992a); Coleman (1990); Granovetter (1985).
4. Burt (1982, 1992a).
5. First, a dominant strand of research on co-operation exchange employs transaction cost analysis (Alvesson and Lindkvist 1993; Barney 1990; Barney and Hansen 1994; Nooteboom, 1996; Williamson 1985; Zajac and Olsen 1993). This work has suggested that the structural features of the exchange are motivated by the desire to minimize cost (Ring and Van de Ven 1992, 1994).
6. See Hirsh and Lounsbury (1996), and North (1990) among others.
7. Williamson (1985).
8. Choi and Lee (1987). Williamson (1985) also noted that *ex ante* bidding competition and faceless contracting is supplanted over time by contracting in which the pair-wise identity of the parties matters.
9. Bradach and Eccles (1989); Choi and Maldoom (1992); Granovetter (1985).
10. Bernstein (1992).
11. Burt (1992a,b).
12. As considered by Boisot and Child (1988).
13. Schelling (1960).
14. Madhok (1995); Kogut (1986).
15. Barzel (1982) has shown that.
16. Hennart (1989, 1990).
17. Indeed, using Australian cases Fletcher (1996) has shown that the networks of relationships in counter-trade transactions are transformed over time by their complexity and reciprocity and by the involvement of government.
18. Abrahamsom and Fombrun (1994) have called such phenomena 'macro-cultures'.
19. Burt (1982); Choi and Lee (1997); Frank (1988); Haunschild (1994); Hosmer (1995); Podolny (1993).
20. Lippman and Rumelt (1982) and Spender and Grant (1996) both noted that.
21. North (1990).
22. This is the line that Williamson (1985) takes. He deals with such considerations implicitly, by treating their unavoidable presence as an example of market failure, which leads to the abandonment of the high-powered incentives of the market for the low-powered incentives available in a hierarchy.
23. The more behaviourally oriented enterprise researchers believe that the partners in co-operative exchange need not be seen as essentially untrustworthy individuals driven solely by self-interest. (Boisot and Child 1988; Burt 1982, 1992a, 1992b; Choi 1994; Donaldson 1990; Dutton and Jackson 1987; Etzioni 1988; Frank 1988; Granovetter 1985; Ouchi 1980; Zajac and Olsen 1993; Zucker 1987).
24. Ellickson (1991).

25. Yoshino and Rangan (1995).
26. Itami and Roehl (1987).
27. As Lippman and Rumelt (1982) and Spender and Grant (1996) both note.
28. This is the thrust of North's (1990) critique of the traditional transaction cost approach.
29. Works by Cadmic (1992), Elsbach and Kramer (1996), Elster (1989), and Haunschild (1993, 1994), Podolny (1993), further developing the earlier works of Bonaich (1987), Burt (1982), Granovetter (1973), Sorensen (1983), White (1970), show that the position of transactors in the social structure not only rewards them directly, but, by institutionalizing their utilizable patterns of relationships, also delineates their capacity to interact with others.
30. Barney and Hansen (1994).
31. Conner and Prahalad (1996) drew attention to this.
32. As Burt (1992a) suggests.
33. Barney and Hansen (1994); Camerer (1988); Schelling (1969); Spence (1973).
34. Jervis (1985).
35. Burt and Knez (1996) have undertaken analysis distinguishing between passive and proactive third parties, and how they affect the interaction between transactors.
36. Burt (1982, 1992a).

## 8 The emergence of a system of dynamic identity

1. Johnson and Burton (1994); Mintzberg and Waters (1990); Stacey (1996a,b).
2. Gell-Mann (1994); Kaufman (1993); Macy (1993).
3. Schumpeter (1942).
4. Hayek (1967); Simon (1992); Vanberg (1994); Winter (1998).
5. Foster and Kaplan (2001). The practical example they quote at length of a corporation which has managed to do this is Johnston and Johnston.
6. Gell-Mann (1994); Sanchez (1997).
7. In this, we agree with Macy (1997).
8. We agree with Macy that theories based on shared identity – the cohesive effects of similarity are not adequate in enhancing 'the capacity of interactants to act collectively in pursuit of common interests' (1997, p. 429). Actors polarize and group together via an emotion of shared identity emanating from salient attributes and characteristics. In this view any sense of self-interest – the attainment of an individualist objective – is lost and substituted by a motivation of pure public spirit, and any attribution of purpose is lost.
9. Kelley and Thibaut (1978).
10. Oberschall and Kim (1996).
11. Macy (1993).
12. Grafstein (1995).
13. Horowitz (1985).
14. Gartner and Segura (1997).
15. As defined by Coleman (1990) and Granovetter (1985).
16. Schelling (1969); Spence (1973).
17. Coleman (1990); Granovetter (1985).
18. Gartner and Siverson (1996); Smith (1996).

19. This overlaps with such works as Cadmic (1992), Carter and Manaster (1990), Haunschild (1994), and Podolny (1993), which developed the earlier works of Bonacich (1987), Dutton and Jackson (1987), and Jackson and Dutton (1988), Simmel (1950), Sorensen (1983), White (1970).
20. Bard and Soderquist (2000).
21. Various works such as Burt (1992), Granovetter (1985), Haunschild (1994), and Podolny (1993), have analysed this.
22. Itami and Roehl (1987).
23. Podolny (1993).
24. Haunschild (1994).
25. D'Aveni (1996).
26. Jones (1995).
27. This also illuminates the behavioural research of Burt (1992), Feld (1981) and Granovetter (1985).
28. A phenomenon adds up to constructing a suitable metaphor or schema, then using the schema to generate a detailed but sufficiently abstract description of the phenomenon to override the limitations posed by the schema (Devlin and Rosenberg 1991).
29. Bourdieu and Wacquant (1992); Coleman (1990); Granovetter (1985).
30. Grant (1991); Wernerfelt (1984).
31. Buzzle and Gale (1987); Porter (1980).
32. Holland (1995).
33. In the terminology of our proposed model it is an attempt to 'generate insight into the agent–artifact space that the agent inhabits and into the way in which control is distributed through that space' (Lane and Maxfield's 1996, p. 226).
34. Lane and Maxfield also suggested this.
35. An enterprise's dynamic identity is a metaphor for its quality and exchange potential in the global system, and it is mediated as a meme (Dawkins 1976).
36. Coveney and Highfield (1995).
37. Macy (1997).
38. The lesson all learned early on in the information age was precisely this, from the effective toppling of 'Big Blue' IBM which refused to abandon its mainframe business in the face of the distributed processing made possible by the micro computer (see the means to deal with this in Foster and Kaplan, 2002).
39. Spender (1997); Spender and Grant (1996).
40. Donaldson and Preston (1995); Dutton and Jackson (1987); Freeman (1984); Jones (1995); Mitchell *et al.* (1987); Rowley (1997); Wood (1991a,b).
41. Foster and Kaplan (2001) for example.
42. Sanchez (1997).
43. Research has been started on this in sociology and other behaviourally oriented disciplines but this has not yet been brought into the mainstream of management research. This was originally suggested by Burt (1992a,b).

## 9 Global diversity, psychic distance and communication costs

1. Schelling (1960) and Riaffa (1982) formulated the fundamentals of rational exchange and co-operation in an international setting with multiple actors.

2. Work such as that of Inkpen and Beamish (1997) and Parkhe (1991) has begun to address the importance of this.
3. Benito and Gripsrud (1992); Hofstede (1980); Kogut and Singh (1998); O'Grady and Land (1996); Peng and Heath (1996).
4. Krugman (1998), for example.
5. We have already alluded to research by North (1990), Olson (1992) and Simon (1991) on how enterprises and institutions influence and change and or are changed by each other. This work is especially relevant for our analysis.
6. Hirschman (1994); Putnam (1996); Rodrik (1997).
7. Ghoshal and Moran (1996); Granovetter (1985); Hill (1995); Nooteboom (1996); Parkhe (1991); Simon (1991); Williamson (1996).
8. North (1990, 1991) and Olson (1992).
9. Research in international business confirms this view and has shown that companies tend to begin their internationalization process, and even continue business exchanges, with countries which are psychically close to them Benito and Gripsrud (1992); Johanson and Vahlne (1977); Kogut and Singh (1988); O'Grady and Lane (1996).
10. Hofstede (1980).
11. Johanson and Vahlne (1977).
12. Gatignon and Anderson (1988); Kogut and Singh (1988); O'Grady and Lane (1996).
13. This deals with what has been called 'alliance-based capitalism': Kogut (1991); North (1990); Olson (1992); Whitley (1992a,b).
14. Beringer and Hebert (1989); Boddewyn (1988); Brouthers and Bamossy (1997); Choi, Lee and Kim (1999); Choi and Lee (1997); Etzioni (1988); Kogut (1991); Lenway and Murtha (1994); Thourow (1992).
15. Inkpen and Beamish (1997); Parkhe (1991).
16. Foster and Kaplan (2001).
17. Albert (1991); Freeman (1984); Hirschman (1994); Putnam (1996).
18. Fruin (1992); Gerlach and Lincoln (1992); Roe (1994).
19. Rostow (1991).
20. This has been the subject of most studies in international business; although emerging economies have been examined by Beamish (1988), Inkpen and Beamish (1997), Landa (1994) and Olson (1992).
21. Simon (1991).
22. It would be possible to think of these stages in Rostow's (1991) terms, but in the light of both Amsden's (1989) review of Korean economic development and the arguments we are setting out here, Gershenkron's (1962) perspective on backwardness seems the most appropriate.

## 10 Bridging the global cultural gap

1. Albert (1991); Brouthers and Bamossy (1997); Choi, Lee and Kim (1999); Freeman (1984).
2. Simon (1991) showed this.
3. Albert (1991); Brothers and Bamossy (1997); Choi, Lee and Kim (1999); Freeman (1984).
4. Hirschman (1994); North (1990); Olson (1992); Simon (1991).

5. North (1990); Simon (1991).
6. Kogurt and Sigh (1988).
7. This way of looking at comparative business systems shows some similarities with past research on institutional aspects of analysis by Hirschman (1994), Johanson and Vahlne (1977); O'Grady and Lane (1996); Putnam (1996) and Whitley (1994). But the difference is that we wish to compare such systems in the context of *globalization*, especially as it effects the creation of co-operative exchange and information-based industries.
8. Johanson and Vahlne (1977); Kogurt and Sigh (1988); O'Grady and Lane (1996).
9. Fruin (1992); Gerlach and Lincoln (1992); Hill (1995).
10. This distinction has been made in both work on comparative business systems and in other social science (Choi and Lee 1997; Fruin 1992; Granovetter 1985; Hirschman 1994; Parkhe 1991; Putnam 1996).
11. Research on international bargaining and co-operative relationships by Beamish (1988); Inkpen and Beamish (1997); Madhok (1995); and Parkhe, (1993); has shown this.
12. All this resembles the communication and co-ordination costs analysed by Raiffa (1982) and Schelling (1960).
13. O'Grady and Lane (1996).
14. Inkpen and Beamish (1987); Raiffa (1982); Schelling (1960, 1966).
15. Choi and Lee (1997); Granovetter (1985); Simon (1991).
16. Kogut and Zander (1996).
17. Boisot and Child (1988).
18. Schelling (1960).
19. Womack and Jones (1991).
20. Benito and Gripsrud (1992); Johanson and Vahlne (1977); Kogurt and Singh (1988); O'Grady and Lane (1997).
21. Gatignon and Anderson (1988); O'Grady and Lane (1996).
22. Albert (1991); Choi, Lee and Kim. (1999); Fruin (1992); Gerlach and Lincoln (1992); Roe (1997); Whitley (1992).

## 11 Knowledge and the emergent global business system

1. Womack and Jones (1996).
2. Fruin (1992).
3. Burt (1992, 1997); Granovetter (1985); Gulati (1995).
4. Polanyi (1957).
5. In addition to the behavioural work already cited, the literature in strategic management has also examined the exchange and exploitation of knowledge (Spender and Grant 1996).
6. Itami and Roehl (1987).
7. Knowledge has become an important topic of research in international business, in the context of multinationals and the transfer of knowledge across borders (Kogut and Zander 1993, 1995; Love 1995; McFetridge 1995). This research has tended to define knowledge generically, and to focus on how markets and enterprises differ in their capacities for transferring knowledge.
8. Choi (1994).

9. First although there is a general interest in knowledge as a resource, there is a gap in conception between international business research and related areas of economics research. This is despite a clear overlap of interests on the major issues: multinationals, global markets, knowledge transfer and public goods. It is also true that although a substantial part of international business research has relied on the methodology of international economics (Dunning 1996) a gap nevertheless exists, because international business has followed a broad interdisciplinary agenda while international economics has pursued the narrower agenda of trade and exchange rate theory. In order to analyse knowledge as a resource there is thus a need to address this gap, and to consider whether other areas of economics might be of value to international business research.
10. The area of economics literature of most relevance for international business in this area is development economics, which has been re-invigorated by the issues raised by economies in transition from central planning to the market. Both the study of emerging economies in Eastern Europe and earlier work on Asia (Amsden 1989; Wade 1985) are relevant.
11. Romer (1986).
12. Choi (1994); Lall (1992, 1995).
13. Kogut and Zander (1993, 1995); Love (1995); McFetridge (1995).
14. Choi (1994); Knack and Keefer (1997); Levine (1997).
15. The definition of knowledge in management and international business research has relied on Polanyi's (1944, 1966, 1971) work.
16. Kogut and Zander (1993, 1995); Nelson and Winter (1982).
17. Choi and Lee (1997); Inkpen and Beamish (1997); Kogut and Zander (1993).
18. Past economics research on intangible resources has been in the context of the New Economic Growth theory (Krugman 1991; Romer 1986).
19. Knack and Keefer (1997); Levine (1997).
20. The economics of knowledge has an extremely broad and deep literature which begins with Schelling (1969) and Spence (1973). The explosive growth in game theoretic models throughout the 1970s and 1980s, along with questions of moral hazard and adverse selection, enabled economists to analyse the nature of markets under imperfect and asymmetric knowledge (Milgrom and Roberts 1992). Like the more recent literature on economic growth, the economics of knowledge has tangential linkages to knowledge research in international business, but it has not developed in a way which offers prospects of cross-fertilization.
21. Rugman (2000).
22. Womack and Jones (1996).
23. Kaplan and Roberts (2001).
24. Kaplan and Roberts (2001).
25. Dunning (1996); Gerlach (1992).
26. Amsden (1989); Lall (1992, 1995); Mody and Yilmaz (1997).
27. Blau (1964); Ekeh (1974); Etzioni (1988); Homans (1974); Mauss (1955); Polanyi (1957).
28. Blau (1993); Cook (1987); Emerson (1976); Fligstein (1996); Hardin (1982, 1997).
29. The reasoning we set out in this chapter is rooted in the concept of 'exchange', as it has been discussed in both the anthropological literature (Alchian 1965; Barzel 1982, 1997; Blau 1964; Bourdieu 1977; Durkheim

1951; Ekeh 1974; Homans 1974; Lévi-Strauss 1969; Sahlins 1972, Simmel 1978; and the 'property rights' literature.

30. Hirsch and Lounsbury (1996); North (1990).
31. Hardin (1982); Olson (1965).
32. No clear common definition exists for exchange across the social science disciplines (Bagozzi 1979; Bearman 1997; Toyne 1989; Uehara 1990).
33. Ostrom (1990).
34. Toyne (1989).
35. Bagozzi (1979); Granovetter (1985).
36. Hart and Moore (1990); Jensen and Meckling (1976); Milgrom and Roberts (1990).
37. Baker, Faulkner and Fisher (1998); Blau (1964); Fligstein (1996); Gouldner (1960); Yamagishi and Cook (1993); Uehara (1990).
38. Etzioni (1988); Hardin (1982, 1997); Olson (1965).
39. Barzel (1982, 1997).
40. Williamson (1985).
41. Etzioni (1988); Hardin (1982); Olson (1965, 1982).
42. There is a vast management literature on networks (Burt 1992a,b; Granovetter 1985; Gulati 1995; Jones 1983), but these issues of exchange and property rights, and the implications for ownership of collectivity, have not as yet been sufficiently analysed.
43. Blau (1964); Ekeh (1974); Lévi-Strauss (1969); Sahlins (1972); Simmel (1978); In law and economics, Alchian (1965); Bernstein (1992); Coase (1960); Landes (1971); Ostrom (1990); Posner (1992); Rubin (1997).
44. Hardin (1982, 1997); Olson (1965); Ostrom (1990).
45. Choi and Lee (1997); Polanyi (1944, 1971); Spender (1996).
46. Bourdieu (1977, 1990); Douglas and Isherwood (1979).
47. Bourdieu (1977, 1990); Douglas and Isherwood (1979).
48. Appadurai (1986); Gregory (1982); Sahlins (1972); Simmel (1978).
49. Granovetter (1985); Marsden and Friedkin (1993); Mizruchi (1996).
50. Barzel (1982); Bernstein (1992); Posner (1992).
51. Polanyi (1944, 1957, 1966, 1971).
52. Choi and Lee (1997); Spender (1997).
53. But, do see Barzel (1997) on this.
54. See the existing research on networks, and on the significance of social structure and relationships among the involved enterprises, (Barney and Hansen 1994; Bradach and Eccles 1989; Burt 1992a,b; Gulati 1998; Zajac and Olsen 1993).
55. For example, in the related research of Bernstein (1992) and Landa (1981).
56. As is well known across the social sciences (Bernstein 1992; Greif 1993; Landa 1981; Posner 1992; Schelling 1960).
57. Hayek (1973); Kornai (1992); Leoni (1961).
58. Burt (1992); Doz (1996); Granovetter (1985); Hennart and Reddy (1997); Nohria and Garcia-Pont (1991); Raub and Weesie (1990); Ring and Van de Ven (1992); Schrum and Withnow (1988); Walker, Kogut and Shan (1996).
59. In the literature on networks (Burt 1992; Gulati 1998) networks rely more on social relationships than they do in traditional neoclassical markets.
60. Barzel (1982, 1997).
61. Mauss (1955); Polanyi (1957).

62. 'Reciprocal exchange, can be defined as those types of exchange in which informally enforced agreements between parties cover the exchange of goods and services' (Choi 1994; Ellickson 1991; Kolm 1984).
63. Bourdieu (1977, 1990); Lévi-Strauss (1969); Malinowski (1961); Mauss (1955); Sahlins (1972).
64. Choi (1994) and Kranton (1996) analysed it in just such a context.
65. Ellickson (1991); Etzioni (1988); MacNeil (1980).
66. Barzel (1982, 1997); Bernstein (1992); Posner (1992).
67. Knight (1921, 1935).
68. Bohm (1980).
69. Bourdieu (1977, 1990).
70. Barzel (1997); Posner (1992).
71. As discussed in the pioneering works by Burt (1982), Coleman (1990) and Granovetter (1985).
72. Itami and Roehl (1987).
73. Spender (1996).
74. Bohm (1980); Eggertson (1990).
75. Mauss (1975), Sahlins (1972) and Simmel (1978) developed in the social anthropological literature.

## 12 Cohesion versus integrity in global knowledge-creating value networks

1. Rugman (2002).
2. Fligstein (1996); Hardin (1982, 1997); Olson (1965, 1982); Sandler (1992).
3. Olson (1965, 1982); Schelling (1960); Sugden (1982).
4. Etzioni (1988); Hardin (1982, 1997); Olson (1965).
5. Baker, Faulkner and Fisher (1998) have analysed in detail the breakup of networks where a sub-group selects the exit option (Hirschman 1970).
6. Blau (1964); Ekeh (1974); Lévi-Strauss (1969).
7. Etzioni (1988); Hardin (1982); Olson (1965).
8. Hardin (1982, 1997); Olson (1965).
9. Etzioni (1988); Olson (1965); Ostrom (1990).
10. As analysed by Baker, Faulkner and Fisher (1998).
11. Blau (1964); Hardin (1982); Sahlins (1978); Simmel (1972).
12. Olson (1965); Ostrom (1990); Sandler (1992).
13. Hardin (1982); Kuran (1989).
14. Olson (1965); Ostrom (1990); Sandler (1992).
15. Bergstrom and Blumeandh (1986); Buchanan (1965).
16. Mauss (1955); Sahlins (1972); Simmel (1978).
17. Hardin (1982); Olson (1965, 1982); Ostrom (1990).

## 13 Socio-economic emergence of man and society

1. Epstein (1995); Greif (1993).
2. Typical in recent years is the explanation of the growth of the 'Tiger Economies' of South-east Asia by 'Asian values'. The Confucian tradition was said to

encourage hard work, savings and investment for the future, and co-operation towards a single end. Interestingly, Weber had argued pointing to China's desolate state at the time, that the same Confucian tradition inhibited economic success because its insistence on obedience to parental authority discouraged competition and innovation.

3. Cheng and Van de Ven (1996).
4. Groener (1999).
5. The New Institutional Economics has introduced the concept of transaction costs (Coase 1937, 1984; Williamson 1985).
6. The concept has found multiple uses: Williamson and Craswell (1993) explained 'trusting behaviour' as the costs of cheating in an environment that is sustained by reputation; Douglass North has rewritten Economic History using a transaction cost approach which explains non-maximizing behaviour such as peasant conservatism by introducing the psychic costs of abandoning ideologies. Ghoshal and Moran (1996) have even argued that transaction cost explanations actually undermine advantageous enterprise practices. There is a certain danger, however, that 'transaction cost' can turn into an ad hoc idea used whenever behaviour does not fit a theory.
7. The philosopher David Gauthier (1986) has taken the utility-maximizing explanation of reciprocity to a level mirrored by Frank in his (1987) paper. Gauthier (1986) argues that a rational person 'chooses on utility-maximizing grounds not to make further choices on those grounds'.
8. An example invented by Parfit elucidates the point. While it may be rational to dispose myself to become a threat fulfiller since anybody threatened by me will then be more likely to comply with my demands, it may not be rational to carry out my threat after it has been ignored (say, blow up the aircraft). Thus one may reject the claim that 'If it is rational for someone to make himself believe that it is rational for him to act in some way, it is rational for him to act in this way' (Parfit, 1984, p. 23).
9. Prisoner's Dilemma games (Axelrod 1986). Others have included a wider range of motivations among the initial preferences of co-operating parties (Olsen 1965).
10. The political scientist Jon Elster (1989) argues trenchantly that norms are 'not merely ex post rationalizations of self-interest' although he expects social and geographical mobility to loosen 'the grip [of social norms] on the mind in the modern world' (1989). Conversely, classical sociology thought that egotistic, self-interested and calculating individuals would not be able to sustain a society at all.
11. Durkheim (1951); Parsons (1937). In pre-structural thinking, social esteem would be explained by the substantial value of solidarity. One could go no further than stipulating that ideas about esteemed behaviour are generated collectively.
12. Max Weber (1968) observed a transition from personal to impersonal trust in which 'there is no brotherliness or reverence, and none of those spontaneous human relations that are sustained by personal unions'. Weber began a more formal type of enquiry in sociology. Rather than holding substantial values directly responsible for social cohesion as Durkheim and Parsons did, he identified structural forces which bring human beings into line with each

other (DiMaggio and Powell 1983), or into competition with each other (Burt 1992).

13. DiMaggio and Powell (1983) and Meyer and Rowan (1977). Thus the main distinctive feature of modern value-driven theories is their rejection of the methodological individualism of rational choice models. Those sociologists (such as Luhmann and Burdieu) who reject direct psychological sources of order and the writers of the New Institutionalist school have, following John Meyer, spoken of the need to reduce 'social complexity by going beyond available knowledge and generalising expectations of behaviour', (Luhmann 1979) something they see achieved by a form of reflexive trust – habitus: a past which survives in the present and tends to perpetuate itself into the future by making itself present in practices structured according to its principles' (Bourdieu 1977, p. 82)

    Institutional Theory sought to understand pressures toward social conformity from ritual, myth and ceremony and developed the notion of coercive, mimetic and normative isomorphism sustaining structure from one period to the next. Value-driven explanations seem far harder to pin down than the calculative deductions of rational choice.
14. This should remind us that co-ordination under the notion of prominence depends on 'imaginative leaps and associations of ideas' (Sugden, 1986) which change with given historical situations.
15. Following philosopher David Lewis (1969), a behavioural regularity *R* is maintained as a convention if:

    (a) everyone conforms to *R*
    (b) everyone expects everyone else to conform to *R*
    (c) everyone *prefers* to conform to *R* since *R* is a *solution to a coordination problem*.

16. Kauffman (1993).
17. This violates the neoclassical economic assumption of diminishing returns which constrain potential solutions to a unique maximum or minimum. Economics argues that profits per unit will eventually fall, as a firm expands into a market (cf. Arthur 1994).

## 14 The paradoxes of global emergence

1. 'Infinitely reflexive mutual expectations' (Schelling 1960, p. 70).
2. Arrow (1974); Elster (1969); Gambetta (1988); Luhmann (1979).
3. Empirical tests have shown that this does happen (Berg, Dickhaut and McCabe 1995). It also appears that trusting and trustworthy behaviour are psychologically linked, (Deutsch 1973, p. 206).
4. Compare Granovetter's related claim that 'social relations, rather than institutional arrangements or generalized morality, are mainly responsible for the production of trust in economic life' (1985, p. 491).
5. As we have seen, a significant portion of extant conceptualizations of economic actions suggests a dichotomy of structural outcomes between hierarchies and markets (Williamson 1975, 1985).
6. Gerlach (1992); Granovetter (1985); Nohria and Eccles (1992a).

7. Begun (1994); Holland (1992); Starbuck (1976).
8. Chakravarthy (1997); Jorde and Teece (1992).
9. Latour (1993, 1996) and Spender (1997) take this view.
10. Nohria and Eccles (1992).
11. But these connections (Giddens 1979; Senge 1990) are also typical of the process of emergence (Jantsch 1980; Morgan 1986; Wheatley 1994).
12. Any attempt to set targets based on attributed direct causality is almost certainly ill-fated (Mintzberg and Waters 1990; Pettigrew 1990).
13. Black and Farias (1996). Latour (1993, 1996) suggested that agents experienced networks because they were part of them, and so they acquired knowledge of acquaintance (James 1950). Similarly, enterprises engage in enacted institutions (Weick 1979) which are simultaneously discovered and created by transactors, in their efforts to exchange with others (Garnsey 1996).
14. Weick (1979); Zohar (1990).
15. Devlin (1991); Hill and Levenhagen (1995); Lakoff and Johnson (1995); McMaster (1996).
16. Goldstein (1994).
17. Luhmann (1992); Stacey (1996b).
18. Such knowing is characterized by recursiveness and bounded knowledge (Drazin and Sandelands 1992) see also Gell-Mann (1994); Kauffman (1995); Macy (1993).
19. Wheatley and Kellner-Rogers (1996).
20. Stacey (1996b).
21. In Arthur, Lee and Rogers (1988); see also Arthur (1994).
22. Drazin and Sandelands (1992).
23. As Devlin and Rosenberg stated (1996, cited by Lissack 1997), understanding a phenomenon adds up to constructing a suitable schema and, based on the schema, generating a detailed but sufficiently abstract description of the phenomenon to override the limitations posed by the schema.
24. Chakravarthy (1997); Granovetter (1992).
25. Ashforth and Humphrey (1997).
26. Gell-Mann (1994).
27. Chakravarthy (1997); Granovetter (1992).
28. Burt (1992a,b).
29. Gell-Mann (1994).

# Bibliography

Abrahamson, E. and Fombrun, C. 1994. 'Macrocultures: Determinants and Consequences', *Academy of Management Review*, 19: 728–755.

Ackerman, R. W. 1975. *The Social Challenge to Business*, Cambridge, MA: Harvard University Press.

Albert, M. 1991. *Capitalism Against Capitalism,* Paris: Centre for Economic Research.

Alchian, A. 1965. *Economic Forces At Work*, Indianapolis: Liberty Press.

Aldrich, H. and Fiol, M. 1994. 'Fools Rush In? The Institutional Context of Industry Creation', *Academy of Management Review*, 19: 645–670.

Alkhafaji, A. F. 1989. *A Stakeholder Approach to Corporate Governance: Managing in a Dynamic Environment*, New York: Quorum Books.

Alvesson, M. and Lindkvist, L. 1993. 'Transaction Costs, Clans and Corporate Culture', *Journal of Management Studies*, 30: 427–452.

Amsden, A. 1989, 'Asia's Next Giant', *Technology Review*, 92(4): 46–54.

Andreoni, J. 1990. 'Impure Altruism and Donations to Public Goods: A Theory of Warm-Glow Giving', *Economic Journal*, 100: 464–477.

Appadurai, A. 1986. *The Social Life of Things: Commodities in Cultural Perspective*, Cambridge: Cambridge University Press.

Arlow, P. and Gannon, M. 1982. 'Social Responsiveness, Corporate Structure, and Economic Performance', *Academy of Management Review*, 7: 235–241.

Arnott, R. and Stiglitz, J. 1990. 'Moral Hazard and Nonmarket Institutions: Dysfunctional Crowding Out or Peer Monitoring', *American Economic Review*, 80: 179–190.

Arrow, K. J. 1974. *The Fels Lectures On Public Policy Analysis*, New York. W.W. Norton.

Arthur, W. B. 1994. *Increasing Returns and Path Dependence in the Economy*, Ann Arbor: University of Michigan Press.

Arthur, W. B. 1996. 'Increasing Returns and the New World of Business', *Harvard Business Review*, 7(4): 100–110.

Arthur, W. B., Lee, R. and Rodgers, G. 1988. *Economics of Changing Age Distributions in Developed Countries*, Oxford: Clarendon.

Ashforth, B. E. and Humphrey, R. H. 1997. 'The Ubiquity and Potency of Labeling in Organizations', *Organization Science* 8(1): 43–58.

Aupperle, K., Carroll, A. and Hatfield, J. 1985. 'An Empirical Examination of the Relationship Between Corporate Social Responsibility and Profitability', *Academy of Management Journal*, 28: 446–463.

Axelrod, R. 1984. *The Evolution of Cooperation*, New York: Basic Books.

Bagozzi, R. 1979. 'Toward A Formal Theory of Marketing Exchange', in S. D. Hunt (ed.), *Marketing Theory: The Philosophy of Marketing Science*, Homewood, IL: Richard D. Irwin.

Bain, J. S. 1956. *Barriers To New Competition*, Cambridge, MA: Harvard University Press.

Bain, J. S. 1959. *Industrial Organization*, New York: Wiley.

Baker, W., Faulkner, R. and Fisher, G. 1998. 'Hazards of the Market: The Continuity and Dissolution of Inter-Organizational Market Relationships', *American Sociological Review*, 63: 147–177.

Bard, A. and Soderquist, J. 2002. *Netocracy*, London: Pearson Education.

Barney, J. 1990. 'The Debate Between Traditional Management Theory and Organizational Economics: Substantive Differences Or Inter-Group Conflict?', *Academy of Management Review*, 15: 382–393.

Barney, J. and Hansen, M. 1994. 'Trustworthiness as a Source of Competitive Advantage', *Strategic Management Journal*, 15: 175–216.

Bartholomew, S. 1997. 'National Systems of Biotechnology Innovation: Complex Interdependence in The Global System', *Journal of International Business Studies*, 28: 241–266.

Barzel, Y. 1982. 'Measurement Cost and the Organisation of Markets', *Journal of Law and Economics*, 25: 27–48.

Barzel, Y. 1997. *Economic Analysis of Property Rights*, Cambridge: Cambridge University Press.

Beale, H. and Dugdale, A. 1975. 'Contracts Between Businessmen: Planning and the Use of Contractual Remedies', *British Journal of Law and Society*, 2: 45–60.

Beamish, P. W. 1988. *Multinational Joint Ventures in Developing Countries*, London: Routledge.

Beamish, P. W. and Banks, J. 1987. 'Equity Joint Ventures and the Theory of the Multinational Enterprise', *Journal of International Business Studies*, 18: 1–16.

Bearman, P. 1997. 'Generalised Exchange', *American Journal of Sociology*, 102: 1383–1415.

Benito, G. and Gripsrud, G. 1992. 'The Expansion of Foreign Direct Investment: Discrete Rational Location Choices or a Cultural Learning Process?', *Journal of International Business Studies*, 23: 461–476.

Bergstrom, T. and Blumeandh, V. 1986. 'On the Private Provision of Public Goods', *Journal of Public Economics*, 29: 25–49.

Berman, H. 1983. *Law and Revolution – The Formation of The Western Legal Tradition*, Oxford: Blackwell.

Bernstein, L. 1992. 'Opting Out of the Legal System: Extralegal Contractual Relations in the Diamond Industry', *Journal of Legal Studies*, 21: 115–157.

Besley, T. 1995. 'Nonmarket Institutions for Credit and Risk Sharing in Low-Income Countries', *Journal of Economic Perspectives*, 9: 115–127.

Blau, J. 1993. *Social Contracts and Economic Markets*, New York: Plenum Press.

Blau, P. 1964. *Exchange and Power in Social Life*, New York: Wiley.

Blau, P. 1975. *Approaches to the Study of Social Structure*, New York: Free Press.

Bobbitt, D. 2002. *The Shield of Achilles*, London: Allen Lane.

Boddewyn, J. 1988. 'Political Aspects of MNE Theory', *Journal of International Business Studies*, 19: 341–363.

Boddewyn, J. J. and Brewer, T. 1994. 'International-Business Political Behavior: New Theoretical Directions', *Journal of International Business Studies*, 19: 119–143.

Bohm, F. 1980. *Freiheit und Ordnung in der Marktwirtschaft*, Baden Baden: Nomos.

Boisot, M. and J. Child 1988. 'The Iron Law of Fiefs: Bureaucratic Failure and the Problem of Governance in the Chinese Economic Reforms', *Administrative Science Quarterly*, 33: 507–527.

Bonacich, P. 1987. 'Power and Centrality: A Family of Measures', *American Journal of Sociology*, 92: 1170–1183.

Bourdieu, P. 1977. *Outline of A Theory of Practice*, Cambridge: Cambridge University Press.
Bourdieu, P. 1990. *Sociology in Question*, London: Sage.
Bourdieu, P. and Wacquant, L. 1992. *An Invitation on Reflexive Sociology*, Chicago: University of Chicago Press.
Bovasso, G. 1996. 'A Network Analysis of Social Contagion Processes in an Organizational Intervention', *Human Relations*, 49(11): 1419–1436.
Bradach, J. and Eccles, R. 1989. 'Price, Authority and Trust: From Ideal Types to Plural Forms', *Annual Review of Sociology*, 15: 97–118.
Brenner, S. N. and Cochran, P. 1991 'The Stakeholder Theory of the Firm: Implications for Business and Society Theory and Research', in J. J. Brummer (ed.), *Corporate Responsibility and Legitimacy: An Interdisciplinary Analysis*, New York: Greenwood Press.
Brewer, T. 1992. 'An Issue-Area Approach to the Analysis of MNE–Government Relations', *Journal of International Business Studies*, 18: 295–309.
Brewer, T. 1993, 'Government Policies, Market Imperfections, and Foreign Direct Investment', *Journal of International Business Studies*, 24: 101–121.
Brockner, J. 1992. 'The Escalation of Commitment to a Failing Course of Action', *Academy of Management Review*, 17: 39–61.
Brouthers, K. and Bamossy, G. 1997. 'The Role of Key Stakeholders in International Joint Venture Negotiations: Case Studies from Eastern Europe', *Journal of International Business Studies*, 23: 285–308.
Buchanan, J. 1965. 'An Economic Theory of Clubs', *Economica*, 32: 1–14.
Buckley, P. 1990. 'Problems and Developments in the Core Theory of International Business', *Journal of International Business Studies*, 21: 657–665.
Buckley, P. 1996, 'The Role of Management in International Business Theory: A Meta-Analysis and Integration of the Literature on International Business and International Management', *Management International Review*, 36: 7–54.
Buckley, F. 1997, 'The Canadian *Keiretsu*', *Journal of Applied Corporate Finance*, 9: 46–56.
Burt, R. 1982. *Toward A Structural Theory of Action*, New York, Academic Press.
Burt, R. 1992a. *Structural Holes: The Social Structure of Competition*, Cambridge, MA: Harvard University Press.
Burt, R. 1992b. 'The Social Structure of Competition', in R. Eccles, and N. Nohria, (eds), *Networks and Organizations*, Cambridge, MA: Harvard University Press.
Burt, R. 1997. 'The Contingent Value of Social Capital', *British Journal of Management*, 8(22): 133–151.
Burt, R. and Knez, M. 1996. 'Trust and Third-Party Gossip', in R. Kramer, and T. Tyler, (eds), *Trust in Organizations*, London: Sage.
Burt, R. and Talmud, I. 1993. 'Market Niche', *Social Networks*, 15: 133–149.
Buzzle, R. D. and Gale, B. J. 1987. 'The PIMS Principle', New York: Free Press.
Cadmic, C. 1992. 'Reputation and Predecessor Selection: Parsons and the Institutionalists', *American Sociological Review*, 57: 421–445.
Camerer, C. 1988. 'Gifts as Economic Signals and Social Symbols', *American Journal of Sociology*, 94: S180–214.
Camerer, C. and Knez, M. 1996. 'Coordination, Organizational Boundaries and Fads in Business Practices', *Industrial and Corporate Change*, 5: 89–112.
Carroll, A. 1979. 'A Three-Dimensional Conceptual Model of Corporate Social Performance', *Academy of Management Review*, 4: 497–505.

Carroll, A. 1989. *Business and Society: Ethics and Stakeholder Management*, Cincinnati: South-Western Publishing Co.

Carroll G. and Hannan, M. 2000. 'Why Corporate Demography Matters: Policy Implications of Organizational Diversity', *California Management Review*, 42(3): 148.

Carter, R. and Manaster, S. 1990. 'Initial Public Offerings and Underwriter Reputation', *Journal of Finance*, 45(1): 1045–1068.

Casson, M. 1996. 'Economics and Anthropology – Reluctant Partners', *Human Relations*, 49(2): 51–118.

Casson, M. and Chukujama, F. 1988. 'Countertrade: Theory and Evidence', unpublished manuscript, University of Reading.

Casson, M. and Lundan, S. 1999. 'Explaining International Differences in Economic Institutions', *International Studies of Management and Organization*, 29(2): 25–42.

Caves, R. and Marin, D. 1992. 'Countertrade Transactions: Theory and Evidence', *Economic Journal*, 102: 1171–1183.

Chakravarthy, B. 1997. 'A New Strategy Framework for Coping with Turbulence', *Sloan Management Review*, 38(2): 69.

Chandler, A. 1990. *Scale and Scope: The Dynamics of Industrial Capitalism*, Cambridge, MA: The Belknap Press.

Chen, M. 1995. *Asian Management Systems: Chinese, Japanese and Korean Styles of Business*, New York: Thomson Business Press.

Cheng, Y. and Van De Ven, A. 1996. 'Learning the Innovation Journey: Order Out of Chaos', *Organization Science*, 7(6): 593–614.

Cheung, S. 1969. *A Theory of Share Tenancy*, Chicago: University of Chicago Press.

Child, J. and Lu, Y. 1995. 'Institutional Constraints on Economic Reform: The Case of Investment in China', Management Studies Research Paper, 8/92, Department of Engineering, University of Cambridge.

Chiles, T. and McMackin, J. 1996. 'Integrating Variable Risk Preferences, Trust, and Transaction Cost Economics', *Academy of Management Review*, 21: 73–99.

Choi, C. 1994. 'Contract Enforcement Across Cultures', *Organization Studies*, 15: 673–682.

Choi, C., Lee, S. and Kim, J. B. 1996. 'Countertrade and International Business Enforcement', paper presented at the Academy of International Business, Vancouver.

Choi, C., Lee, S. and Kim, J. 1999. 'Countertrade, and Contractual Governance in Emerging Markets', *Journal of International Business Systems*, 30(1): 120–132.

Choi, C. and Maldoom D. 1992. 'A Simple Model of Buybacks', *Economics Letters*, 40: 77–82.

Chamberlin, E. 1933. *The Theory of Monopolistic Competition*, Cambridge, MA: Harvard University Press.

Clarkson, M. 1991. 'Defining, Evaluating, and Managing Corporate Social Performance: A Stakeholder Management Model', in J. E. Post (ed.), *Research in Corporate Social Performance and Policy*, Greenwich, CT: JAI Press: 331–358.

Coase, R. 1937. 'The Contractual Nature of the Firm', *Journal of Law and Economics*, 4: 386–405.

Coase, R. 1960. 'The Problem of Social Cost', *Journal of Law and Economics*, 3: 1–44.

Cochran, P. L. and Wood, R. A. 1984. 'Corporate Social Responsibility and Financial Performance', *Academy of Management Journal*, 27: 42–56.

Coleman, J. 1990a. 'Social Capital in The Creation of Human Capital', *American Journal of Sociology*, 94: 95–120.
Coleman, J. 1990b. *Foundations of Social Theory*, Cambridge, MA: The Belknap Press.
Coleman, L. 1987. 'What is meant by global marketing?', *Academy of Marketing Science Journal*, 10: 176–181.
Collins, R. 1992. *Sociological Insight*, Oxford: Oxford University Press.
Conner, K. and Prahalad, C. 1996. 'A Resource-Based Theory of The Firm: Knowledge Versus Opportunism', *Organization Science*, 7: 477–501.
Cook, K. 1987. 'Social Exchange Theory', *Journal of Institutional and Theoretical Economics*, 152: 7–29.
Cornell, B. and Shapiro, A. 1987. 'Corporate Stakeholders and Corporate Finance', *Financial Management*, 16(2): 5–14.
Coveney, P. and Highfield, R. 1995. *Frontiers of Complexity: the Search for Order in a Chaotic World*, New York: Ballantine Books.
Crozier, M. 1964. *The Bureaucratic Phenomenon*. London: Tavistock.
D'Aveni, R. 1996. 'A Multiple-Constituency, Status-Based Approach to Inter-organizational Mobility of Faculty and Input–Output Competition among Top Business Schools', *Organization Science*, 7: 166–189.
Davis, K. 1973. 'The Case for and against Business Assumption of Social Responsibilities', *Academy of Management Journal*, 16: 312–322.
Dawkins, R. 1976. *The Selfish Gene*, Oxford: Oxford University Press.
Devlin, K. and Rosenberg, D. 1991. *Logic and Information*, Cambridge: Cambridge University Press.
Devlin, K. and Rosenberg, D. 1996. *Language at Work: Analyzing Communication Breakdown in the Workplace to Inform Systems Design*, Stanford, CA: CSLI Publications.
Dickhaut, B., Hughes, J., McCabe, K. and Rayburn, J. 1995. 'Capital Market Experience for Financial Accounting Students', *Contemporary Accounting Research*, 11(2): 941–959.
DiMaggio, P. and Powell, W. 1983. 'The Iron Cage Revisited: Institutional Isomorphism, Collective Rationality in Organizational Fields', *American Sociological Review*, 48: 147–160.
Donaldson, L. 1990. 'A Rational Basis For Criticisms of Organizational Economics: A Reply To Barney', *Academy of Management Review*, 15: 394–401.
Donaldson, T. and Preston, L. 1995. 'The Stakeholder Theory of the Corporation: Concepts, Evidence and Implications', *Academy of Management Review*, 20: 65–91.
Dore, R. 1983. 'Goodwill and the Spirit of Market Capitalism', *British Journal of Sociology*, 34: 459–82.
Douglas, M. and Isherwood, B. 1979. *The World of Goods: Towards An Anthropology of Consumption*, London: Allen Lane.
Doz, Y. 1996. 'The Evolution of Co-Operation in Strategic Alliances: Initial Conditions of Learning Processes', *Strategic Management Journal*, 17: 55–83.
Doz, Y. and Prahalad, C. K. 1984. 'Patterns of Strategic Control Within Multinational Corporations', *Journal of International Business Studies*, 15: 55–72.
Drazin, R. and Sandelands, L. 1992. 'Autogenesis: A Perspective on the Process of Organizing', *Organization Science*, 3(2): 230–249.
Dutton, J. E. and Jackson, S. E. 1987. 'Categorizing Strategic Issues: Links to Organizational Action', *Academy of Management Review*, 12(1): 76–90.

Dunning, J. 1996. 'Reappraising the Eclectic Paradigm in an Age of Alliance Capitalism', *Journal of International Business Studies*, 26: 461–491.
Durkheim, E. 1951. *Suicide: A Study in Sociology*, New York: Free Press.
Dutton, J. E. and Jackson, S. 1987. 'Categorizing Strategic Issues: Links to Organizational Action', *Academy of Management Review*, 12: 76–90.
Easterbrook, F. 1997. 'International Corporate Differences: Markets Or Law?', *Journal of Applied Corporate Finance*, 9: 23–29.
Eggertsson, T. 1990. *Economic Behaviour and Institutions*, Cambridge: Cambridge University Press.
Eisenhardt, K. M. 1989. 'Agency Theory: an Assessment and Review', *Academy of Management Review*, 14: 57–74.
Ekeh, P. 1974. *Social Exchange Theory: The Two Traditions*, Cambridge, MA: Harvard University Press.
Ellickson, R. 1991. *Order Without Law*. Cambridge, MA: Harvard University Press.
Elsbach, K. and Kramer, R. 1996. 'Members' Responses to Organizational Identity Threats: Encountering and Countering the *Business Week* Rankings', *Administrative Science Quarterly*, 41: 442–476.
Elster, J. 1989. *The Cement of Society: A Study of Social Order*, Cambridge: Cambridge University Press.
Elster, J. and Moene, K. 1989. *Alternatives to Capitalism*, Cambridge: Cambridge University Press.
Emerson, R. 1976. 'Social Exchange Theory', *Annual Review of Sociology*, 2: 335–362.
Epstein, S. 1994. 'Regional Fairs, Institutional Innovation, and Economic-Growth in Late Medieval Europe', *Economic History Review*, 47(3): 459–482.
Etzioni, A. 1988. *The Moral Dimension: Toward A New Economics*, New York: Free Press.
Etzioni, A. 1996. 'The Responsive Community: A Communitarian Perspective', *American Sociological Review*, 61: 1–11.
Evan, W. M. and Freeman, R. E. 1988. 'A Stakeholder Theory of the Modern Corporation: Kantian Capitalism', in T. Beauchamp and N. Bowie (eds), *Ethical Theory and Business*, Englewood Cliffs, NJ: Prentice-Hall: 75–93.
Fahey, L. and Narayanan, V. K. 1986. *Macroenvironmental Analysis for Strategic Management*, St Paul, MN: West.
Feld, S. 1981. 'The Focused Organization of Social Ties', *American Journal of Sociology*, 86: 1015–1034.
Fletcher, R. 1996. 'Network Theory and Countertrade Transactions', *International Business Review*, 5: 167–189.
Fleming, J. E. 1981. 'Public Issues Scanning', in L. E. Preston (ed.), *Research in Corporate Social Performance and Policy*, Vol. 3, Greenwich, CT: JAI Press: 154–174.
Fligstein, N. 1996. 'Markets as Politics: A Political–Cultural Approach to Market Institutions', *American Sociological Review*, 61: 656–673.
Fombrun, C. J. and Shanley, M. 1990. 'What's in A Name? Reputation-Building and Corporate Strategy', *Academy of Management Journal*, 33: 233–258.
Foss, N. 1999. 'Perspectives on Business Systems', *International Studies of Management and Organization*, 29(2): 3–8.
Foster, R. and Kaplan, S. 2001. *Creative Destruction*, London: Pearson Education.
Frank, R. 1987. 'If *Homo Economicus* Could Choose his own Utility Function, Would He Want One with a Conscience?', *American Economic Review*, 77: 593–605.
Frank, R. 1988. *Passions Within Reason*, New York: W.W. Norton.

Frank, R. and Cook, P. J. 1995. *The Winner-Take-All Society*, New York: Free Press.
Franks, J. and Mayer C. 1997. 'Corporate Ownership and Control in the UK, Germany and France', *Journal of Applied Corporate Finance*, 9: 30–45.
Frederick, W. 1986. 'Theories of Corporate Social Performance: Much Done, More To Do', Working Paper, University of Pittsburgh, Graduate School of Business.
Freeman, R. 1984. *Strategic Management: A Stakeholder Approach*, New York: Free Press.
Freeman R. and Reed D. 1983. 'Stockholders and Stakeholders – A New Perspective on Corporate Governance', *California Management Review*, 25(3): 88–106.
Fruin, M. 1992. *The Japanese Enterprise System*, Oxford: Oxford University Press.
Gambetta, D. 1988. *Trust: Making and Breaking Cooperative Relations*, New York: Basil Blackwell.
Garnsey, E. 1996. 'Location of the High Technology Milieu: A Systems Approach', *Research papers in management studies*, 6/96, Judge Institute of Management Studies, Cambridge.
Gartner, S. S. and Segura, G. M. 1997. 'Appearances Can be Deceptive: Self-Selection, Social Group Identification and Political Mobilization', *Rationality and Society*, 9(2): 131–161.
Gartner, S. S. and Siverson, R. M. 1996. 'War Outcome and War Expansion', *Journal of Conflict Resolution*, 40(2): 4–15.
Gatignon, H. and Anderson, E. 1988. 'The Multinational Corporation's Degree of Control Over Foreign Subsidiaries', *Journal of Law, Economics and Organization*, 4: 305–336.
Gauthier, D. P. 1986. *Morals By Agreement*, Oxford: Clarendon Press.
Geertz, C. 1978. 'The Bazaar Economy: Information and Search in Peasant Marketing', *American Economic Review*, 68: 28–32.
Gell, A. 1982. 'The Market Wheel: Symbolic Aspects of an Indian Tribal Market', *Man*, 17: 470–491.
Gell-Mann, M. 1994. *The Quark and The Jaguar: Adventures in the Simple and the Complex*, London: Little, Brown.
Geringer, M. and Herbert, L. 1989. 'Control and Performance of International Joint Ventures', *Journal of International Business Studies*, 20(2): 235–255.
Geringer, J. and Louis, H. 1991. 'Strategic Determinants of Partner Selection Criteria in International Joint Ventures', *Journal of International Business Studies*, 22(2): 23–39.
Gerlach, M. L. 1992. 'The Japanese Corporate Network: A Blockmodel Analysis', *Administrative Science Quarterly*, 37(1): 105.
Gerlach, M. and Lincoln, J. 1992. 'The Organization of Business Networks in the US and Japan', in R. Eccles and N. Nohria (eds), *Networks and Organizations*, Boston, MA: Harvard Business School Press.
Gershenkron, A. 1962. *Economic Backwardness in Historical Perspective*, Cambridge, MA: The Belknap Press.
Ghoshal, S. and Moran, J. 1996. 'Bad For Practice: A Critique of the Transaction Cost Theory', *Academy of Management Review*, 21: 13–45.
Giddens, A. 1971. *Capitalism and Modern Social Theory*, Cambridge: Cambridge University Press.
Giddens, A. 1979. *Central Problems in Social Theory*, London: Macmillan.
Goldstein, J. 1994. *The Unshackled Organization: Facing the Challenge of Unpredictability through Spontaneous Reorganization*, Portland, OR: Productivity.

Gomes-Casseres, B. 1990. 'Firm Ownership Preferences and Host Government Restrictions: An Integrated Approach', *Journal of International Business Studies*, 21(1): 1–22.

Goodpaster, K. E. 1991. 'Business Ethics and Stakeholder Analysis', *Business Ethics Quarterly*, 1(1): 53–73.

Gouldner, A. 1960. 'The Norm of Reciprocity: A Preliminary Statement', *American Sociological Review*, 25: 161–178.

Grafstein, R. 1995. 'Group Identity, Rationality and Electoral Mobilization', *Journal of Theoretical Politics*, 7(2): 181–200.

Granovetter, M. 1973. 'The Strength of Weak Ties', *American Journal of Sociology*, 78: 1360–1380.

Granovetter, M. 1985. 'Economic Action and Social Structure: The Problem of Embeddedness', *American Journal of Sociology*, 91: 481–510.

Granovetter, M. and Swedberg, R. (eds) 1992. *The Sociology of Economic Life*, Boulder, CO and Oxford: Westview Press.

Grant, R. 1991. 'The Resource Based View of the Firm', *Strategic Management Journal*, 5: 171–180.

Grant, R. 1996. 'Knowledge, Strategy and the Theory of the Firm', *Strategic Management Journal*, 17: 109–122.

Grant, R. and Spender, J. 1996. 'Knowledge and the Firm: Overview', *Strategic Management Journal*, 17.

Graves, S. and Waddock, S. 1994. 'Institutional Owners and Corporate Social Performance', *Academy of Management Journal*, 37: 1034–1046.

Gray, B. 1989. *Collaborating: Finding Common Ground for Multiparty Problems*, San Francisco: Jossey-Bass.

Gregory, C. A. 1982. *Gifts and Commodities*, London: Academic Press.

Greif, A. 1989. 'Reputation and Coalitions in Medieval Trade: Evidence on the Maghribi Traders', *Journal of Economic History*, 49: 857–882.

Greif, A. 1993. 'Contract Enforceability and Economic Institutions in Early Trade: The Maghribi Traders' Coalition', *American Economic Review*, 102, 912–950.

Greif, A., Milgrom, P. and Weingast, B. R. 1994. 'Coordination, Commitment, and Enforcement – The Case of The Merchant Guild', *Journal of Political Economy*, 102(4): 745–776.

Groerner, S. 1999. *The Ending of the Clockwork Universe*, Edinburgh: Floris.

Grossman, S. and Hart, O. 1986. 'The Costs and Benefits of Ownership: A Theory of Vertical and Lateral Integration', *Journal of Political Economy*, 94: 691–719.

Gudeman, S. 1986. *Economics as Culture: Models and Metaphors of Livelihood*, London, Routledge Kegan Paul.

Gulati, R. 1995. 'Social Structure and Alliance Formation Pattern: A Longitudinal Analysis', *Administrative Science Quarterly*, 40, 619–652.

Gulati, R. 1998. 'Alliances and Networks', *Strategic Management Journal*, 19, 93–317.

Gurjewitsch, A. 1987. *Mittelalterliche Volkskultur*, Munich: Beck.

Haber, S., North, D. and Weingast, B. R. 2002. 'The Poverty Trap', *Hoover Digest*, 4(online).

Hammond, G. T. 1990. *International Business – Counter-trade Offsets and Barter in International Political Economy*, New York: St Martin's Press.

Hannan, M. 1997. 'Inertia, Density and the Structure of Organizational Populations: Entries in European Automobile Industries, 1886–1981', *Organization Studies*, 18(2): 193–228.

Hardin, R. 1982. *Collective Action*, Baltimore, MD: Johns Hopkins University Press.
Hardin, R. 1997. *One For All. The Logic of Group Conflict*, Princeton, NJ: Princeton University Press.
Harrison, J. S. and Freeman, R. E. 1999. 'Stakeholders, Social Responsibility, and Performance: Empirical Evidence and Theoretical Perspectives', *Academy of Management Journal*, Oct 42(5): 479–485
Hart, H, 1997. 'The Concept of Law', *Clarendon Law Series*, 2nd edn. London.
Hart, O. and Moore, J. 1990. 'Property Rights and the Nature of the Firm', *Journal of Political Economy*, 48: 1119–1158.
Hartford, K. 1990. 'The Double Dilemma of China, Economic Reforms', *Socialist Review*, 20(4): 95–114.
Haunschild, P. 1993. 'Inter-Organizational Imitation: The Impact of Interlocks on Corporate Acquisition Activity', *Administrative Science Quarterly*, 38: 564–592.
Haunschild, P. 1994. 'How Much Is That Company Worth?: Inter-Organizational Relationships, Uncertainty and Acquisition Premiums', *Administrative Science Quarterly*, 39: 391–411.
Hayek, F. Von 1945. 'Individualism and Economic Order', *American Economic Review*, 35: 519–530.
Hayek, F. Von 1967. *Studies in Philosophy, Politics and Economics*, Chicago: University of Chicago Press.
Hayek, F. Von 1973. *Law, Legislation and Liberty: Rules and Order*, Chicago: University of Chicago Press.
Hedlund, G. 1994. 'A Model of Knowledge Management and The N-Form Corporation', *Strategic Management Journal*, 15: 73–90.
Heil, O. and Robertson, T. 1991. 'Towards A Theory of Competitive Market Signaling: A Research Agenda', *Strategic Management Journal*, 12(2): 403–418.
Hennart, J. 1989. 'The Transaction Costs Rationale for Countertrade', *Journal of Law, Economics and Organization*, 5: 127–53.
Hennart, J. 1990. 'Some Empirical Dimensions of Countertrade', *Journal of International Business Studies*, 21: 243–270.
Hennart, J. and Anderson, E. 1993. 'Countertrade and the Minimization of Transaction Costs: An Empirical Examination', *Journal of Law, Economics and Organization*, 9: 290–313.
Hennart, J. and Reddy, S. 1997. 'The Choice Between Mergers–Acquisitions and Joint Ventures: The Case of Japanese Investors in the United States', *Strategic Management Journal*, 18: 1–12.
Hill, C. 1995. 'National Institutional Structures, Transaction Cost Economizing and Competitive Advantage', *Organization Science*, 6: 119–131.
Hill, C. and Jones, T. M. 1992. 'Stakeholder-Agency Theory', *Journal of Management Studies*, 29(1): 131–154.
Hill, R. C. and Levenhagen, H. 1995. 'Metaphors and Mental Models: Sense Making and Sense Giving in Innovative and Entrepreneurial Activities', *Journal of Management*, 21(6): 1057–1074.
Hillman, A. and Keim, G. 1995. 'International Variation in the Business–Government Interface – Institutional and Organizational Considerations', *Academy of Management Review*, 20(1): 193–214.
Hirsch, P. and Lounsbury, M. 1996. 'Rediscovering Volition: The Institutional Economics of Douglass C. North', *Academy of Management Review 21*, Book Review Essay, 872–884.

Hirschman, A. O. 1970. *Exit, Voice and Loyalty*, Cambridge, MA: Harvard University Press.

Hirschman. A. O. 1982. 'Shifting Involvements: Private Interest and Public Action', Oxford: Robertson.

Hirschman. A. O. 1984. *Getting Ahead Collectively: Grassroots Experiences in Latin America*, London. Pergamon Press.

Hirschman, A. O. 1994. 'Social Conflict as a Pillar of Democratic Society', *Political Theory*, 22: 15–27.

Hirshleifer, J. 1980. *Price Theory and Applications*, Englewood Cliffs, NJ: Prentice-Hall.

Hofstede, G. 1980. *Culture's Consequences: International Differences in Work Related Values*, Beverly Hills, CA: Sage.

Holland. J. H. 1992. Adaptation in Natural and Artificial Systems: An Introductory Analysis with Applications to Biology, Control, and Artificial Intelligence, Cambridge, MA: MIT Press.

Holland, J. H. 1995. *Hidden Order: How Adaptation Builds Complexity*, Reading, MA: Addison-Wesley.

Homans, G. 1974. *Social Behavior: Its Elementary Forms*, New York: Harcourt Brace Jovanovich.

Horowitz, D. L. 1985. *Ethnic Groups in Conflict*, Berkeley, CA: University of California Press.

Hosmer, L. 1995. 'Trust: The Connecting Link Between Organizational Theory and Philosophical Ethics', *Academy of Management Review*, 20: 379–403.

Humphrey, C. and Hugh-Jones S. 1992. *Barter, Exchange and Value*, Cambridge: Cambridge University Press.

Inkpen, A. and Beamish, P. 1997. 'Knowledge, Bargaining Power, and the Instability of International Joint Ventures', *Academy of Management Review*, 22: 177–202.

Itami, H. and Roehl, T. 1987. *Mobilizing Invisible Assets*, Cambridge, MA: Harvard University Press.

Jackson, S. E. and Dutton, J. E. 1988. 'Discerning Threats and Opportunities', *Administrative Science Quarterly*, 33(2): 370–387.

Jacobs, J. 1994. *Systems of Survival*, Toronto: First Vintage Books.

James, W. A. 1950. *Selection From His Writings on Psychology* (edited with a commentary by Margaret Knight), Harmondsworth: Penguin Books.

Jantsch, E. 1980. *The Self-Organizing Universe: Scientific and Human Implications of the Emerging Paradigm of Evolution*, Oxford: Pergamon.

Jensen, M. and Meckling, W. 1976. 'Theory of the Firm: Managerial Behaviour, Agency Costs and Ownership Structure', *Journal of Financial Economics*, 3: 305–360.

Jervis, R. 1985. *The Logic of Images in International Relations*, Princeton, NJ: Princeton University Press.

Johanson, S. and Vahlne, J. 1977. 'The Internationalization Process of the Firm – A Model of Knowledge Development and Increasing Foreign Market Commitments', *Journal of International Business Studies*, 8: 22–32.

Johnson, J. L. and Burton, B. K. 1994. 'Chaos and Complexity Theory for Management: Caveat Emptor', *Journal of Management Enquiry*, 3(4): 320–328.

Jones, C., Hesterly, W. and Borgatti, S. 1997. 'A General Theory of Network Governance: Exchange Conditions and Social Mechanisms', *Academy of Management Review*, 22: 911–945.

Jones, G. 1983. 'Transaction Costs, Property Rights and Organisational Culture: An Exchange Perspective', *Administrative Science Quarterly*, 23: 454–467.

Jones, T. M. 1995. 'Instrumental Stakeholder Theory: A Synthesis of Ethics and Economics', *Academy of Management Review*, 20: 404–437.
Jorde, T. M. and Teece. D. J. (ed). 1992. *Antitrust, Innovation and Competitiveness*, Oxford: Oxford University Press.
Kaplan, S. 1997, 'Corporate Governance and Corporate Performance: A Comparison of Japan, Germany and the US', *Journal of Applied Corporate Finance*, 9: 86–93.
Kaufer, E. 1996. 'The Evolution of Governance Structures: Entrepreneurs and Corporations', *Journal of Institutional and Theoretical Economics*, 152: 7–29.
Kauffman, S. 1993. The *Origins of Order*, Oxford: Oxford University Press.
Kauffman, S. 1995. *At Home in the Universe: The Search for Laws of Self-Organization and Complexity*, New York and Oxford: Oxford University Press.
Kelley, H. and Thibaut, J. 1978. *Interpersonal Relations: A Theory of Interdependence*, New York: Wiley.
Knack, S. and Keefer, P. 1997. 'Why Don't Poor Countries Catch Up? A Cross-National Test of an Institutional Explanation', *Economic Inquiry*, 35(3): 590–602.
Knight, F. 1921. *Risk, Uncertainty and Profit*, Boston MA: Houghton-Mifflin.
Knight, F. 1935. *The Ethics of Competition*, New York: Harper and Bros.
Kogut, B. 1986. 'On Designing Contracts to Guarantee Enforceability: Theory and Evidence From East–West Trade', *Journal of International Business Studies*, 17: 47–62.
Kogut, B. 1991. 'Country Capabilities and the Permeability of Borders', *Strategic Management Journal*, 12: 33–47.
Kogut, B., 1993. *Country Competitiveness: Technology and the Organizing of Work*, Oxford: Oxford University Press.
Kogut, B. and Singh, H. 1988. 'The Effect of National Culture on the Choice of Entry Mode', *Journal of International Business Studies*, 19: 411–432.
Kogut, B. and Zander, U. 1992. 'Knowledge of the Firm, Combinative Capabilities, and the Replication of Technology', *Organization Science*, 3: 383–397.
Kogut, B. and Zander, U. 1993. 'Knowledge of the Firm and the Evolutionary Theory of the Multinational Corporation', *Journal of International Business Studies*, 24: 625–645.
Kogut, B. and Zander, U. 1995. 'Knowledge, Market Failure and the Multinational Enterprise: A Reply', *Journal of International Business Studies*, 26(2): 417–427.
Kogut, B. and Zander, U. 1996. 'What Firms Do, Co-ordination, Identity, and Learning', *Organization Science*, 7: 502–518.
Kolm, S. C. 1984. *La Bonne Economie*, Paris: Presses Universitares de France.
Kornai, J. 1992. 'The Postsocialist Transition and the State: Reflections in the Light of Hungarian Fiscal Problems', *American Economic Review*, 82: 1–21.
Kotler, P. 1976. *Marketing Management: Analysis, Planning, Control*, Englewood Cliffs, NJ: Prentice-Hall.
Kranton, R. 1996, 'Reciprocal Exchange: A Self-Sustaining System', *American Economic Review*, 86: 830–851.
Kreps, D. 1990. 'Corporate Culture and Economic Theory', in J. Alt and K. Shepsle (eds), *Perspectives on Positive Political Economy*, Cambridge: Cambridge University Press.
Krugman, P. 1998. 'What Happened To Asia?' Department of Economics, MIT, Mimeo.
Krugman, P. 1991a. 'Increasing Returns and Economic Geography' *The Journal of Political Economy*, 99: 483–500.
Krugman, P. 1991b. 'History and Industry Location: The Case of the Manufacturing Belt' *American Economic Review*, 81(2): 80–84.

Kuran, T. 1989. 'Sparks and Prairie Fires: A Theory of Unanticipated Political Revolution', *Public Choice* 61(1): 41–74.

Lakoff, G. and Johnson, M. 1995. *Metaphors We Live By*, Chicago: University of Chicago Press.

Lall, S. 1992. 'Technological Capabilities and Industrialization', *World Development*, 20(2): 165.

Landa, J. 1981. 'A Theory of the Ethnically Homogeneous Middleman Group: An Institutional Alternative to Contract Law', *Journal of Legal Studies*, 10, 349–362.

Landa, J. 1994. *Trust, Ethnicity, and Identity*, Michigan: University of Michigan Press.

Landa, J. and Grofman, B. 1983. 'The Development of Trading Networks Among Spatially Separated Traders as a Process of Proto-Coalition Formation – The Kula Trade', *Social Networks* 5(4): 347–365.

Landes, W. 1971. 'An Economic Analysis of The Courts', *Journal of Law and Economics*, 14: 61–108.

Lane, D. and Maxfield, R. 1996. 'Strategy Under Complexity: Fostering Generative Relationships', *Long Range Planning*, 29(2), 215–231.

Langlois, R. 1992. 'Transaction-Cost Economics in Real Time', *Industrial and Corporate Change*, 1: 99–127.

Latour, B. 1993. *We Have Never Been Modern*, trans by Catherine Porter, New York and London: Harvester Wheatsheaf.

Latour, B. 1996. *Aramis, or, The Love of Technology*, trans by Catherine Porter, Cambridge, MA: Harvard University Press.

Lecraw, D. 1989. 'The Management of Countertrade: Factors Influencing Success', *Journal of International Business Studies*, 20: 41–59.

Lenway, S. and Murtha, T. 1991. 'The Idea of the State in the International Business Literature', Division of Research, School of Business Administration, University of Michigan, Ann Arbor.

Lenway, S. and Murtha, T. 1994. 'The State as Strategist in International Business Research Literature', *Journal of International Business Studies*, 25: 513–536.

Lenz, R. T. 1980. 'Strategic Capability: A Concept and Framework for Analysis', *Academy of Management Review*, 5: 225–234.

Leoni, B. 1961. *Freedom and the Law*, Indianapolis: Liberty Fund.

Levine, D. I. 1997. 'Reinventing Workplace Regulation' *California Management Review*, 39(4): 98.

Levi-Strauss, C. 1969. *The Elementary Structure of Kinship*, Boston, MA: Beacon Press.

Lewis, D. 1969. *Convention: A Philosophical Study*, Cambridge, MA: Harvard University Press.

Lippman, S. and Rumelt, R. 1982. 'Uncertain Imitability: An Analysis of Interfirm Differences in Efficiency Under Competition', *Rand Journal of Economics*, 13(2): 418–439

Lissack, M. 1997. 'Mind Your Metaphors: Lessons from Complexity Science', *Long Range Planning*, 30(2): 294–299.

Love, J. H., 1995. 'Knowledge, Market Failure and the Multinational Enterprise: A Theoretical Note', *Journal of International Business Studies*, 26(2): 399–408.

Luhmann, N. 1979. *Trust and Power*, New York: Wiley.

Luhmann, N. 1992. *Die Wissenschaft der Gesellschaft*, Frankfurt am Main: Suhrkamp.

Macaulay, S. 1963. 'Non-Contractual Relations in Business: A Preliminary Study', *American Sociological Review*, 45: 55–69.

MacNeil, I. R. 1974. 'The Many Futures of Contract', *Southern California Law Review*, 47: 692–738.
MacNeil, I. R. 1980. *The New Social Contract*, New Haven: Yale University Press.
Macy, M. W. 1993. 'Social Learning and the Structure of Collective Action', in E. Lawler *et al.* (eds),' *Advances in Group Processes*, Greenwich, CT: JAI Press: 1–36.
Macy, M. W. 1997. 'Identity, Interest and Emergent Rationality: An Evolutionary Synthesis', *Rationality and Society*, 9(4): 427–448.
Madhok, A. 1995. 'Revisiting Multinational Firms' Tolerance for Joint Ventures: A Trust-Based Approach', *Journal of International Business Studies*, 26: 117–37.
Mahoney, J., Huff, A. and Huff, J. 1994 . 'Toward a New Social Contract Theory in Organization Science', *Journal of Management Inquiry*, 3: 153–168.
Malinowski, B. 1961. *Argonauts of the Western Pacific*, New York: Dutton.
Mallott, M. J. 1990. 'Mapping Stakeholder Patterns', paper presented at the Annual Meeting of the Academy of Management, San Francisco.
Mansfield, E. 1989. 'The Diffusion of Industrial Robots in Japan and The United States', *Research Policy*, 18: 183–192.
Marcus, A. A. 1993. *Business and Society: Ethics, Government and The World Economy*, Homewood, IL: Irwin.
Marin, D. and Schnitzer, M. 1995. 'Tying Trade Flows: A Theory of Countertrade with Evidence', *American Economic Review*, 85: 1047–1064.
Marsden, P. V. and N. E. Friedkin 1993. 'Network Studies of Social Influence', *Sociological Methods and Research*, 22: 127–151.
Marwell, G., Oliver, P. and Prahl, R. 1989. 'Social Networks and Collective Action: A Theory of the Critical Mass, III', *American Journal of Sociology*, 94: 100–120.
Marx, K. 1887. *Das Kapital*, Moscow: English Progress Publishing.
Mason, E. S. 1939. 'Price and Production Policies of Large Scale Enterprises', *American Economic Review*, 29(1): 61–74.
Mauss, M. 1955. *The Gift – Forms and Functions of Exchange in Archaic Societies*, London: Cohen & West.
McFetridge, D. G. 1995. 'Knowledge, Market Failure and the Multinational Enterprise: A Comment', *Journal of International Business Studies*, 26(2): 409–416.
Meyer, J. W. and Rowan, B. 1977. 'Institutionalised Organizations. Formal Structure as Myth and Ceremony', *American Journal of Sociology*, 83: 340–363.
Meyer, J. W. and Scott, R. W. 1983. *Organizational Environments Ritual and Rationality*, Beverly Hills, CA: Sage.
Milgrom, P. and Roberts, J. 1990. 'The Economics of Modern Manufacturing: Technology Strategy and Organization', *American Economic Review*, 80: 511–528.
Milgrom, P. and Roberts, J. 1992. *Economics, Organization and Management*, New York: Prentice-Hall.
Mintzberg, H. and Waters, J. 1990. 'Does Decision Get in The Way?' *Organization Studies*, 11(1): 1–6.
Mirus, R. and Yeung, B. 1986. 'Economic Incentives for Countertrade', *Journal of International Business Studies*, 17: 27–40.
Mitchell, P., Sault, J. Smith, P. and Wallis, K. 1998. 'Comparing Global Economic Models', *Economic Modelling*, 51: 1–49.
Mitchell, R. K., Agle, B. R. and Wood, D. J. 1997. 'Toward a Theory of Stakeholder Identification and Salience: Defining the Principle of Who and What Really Counts', *Academy of Management Review*, 22: 853–886.

Mizruchi, M. S. 1996. 'What Do Interlocks Do', *Annual Review of Sociology*, 22: 271–298.
Mobley, C. and Mobey, S. 1987. 'Restructuring: Bond is Backed', *International Financial Law Review*, 6(4): 24–26.
Mody, A. and Yilmaz, K. 1997. 'Is There Persistence in the Growth of Manufactured Exports? Evidence from Newly Industrializing Countries', *Journal of Development Economics*, 5(2): 447.
Murrell, P. 1982. 'Product Quality, Market Signaling, and the Development of East–West Trade', *Economic Inquiry*, 20: 589–603.
Murtha, T. and Lenway, S. 1994. 'Country Capabilities and the Strategic State: How National Political Institutions Affect Multinational Corporations' Strategies', *Strategic Management Journal*, 15: 110–131.
Nahapiet, J. and Ghoshal, S. 1988. 'Social Capital, Intellectual Capital, and the Organizational Advantage' *Academy of Management Review*.
Nalebuff, B. J. and Brandenburger, A. M. 1996. *Co-opetition*, New York: Doubleday.
Nelson, R., 1992. 'Recent Writings on Competitiveness: Boxing the Compass', *California Management Review*, 34(2): 117–125.
Nelson. R. and Winter, S. 1982. *An Evolutionary Theory of Economic Change*, Cambridge, MA and London: The Belknap Press.
Newgren, K. E., Rasher, A. A., Laroe, M. E., and Szabo, M. R. 1985. 'Environmental Assessment and Corporate Performance: A Longitudinal Analysis Using A Market-Determined Performance Measure', in L. E. Preston (ed.), *Research in Corporate Social Performance and Policy*, 7, Greenwich, CT: JAI Press, 23(2): 153–164.
Nohria, N. and Eccles, R. 1992. *Networks and Organizations: Structure, Form and Action*, Cambridge, MA: Harvard Business School Press.
Nohria, N. and Garcia-Pont, C. 1991. 'Global Strategic Linkages and Industry Structure', *Strategic Management Journal*, 12: 105–124.
Nonaka, I. and Takeuchi, H. 1995. The *Knowledge-Creating Company*; Oxford, Oxford University Press,.
Noorderhaven, N., 1995. 'Trust and Transactions: Towards Transaction Cost Analysis with a Differential Behavioral Assumption', *Tijdschrift Voor Economies En Management*, 15: 5–18.
Nooteboom, B. 1996. 'Trust, Opportunism and Governance: A Process and Control Model', *Organization Studies*, 17: 985–1010.
North, D. 1990. *Institutions, Institutional Change and Economic Performance*, Cambridge: Cambridge University Press.
North, D. C. 1991. 'Institutions', *Journal of Economic Perspectives*, 5: 97–112.
North, D. C. 1994. 'Economic Performance through Time', *American Economic Review*, 84: 359–368.
North, D. and Douegass, C. 1981. *Structure and Change in Economic History*, New York and London: W.W. Norton.
Oberschall, A. and Kim, H. 1996. 'Identity and Action', *Mobilization*, 1(2): 63–86.
Ohmae, K. 1995. *The End of The Nation State*, London: HarperCollins, McKinsey and Co.
O'Grady, S. and Lane, H. 1996. 'The Psychic Distance Paradox', *Journal of International Business Studies*, 27: 305–333.
Oliver, C. 1990. 'Determinants of Interorganisational Relationships: Integration and Future Directions', *Academy of Management Review*, 15: 241–265.

Oliver, P. and Marwell, G. 1987. 'The Paradox of Group Size in Collective Action: A Theory of the Critical Mass II', *American Sociological Review*, 53: 1–8.
Oliver, P., Marwell, G. and Teixeria, R. 1985. 'A Theory of The Critical Mass I', *American Journal of Sociology*, 91: 522–556.
Olson, M. 1965. *The Logic of Collective Action*, Cambridge, MA: Harvard University Press.
Olson, M. 1991. 'Autocracy, Democracy, and Prosperity', in R. Zeckhauser (ed.) *Strategy and Choice*, Cambridge, MA: MIT Press.
Olson, M. 1992. 'The Hidden Path to a Successful Economy', in C. Clague and G. Rausser, (eds), *The Emergence of Market Economies in Eastern Europe*, London: Blackwell.
Orbell, J. and Dawes, R. 1991. 'A "Cognitive Miser" Theory of Cooperators' Advantage', *American Political Science Review*, 85(3): 515–28.
Orru, M., Biggart, N. and Hamilton, G. 1997. *The Economic Organization of East Asian Capitalism*, New York: Sage.
Ostrom, E. 1990. *Governing the Commons: The Evolution of Institutions for Collective Action*, Cambridge: Cambridge University Press.
Ouchi, W. 1980. 'Markets, Bureaucracies and Clans', *Administrative Science Quarterly*, 25: 121–141.
Ouchi. W. 1981. *Theory* Z: How *American Business Can Meet the Japanese Challenge*, Reading, MA: Addison-Wesley.
Parasuraman, A., Zeithaml, V. and Berry, L. 1985. 'A Conceptual Model of Service Quality and Its Implications for Future Research', *Journal of Marketing*, 4(1): 41–50.
Parfit, D. 1984. *Reasons and Persons*, Oxford: Oxford University Press.
Parkhe, A. 1991. 'Interfirm Diversity, Organisational Learning, and Longevity in Global Strategic Alliances', *Journal of International Business Studies*, 22: 579–602.
Parkhe, A. 1993. 'Strategic Alliance Structuring: A Game Theoretic and Transaction Cost Examination of Interfirm Cooperation', *Academy of Management Journal*, 36(4): 794–830.
Parsons, T. 1960. *Structure and Process in Modern Societies*. Glencoe, IL: Free Press.
Pedersen, T. and Thomsen, S. 1999. 'Business Systems and Corporate Governance', *International Studies of Management and Organization*, 29(2): 43–59.
Peng, M. and Heath, P. 1996. 'The Growth of the Firm in Planned Economies in Transition: Institutions, Organizations and Strategic Choice', *Academy of Management Review*, 2: 492–528.
Podolny, J. 1993. 'A Status-Based Model of Market Competition', *American Journal of Sociology*, 98: 829–872.
Polonsky, M. 1995. 'A Stakeholder Theory Approach to Designing Environmental Marketing Strategy', *Journal of Business and Industrial Marketing*, 10(1): 29–46.
Polanyi, K. 1944. The *Great Transformation*. New York and Boston, MA: Rinehart and Co.
Polanyi, K. 1957. *Trade and Markets in The Early Empires*, with C. Arensberg, and H. Pearson, New York: Free Press.
Polanyi, K. 1966a. *Dahomey and the Slave Trade: An Analysis of an Archaic Economy*, in collaboration with A. Rotspein, Washington, DC: University of Washington Press.
Polanyi, M. 1966b. *The Tacit Dimension*, New York: Anchor Day.
Polanyi, K. 1968. *Primitive, Archaic and Modern Economies: Essays of Karl Polanyi*, with Dalton, Boston, MA: Beacon Press.

Porac, J. F., Thomas, H. and Baden-Fuller, C. 1989. 'Competitive Groups as Cognitive Communities: The Case of Scottish Knitwear Manufacturers', *Journal of Management Studies*, July.

Porter, M. E. 1980. *Competitive Strategy*, New York: Free Press.

Porter, M. E. 1981. 'The Contribution of Industrial Organization to Strategic Management', *Academy of Management Review*, 6: 609–620.

Porter, M. E. 1990. *The Competitive Advantage of Nations*, New York: Free Press.

Posner, R. 1980. 'A Theory of Primitive Society, With Special Reference to Law', *Journal of Law and Economics*, 23: 1–53.

Posner, R. 1992. *Economic Analysis of Law*, Boston, MA: Little, Brown.

Post, J., Murray, E., Dickie, R. and Mahon, J. 1983. 'Managing Public Affairs – The Public Affairs Function', *California Management Review*, 26(1): 135–150.

Pouder, R. and St John, C. H. 1996. 'Hot Spots and Blind Spots: Geographical Clusters of Firms and Innovation', *Academy of Management Review*, 21(4): 1192–1126.

Powell, W. 1990. 'Neither Market nor Hierarchy: Network Forms of Organization', *Research in Organizational Behaviour*, 12: 295–336.

Prahalad, C. K. 2002. 'Serving the World's Poor, Profitably', *Harvard Business Review*, 80(9): 48–52.

Prahalad C. and Hamel, G. 1994. 'Competing for the Future', *Harvard Business Review*, 72(4): 122–129.

Preston, L. 1994. 'Stakeholder Issues: Four Essays', Working Paper, Center for International Business Education and Research, College of Business and Management, University of Maryland.

Preston, L. and Post, J. E. 1975. *Private Management and Public Policy: The Principle of Public Responsibility*, Englewood Cliffs, NJ: Prentice-Hall.

Preston, L. and Sapienza, H. 1990. 'Stakeholder Management and Corporate Performance', *Journal of Behavioral Economics*, 19(4): 361–375.

Putnam, R. 1996. 'The Strange Disappearance of Civic America', *The American Prospect*, 24: 34–48.

Raiffa, H. 1982. *The Art and Science of Negotiation*, Cambridge, MA: Harvard University Press.

Raub, W. and Weesie, J. 1990. 'Reputation and Efficiency in Social Institutions: An Example of Network Effects', *American Journal of Sociology*, 96: 626–654.

Rausser and Clague, C. K. (eds), 1990. *The Emergence of Market Economies in Eastern Europe*, Cambridge, MA: Blackwell.

Reich, R. B. 1991. *The Work of Nations: Preparing Ourselves for 21st Century Capitalism*, New York: Alfred Knopf.

Ring, P. and Van De Ven, A. 1992. 'Structuring Cooperative Relationships between Organizations', *Strategic Management Journal*, 13: 483–498.

Ring, P. and Van De Ven A. 1994. 'Developmental Processes of Cooperative Inter-Organizational Relationships', *Academy of Management Review*, 19: 90–118.

Robinson, J. 1933. *The Economics of Imperfect Competition*, London: Macmillan.

Rodrik, D. 1997. 'Has Globalization Gone Too Far?', *California Management Review*, 39: 29–53.

Roe, M. 1994. *Strong Managers, Weak Owners: The Political Roots of American Corporate Finance*, Princeton, NJ: Princeton University Press.

Roe, M., 1997 'The Political Roots of American Corporate Finance', *Journal of Applied Corporate Finance*, 9: 8–22.

Romer, P. 1986, 'Increasing Returns and Long-Run Growth', *Journal of Political Economy*, 94(5): 1002–1038.

Rostow, M. 1991. *The Stages of Economic Growth*, Cambridge: Cambridge University Press, 3rd edn.

Rowley, T. J. 1997. 'Moving Beyond Dyadic Ties: A Network Theory of Stakeholder Influences', *Academy of Management Review*, 22: 887–910.

Rugman, A. 2002. *The End of Globalization*, New York: Random House.

Sahlins, M. 1965. 'On The Sociology of Primitive Exchange', in M. Banton, (ed.) *The Relevance of Models for Social Anthropology*, London: Tavistock Publications.

Sahlins, M. 1972. *Stone Age Economics*, Chicago: Aldine Atherton.

Sanchez, R. 1997. 'Strategic Management at the Point of Inflection: Systems, Complexity and Competence Theory', *Long Range Planning*, 30(6): 939–946.

Sandler, T. 1992. 'After the Cold War, Secure the Global Commons', *Challenge*, 35(4): 16–24.

Saxenian, A. L. 2002. 'Transnational Communities and, the Evolution of Global Production Networks: The Cases of Taiwan, China and India', *Industry and Innovation*, 9(3): 183–204.

Schelling, T. C. 1960. *The Strategy of Conflict*. Cambridge, MA: Harvard University Press.

Schelling, T. C. 1966. *Arms and Influence*, New Haven: Yale University Press.

Schelling, T. C. 1969. 'Neighborhood Tipping and Discrimination', Working Paper, Kennedy School of Government Harvard University.

Schelling, T. C. 1978. *Micromotives and Macrobehavior*, New York: W.W. Norton.

Schrum, W. and Withnow, R. 1988. 'Reputational Status of Organizations in Technical Systems', *American Journal of Sociology*, 94: 882–912.

Schumpeter, J. A. 1950 [1942]. *Capitalism, Socialism and Democracy*, New York: Harper.

Senge, P. M. 1990. *The Fifth Discipline: The Art and Practice of the Learning Organization – The Social Psychology of Organizing*, New York: Doubleday.

Shan, W. and Hamilton, W. 1991. 'Country-Specific Advantage and International Cooperation', *Strategic Management Journal*, 12: 419–432.

Simmel, G. 1950. 'Superordination and Subordination', in K. Wolf, trans, *The Sociology of Georg Simmel*, Homewood, IL: Free Press.

Simmel, G. 1978. *The Philosophy of Money*, London: Routledge.

Simon, H. 1991. 'Organizations and Markets', *Journal of Economic Perspectives*, 5: 25–44.

Simon, H. 1992. 'Decision-Making and Problem-Solving', in M. Zey (ed.), *Decision Making: Alternatives to Rational Choice Models*, Newbury Park, CA: Sage.

Sirgy, M. 2002. 'Measuring Corporate Performance by Building on the Stakeholders' Model of Business Ethics', *Journal of Business Ethics*, 35(3): 143–162

Smith, A, 1776. *The Wealth of Nations*, London: Methuen, 1904, 3rd edn.

Smith, A. 1996. 'To Intervene or not to Intervene: A Biased Decision', *Journal of Conflict Resolution*, 40(1): 16–40.

Soh, J. 1994. 'Social Knowledge as a Control System: A Proposition and Evidence from the Japanese FDI Behavior', *Journal of International Business Studies*, 25: 295–324.

Sorensen, A. 1983. 'Processes of Allocation to Open and Closed Positions in Social Structure', *Zeitschrift Für Soziologie*, 12: 203–224.

Sorge, A. 1991. 'Strategic Fit and the Societal Effect: Interpreting Cross-National Comparisons of Technology, Organization, and Human Resources', *Organization Studies*, 12: 161–190.

Spence, M. 1973. *Market Signalling*, Cambridge, MA: Harvard University Press.
Spencer, B. A. and Taylor, G. S. 1987. 'A Within and Between Analysis of the Relationship Between Corporate Social Performance and/Financial Performance', *Akron Business and Economic Review*, 18(1): 7–18.
Spender, J. C. 1997. 'Making Knowledge the Basis of a Dynamic Theory of the Firm', *Strategic Management Journal*, 17(4): 45–62.
Spender, J. C. and Grant. R. 1996. 'Knowledge and the Firm: Overview', *Strategic Management Journal*, 17: 5–9.
Stacey, R. D. 1995. 'The Science of Complexity: An Alternative Perspective for Strategic Change Processes', *Strategic Management Journal*, 16(6): 477–496
Stacey, R. D. 1996a. *Strategic Management and Organizational Dynamics*, London: Pitman.
Stacey, R. D. 1996b. *Complexity and Creativity in Organizations*, San Francisco: Berrett Koehler.
Starbuck, W. 1976. 'Organizations and their Environments', in M. Dunnette (ed.), *Handbook of Industrial and Organizational Psychology*, Chicago: Rand McNally: 1069–1123.
Stevenson, H. 1976. 'Defining Corporate Strengths and Weaknesses', *Sloan Management Review*, 17(3): 51–68.
Stigler, G. 1966. *The Theory of Price*, New York: Macmillan.
Stinchcombe, A. 1965. 'Social Structure and Organizations', in J. G. March (ed.), *Handbook of Organizations*, Chicago: Rand McNally.
Stopford, J. and Strange, S. 1993. *Rival States, Rival Firms*, Cambridge: Unwin.
Strand, R. 1983. 'A Systems Paradigm of Organizational Adaptations to the Social Environment', *Academy of Management Review*, 8: 90–96.
Sugden, R. 1982. 'On the Economics of Philanthropy', *Economic Journal* 92(366): 341–351.
Swanson, D. 1995. 'Addressing a Theoretical Problem by Reorienting the Corporate Social Performance Model', *Academy of Management Review*, 20: 43–64.
Takeuchi, M. and Ikyiro, N. 1995. *The Knowledge-Creating Company*, Oxford: Oxford University Press.
Thurow, L. 1992. *Head To Head: The Coming Economic Battle Among Japan, Europe and America*, New York: Edward Morrow.
Toyne, B. 1988. 'International Exchange: A Foundation for Theory Building in International Business', *Journal of International Business Studies*, 13: 1–17.
Uehara, E. 1990. 'Dual Exchange Theory, Social Networks, and Informal Social Support', *American Journal of Sociology*, 96: 521–557.
Ullman, A. 1985. 'Data in Search of a Theory: A Critical Examination of the Relationships Among Social Performance, Social Disclosure, and Economic Performance', *Academy of Management Review*, 10: 540–577.
Uzzi, B. 1997. 'Social Structure and Competition in Interfirm Networks: The Paradox of Embeddedness', *Administrative Science Quarterly*, 42: 35–67.
Vanberg, V. 1994. *Rules and Choice in Economics*, London: Routledge.
Van de Ven, A. 1993. 'The Development of an Infrastructure for Entrepreneurship', *Journal of Business Venturing*, 3: 211–231.
Wade, R. 1985. 'East Asian Financial Systems as a Challenge to Economics: Lessons from Taiwan', *California Management Review*, 4: 106-128.
Wade, R. 1996. 'Japan, The World Bank, and the Art of Paradigm Maintenance: The East Asian Miracle in Political Perspective', *New Left Review*, 17: 3–36.

Walker, G., Kogut, B. and Shan, W. 1996 . 'Social Capital, Structural Holes and the Formation of an Industry Network', *Organization Science*, 8: 109–126.
Wallis, K., Mitchell, P., Sault, J. and Smith, P. 1998. 'Comparing Global Economic Models', *Economic Modelling*, 15(1): 1–49.
Wallis, R., Baden-Fuller C., Kretschmer, M. and Klimis, G. M. 1999. 'Contested Collective Administration of Intellectual Property Rights in Music – The Challenge to the Principles of Reciprocity and Solidarity', *European Journal of Communication*, 14(1): 5–35.
Weber, M. 1968. *Economy and Society*, New York: Bedminster Press.
Weber, M. 1979. *Economy and Society: An Outline of Interpretive Sociology*, C. T. Roth, and G. Wittich, eds, trans by E. Fischof *et al*. London: University of California Press.
Weick, K. 1979. *The Social Psychology of Organising*, Reading, MA and London: Addison-Wesley.
Weingast, B. 1995. 'The Economic Role of Political Institutions: Market-Preserving Federalism and Economic Development', *Journal of Law, Economics and Organization*, 5: 1–31.
Weitzman, M.-L. 1984a. 'The Simple Macroeconomics of Profit Sharing', *American Economic Review*, 75: 937–953.
Weitzman, M.-L. 1984b. *The Share Economy*, Cambridge, MA: Harvard University Press.
Wernerfelt, B. 1984. 'A. Resource Based View of the Firm', *Strategic Management Journal*, 5: 171–180.
Wheatley, M. J. 1992. *Leadership and the New Science: Learning about Organization from an Orderly Universe*, San Francisco: Berrett-Koehler.
Wheatley, M. and Kellner-Rogers, M. 1996. *A Simpler Way*, San Francisco: Berrett-Koehler.
White, H. 1970. *Chains of Opportunity: System Models of Mobility in Organisations*, Cambridge, MA: Harvard University Press.
Whitley, R. 1990. 'Eastern Asian Enterprise Structures and the Comparative Analysis of Forms of Business Organisations', *Organization Studies*, 11: 47–74.
Whitley, R. 1992a. *Business Systems in East Asia: Firms, Markets and Societies*, Oxford: Clarendon Press.
Whitley, R. 1992b. *European Business Systems: Firms and Markets in Their National Contexts*, London: Sage.
Whitley, R. 1992c. *East Asian Business Systems*, London: Sage.
Whitley, R. 1994. Dominant Forms of Economic Organisation in Market Economies,; *Organization Studies*, 15: 153–183.
Williamson, O. E. 1975. *Markets and Hierarchies: Analysis and Antitrust Implications – A Study in the Economics of Internal Organization*, New York: Free Press, London: Collier Macmillan.
Williamson, O. 1983. 'Credible Commitments: Using Hostages to Support Exchange', *American Economic Review*, 73: 519–40.
Williamson, O. E. 1985. *The Economic Institutions of Capitalism*, New York: Free Press.
Williamson, O. E. 1994. 'Transaction Costs Economics and Organization', in N. Smelser and R. Swedberg (eds), *The Handbook of Economic Sociology*, Princeton, NJ: Princeton University Press.
Williamson, O. E. 1996. 'Economic Organization: The Case for Candor', *Academy of Management Review*, 21: 48–57.

Williamson, O. E. and Craswell, R. 1993. 'Calculativeness, Trust, and Economic Organization', *Journal of Law and Economics*, 36(1): 453.

Wilson, I. H. 1977. 'Socio-Political Forecasting: A New Dimension To Strategic Planning', in A. B. Carroll (ed.), *Managing Corporate Social Responsibility*, Boston: Little, Brown: 159–169.

Winter, S. 1998. 'Comments on Arrow and on Lucas', in R. Hogarth and M. Reder (eds), *Rational Choice: The Contrast Between Economics and Psychology*, Chicago: University of Chicago Press: 243–250.

Womack, J. P., Jones, D. T. and Roos, D. 1991. *'The Machine that Changed The World'*, London: HarperBusiness.

Wood, D. J. 1991a. 'Corporate Social Performance Revisited', *Academy of Management Review*, 16: 691–718.

Wood, D. J. 1991b. 'Social Issues in Management: Theory and Research in Corporate Social Performance', *Journal of Management*, 17(2): 383–406.

World Bank, 1993. The *World Development Report*, Oxford: Oxford University Press.

World Bank, 1997. The *World Development Report – 1997: The State in a Changing World*, Oxford: Oxford University Press.

Yamagishi, T. and Cook, K. 1993. 'Generalized Exchange and Social Dilemmas', *Social Psychological Quarterly*, 56: 235–248.

Yarbrough, B. and Yarbrough, R. 1992. *Co-Operation and Governance in International Trade*, Princeton, NJ: Princeton University Press.

Yoffie, D. 1984. 'Profiting from Countertrade', *Harvard Business Review*, May–June: 8–12.

Yoshino, M. and Rangan, U. S. 1995. *Strategic Alliances: An Entrepreneurial Approach To Globalization*, Boston, MA: Harvard Business School Press.

Zajac, E. and Olsen. C. 1993. 'From Transaction Cost to Transaction Value Analysis: Implications for the Study of Interorganizational Strategies', *Journal of Management Studies*, 30: 131–145.

Zohar, D., 1990. *The Quantum Self*, London: Flamingo.

Zubkin, S. and DiMaggio, P. 1990. *Structures of Capital: The Social Organization of the Economy*, New York: Cambridge University Press.

Zucker, L. 1987. 'Institutional Theories of Organization', *Annual Review of Sociology*, 13: 443–464.

Zucker, L. 1989. 'Combining Institutional Theory and Population Ecology – No Legitimacy, No History', *American Sociological Review*, 54(4): 542–545.

# Index

The manufacturer's authorised representative in the EU is Springer Nature Customer Service Centre GmbH, Europaplatz 3, 69115 Heidelberg, Germany. If you have any concerns regarding our products, please contact ProductSafety@springernature.com

Printed and bound by CPI Group (UK) Ltd, Croydon, CR0 4YY
10/10/2026
02231228-0001